LECTURES ON
THE HISTORY AND ART
OF MUSIC

The Louis Charles Elson Memorial Lectures
at the Library of Congress, 1946-1963

Da Capo Press Music Reprint Series
GENERAL EDITOR: FREDERICK FREEDMAN
Vassar College

LECTURES ON
THE HISTORY AND ART
OF MUSIC

*The Louis Charles Elson Memorial Lectures
at the Library of Congress, 1946-1963*

Preface by IRVING LOWENS, Music Critic
Washington Evening Star

𝄐 DA CAPO PRESS · NEW YORK · 1968

The Louis Charles Elson Memorial Fund was established at the Library of Congress in 1945 to provide for a continuing series of lectures on music and musical literature. The first lecture, delivered by Otto Kinkeldey, took place in April, 1946, and there now have been fifteen in all. Eleven of these have been published by the Library of Congress in separate pamphlets and are gathered for the first time in the present volume. The following four Elson Fund lectures remain unpublished:

Otto Kinkeldey, *Early Ensembles: The Forerunners of the Orchestra* (delivered April 25, 1946)

Helen Hartness Flanders, *New England Balladry* (delivered February 27, 1948)

Marious Barbeau, *Canadian Folk and Indian Music* (delivered May 10, 1948)

Gustave Reese, *The Renaissance Attitude Toward Music* (delivered December 17, 1952)

To facilitate reference to the pamphlets as originally published, the pagination of the separate pamphlets has been included in this edition in square brackets.

Library of Congress Catalog Card Number 68-55319

PREFACE

L OUIS CHARLES ELSON (born April 17, 1848, Boston; died there, February 14, 1920) was educated in the public schools of Boston. He received his first music lessons from his mother, later took vocal instruction from August Kreissmann, leader of the Orpheus Club chorus, and finally gravitated to Leipzig, where he studied music theory in the Conservatory with Carl Gloggner-Castelli. Upon his return to the United States in 1876, his first professional activity — quite unusual for the period — was in the field of music criticism. By 1880, he was the editor of *Vox Humana* and of the *Musical Herald*. His first contributions to the press appear to have been to the *Boston Courier*, and during an extended trip to Europe in 1883–84, he served as European correspondent for the *Boston Transcript*. He joined the staff of the *Boston Advertiser* in 1886, became its music editor in 1888, and retained that position until his death in 1920. Although not so polished a stylist as William Foster Apthorp (1848–1913) of the *Boston Evening Transcript* or Philip Hale (1854–1934), first of the *Boston Journal* and, after 1903, with the *Boston Herald,* Elson led the way in writing detailed and thorough estimates of musical works and performances, and was, in this sense, Boston's first genuinely modern critic.

But it was really as a lecturer and teacher that Elson made his deepest impact on the development of musical literacy in the United States. He became a member of the Boston University faculty shortly after his return home from Leipzig and in 1880 switched his allegiance to the

New England Conservatory of Music, where he remained as head of the theory department for forty years. He was largely responsible for developing the school's courses to the point where they were as thorough and detailed as any offered by a European conservatory. The theory curriculum under Elson included careful study of form and analysis, which he supplemented by delivering two sets of lectures, one dealing with orchestral instruments and their particular characteristics, the other with the history of music and the stylistic development of the great composers. Elson's students took away from the New England Conservatory a keen appreciation of his masterful lectures, and as a result, he was invited to talk on music at such schools as Harvard, Cornell, Brown, Vassar, Yale, Tulane, and Pennsylvania.

Elson's most spectacular achievement as a lecturer undoubtedly was his appointment in 1907 as lecturer on music for the city of Boston. The forty lectures he delivered annually for some seven years were of especial value in developing the musical taste of the Boston public. They were given in various public halls and schools in connection with concerts by a small but excellent orchestra and occasional vocal and instrumental soloists. Elson chose the programs, beginning with the music of Mozart, and progressing through the compositions of Schubert, Beethoven, the romanticists, the operatic composers, Liszt, Wagner, and the contemporaries. The Elson municipal lectures were, in effect, a successful experiment in the adult education which was so much in vogue in the early years of the century thanks to such institutions as the Chautauquas.

Elson wrote, of course — voluminously. Beginning with his *Curiosities of Music* of 1883, few years passed without an Elson title in the lists. His best works were perhaps *The National Music of America and Its Sources* (1899) and *A History of American Music* (1904), the definitive treatment of the subject which supplanted F. L. Ritter's *Music In America* (1883) and held the field, virtually unchallenged, until the appearance of John Tasker Howard's *Our American Music* in 1929. To catch the flavor of Elson the man, and to experience some of the magic he evidently exercised as a lecturer, it is necessary to go to his almost forgotten *European Reminiscences, Musical and Otherwise* (1891), an informal record of several vacation tours he took during the 1880's. Here you can feel the genial personality of the man, his commanding presence, his wit and felicity of expression, his mastery of the anecdote, his thorough comprehension of the subject at hand, and even, to a certain extent, his style of delivery. In its broad humor and invariable high spirits, the book is often reminiscent of Mark Twain's *Innocents Abroad,* and I would recommend it to the reader as a totally forgotten minor classic of American travel literature, of particular interest because of Elson's insatiable curiosity about what the people of other countries thought of the music and music-making of his own.

Elson should probably be remembered as a popularizer, in the best sense of the word, and thus it was a particularly thoughtful and appropriate gesture on the part of his widow, Mrs. Bertha L. Elson, to bequeathe to the Library of Congress, upon her death in 1945, a sum of money to provide for lectures on music and musical literature in memory of her husband. Her intent was to preserve the memory of Louis Charles Elson's name by insuring a continuing tradition of lectures by other men naturally gifted in the difficult art of talking intelligently to laymen about music. This book shows how successful she was.

The Elson Fund lectures at the Library of Congress have been noteworthy musical events. Non-technical in nature and generally philosophical in bent, they have brought some of the finest minds in music to Washington audiences, and as a modern adaptation of the sort of adult education which was so popular when ours was still an inner-directed civilization, they follow very directly in the tradition of Elson himself.

The Louis Charles Elson Memorial Fund in the Library of Congress has enabled the institution not only to engage lecturers, but also, for the most part, to publish their lectures so that those not present in the Whittall Pavilion (where they customarily are delivered) can enjoy the comments of the speakers. And what a distinguished roster of names the lecturers represent! Glen Haydon, Curt Sachs, Carroll C. Pratt, Jacques Barzun, Archibald T. Davison, Karl Geiringer, Jaap Kunst, Egon Wellesz, Marc Pincherle, Anthony van Hoboken, Sir Jack Westrup — here is a virtual honor roll of twentieth-century musical scholarship.

Unfortunately, the Elson Fund is not large enough to allow the Library of Congress to reprint lectures, and since the initial printing is small and copies are distributed free upon request while the supply lasts, individual lectures go out of print quite rapidly. The Da Capo Press is doing the world of music a considerable favor by making available under a single cover, for the first time, all previously published Elson Fund lectures. In this form, they will memorialize the name of Louis Charles Elson even more eloquently than they did before they were collected, and they will illustrate vividly how a creative idea can be transformed into a brilliant reality by an institution devoted to scholarship and the humanities.

Washington, D.C.
June 1968

IRVING LOWENS

CONTENTS

LECTURES ON
THE HISTORY AND ART
OF MUSIC

The Louis Charles Elson Memorial Lectures
at the Library of Congress, 1946-1963

THE LIBRARY OF CONGRESS

THE LOUIS CHARLES ELSON MEMORIAL FUND

ON THE MEANING OF MUSIC

A LECTURE DELIVERED BY

GLEN HAYDON

Professor of Music, University of North Carolina

IN

THE COOLIDGE AUDITORIUM

OF THE LIBRARY OF CONGRESS

NOVEMBER 28, 1947

Washington, D. C.

1948

ON THE MEANING OF MUSIC

ANYONE undertaking a discussion of such a problem as the meaning of music is faced with two major difficulties: the complicated nature of the realities under consideration and the ambiguities of language. One's success in dealing with the former will depend in large measure on his ability to surmount the latter. A preliminary survey of certain matters pertinent to these difficulties seems advisable in order to clear the way for a more detailed investigation of the problem.

Art as Experience

All art may, for purposes of understanding, be conveniently regarded as a process involving the human organism and its environment. The several arts may be distinguished by the aspects of the environment or of the organism which come into play. The process may be thought of as an event requiring activity on the part of the organism related to an external stimulus, or as an interplay between the organism and its environment. One ordinarily thinks of the object of art as "the thing out there"—the painting, statue, or the vibratory motion in the air; but the science of aesthetics points out that the work of art is more than the physical object.

What any individual appreciates is not, strictly speaking, "the thing out there" but the thing-as-perceived; it is the perception plus all relevant elaboration by the organism. This fact is of particular importance for the study of meaning. Suppose two individuals attend a symphony concert. One, because of his natural endowments, training, and experience in music, has a profound response; the other, because of his lack of musical gift, training, and experience, is little affected by the music. The objective stimulus in both instances is the same; the sense of hearing may be equally good. One person hears a highly organized work of art, rich in musical meanings; the other, a meaningless cacophony of sounds. The point I wish to emphasize is that the organism is always an implicit causal factor in any meaning situation.

Denotative and Connotative Definitions of Music

When we speak of the problem of meaning in music, we do not ordinarily refer primarily to the meaning of the term *music;* nevertheless a consideration of the term itself is not without significance for the more general problem. In this connection it is interesting to note that most of our dictionaries of music omit *music* itself from the word list. Is this an oversight, or is the meaning of the term so obvious that it need not be included? Or could it be because of the difficulties of formulating a satisfactory definition? Definitions are logically of two types—denotative and connotative. Denotative definitions are extensive, and tend to point to particular instances to which a term is applied. Connotative definitions, on the other hand, are intensive, and try to specify the characteristics common to all particular instances. Most of our concepts of the meaning of terms are acquired by the denotative method. We point to the leaves of a tree, for example, and say: "The leaves on that tree are green." Thus we may come to know the meaning of the word *green*. Dictionary definitions are necessarily essentially connotative, and this is their essential weakness; in referring to qualities common to many particular instances, individual differences tend to get lost, meanings become abstract, and with the increasing abstractness they tend to get more and more ambiguous.

A denotative definition of music points to particular instances of music: a particular piece is played by a particular musician, to a particular listener. A connotative definition of music, always incomplete and ambiguous, tries to comprehend under one formulation the common qualities of all instances. Such a definition might run somewhat as follows: *Music is the interplay of the organism with its environment in the organization and manipulation of the sensory materials of sound in which the values involved have to do with the pleasurable aspect of the experience as such.* Obviously the difficulties of formulating any such definition lie not only in the complicated nature of the realities referred to, but also in the inevitable ambiguities of language. The definition suggested does not sound very much like the ordinary dictionary definition, which, according to Webster, reads: "The science or art of pleasing, expressive, or intelligible combination of tones"; but it does have the merit of stressing the nature of music as an experience.

The Structure of the Musical Process

Before proceeding to a discussion of the problem of meaning let us pause briefly to consider some of the salient features of the process, activity, or event which we may refer to as an instance of music. The part of the event which occurs outside the organism is the physical aspect of music, the study of which falls primarily into the province of the branch of physical science which is known as acoustics. This science attempts the descriptive analysis of everything pertaining to the origin and transmission of sound impulses. The particular set of sound impulses in a given instance of music is normally a performer's realization of a design set down in a musical score which is the composer's "blueprint" of his musical composition. At the other end of the process, so to speak, is the auditor. At this stage it is the function of the sciences of physiology and psychology to study and account for the behavior of the organism whether as listener, performer, or composer. This is done primarily through the study of the sensory, perceptual, and meaningful aspects of the experience as manifested in the stream of consciousness. Closely related in the consideration of the aesthetic experience are the correlative concepts of material, form, and expression.

In music the interplay between the organism and its environ-

[9]
5

ment takes place in terms of two complementary principles which philosophers have called the principles of *acquiescence* and *transformation*. Simply stated, the principle of acquiescence means that in the musical process the organism accommodates itself to the nature of the physical materials of music; the principle of transformation means that in the musical process the physical materials undergo a kind of metamorphosis which is determined by the nature of the organism. For example, although the composer cannot modify the inherent physical nature of his materials, nevertheless the musical composition is the result of his contrivance. I have mentioned the composer as an example, but it should be noted that the same principles apply, with necessary changes, to the activities of the performer and listener. We may say that a musical composition is the product of the individual's conception or imagination; within limits it assumes such form or design as he imposes on the raw material, and represents whatever meaning or purpose he may be able to realize creatively.

There remains to mention one more important aspect of the process: namely, that in the course of the experience the organism senses a certain kind of value. Here we come to the proper field of aesthetics; and here, too, we find ourselves confronted with the problem of meaning, for one's conception of aesthetic value in any art seems to hinge largely on one's interpretation of the problem of meaning in that art.

The Meaning of Meaning in Language

The meanings of meaning in language are not directly applicable without appropriate modifications in art in general or in music in particular. By this I mean especially that the meanings of meaning derived from the study of language cannot be applied to the arts without due regard for the differences in the materials of the several arts. For example, words have chiefly conventional meanings; that a word like *chair* should refer to the particular objects it does refer to and not to others, is a matter of social usage and agreement. There is nothing intrinsic in the word itself that would lead one to its meaning. If we may take the individual musical tone as the equivalent of the sound of the word, we find there is little if any meaning in music; the sound itself has no conventional referent. Sounds not constituting words are frequently used like words to represent meanings in this sense: for example, to cite only a few instances, the conductor's clang of a streetcar bell, the starter's pistol shot at a track meet, and the timekeeper's shot at the close of a football game. But these are not the sounds of music. However, musical sounds are used as signals too: chimes used as door bells, the radio's signal "At the sound of the musical tone it will be 12 o'clock," etc. In the case of bugle calls we have musical patterns similarly used as signals; but in general the use of meaning in this sense is rare in music.

The symbols of musical notation, however, are used to convey conventional musical meanings. The meaningful relation of the written or printed musical notes to the sounds for which they stand is analogous to the relation between written or printed words and spoken word-sounds, or vocables. But it should be carefully noted that the analogy ceases at that point, for the musical sound does not normally evoke any further conventional meaning as does a word.

If at this stage of our discussion the question were raised: "What is the meaning of music?" in the same sense as the question might be asked "What is the meaning of language?" I should have to say that both questions are ambiguous, vague to a point that one would seem warranted to conclude that in either case the question has no meaning. It is simply a series of words with a question mark at the end. If the question should be worded: "What is meaning in music?" in the sense that one might ask "What is meaning in language?" referring to the previously discussed idea of conventional meaning, the answer would necessarily be that there is no meaning of this sort in music.

Various other meanings of meaning have been pointed out by writers on the subject: for example, *value* ("His friendship means a great deal to me."), *intention* ("He means well."), *significance* in the sense of place of anything in a system ("What is the meaning of life?"), and *logical entailment* ("That means that I shall not be able to go.") Some of these meanings of meaning might be implied in the question as to the meaning of music; and if one could discover which meaning was intended one might be able to attempt a reasonable answer. For example, if it is a question as to the value of music to an individual or to a people, or if it is a question as to its significance as a cultural element, a valid answer might be forthcoming. The other meanings seem less applicable.

Another important problem of meaning in language is that of the uses of language in communication. Two types of uses may be distinguished: the one is called *informative* or *symbolic;* the other *dynamic* or *emotive*. The former use of words is to make statements; the latter, to evoke feelings and attitudes. Often the two uses occur simultaneously. If I say: "The moon will be full tonight," my intention is informative; if I say: "Do wait for the full moon!" my intention is dynamic; but if I say: "What a sight the full moon will be tonight!" my intention is of the two sorts at once. Except in the language of academic and technical information and business, almost every sort of language is permeated by emotive meanings. Furthermore it should be noted that in spoken language innumerable changes in meaning are effected, not by changes in the words used, but by the inflections of the voice or by accompanying gestures. We cannot dwell further on these problems of language, interesting as they may be in themselves; we must turn to a consideration of some of the musical implications of our discussion to this point.

Communication in Language and Music Compared

Music and language each has its own characteristic problems of material, form, and meaning or content. Some comparisons as to material and meaning have already been made; others have been hinted at; while still others will be considered later. At the moment it seems important to compare briefly communi-

[12]

cation in language and music. It has been suggested that, with comparatively few exceptions, words have primarily conventional meanings. This is especially true in the informative use of language; but in the artistic use of language as in poetry, for example, the situation is radically changed. Insofar as the poet's purpose is emotive rather than informative, he tends to the dynamic use of language. He attains his objectives largely by his choice of words not merely for their conventional meanings but also with a consideration of the range of emotional overtones which they tend to evoke. He further effects his purpose by the description of feelings by various methods: the use of names for emotions and attitudes (*anger, fear, joy*); the use of derivatives of such substantives and emotive adjectives (*passionate, tender, pretty, lovely, sublime*); and by various other similar methods but especially by the use of metaphor (*fleeting, massive, lofty, profound*). In the last instance it is important to notice that the use of metaphor depends on a supposed similarity between the feeling to be described and something in itself quite different; or between it and another feeling which is described by reference to its cause or object.[1]

In music the situation is very different. Informative communication is almost entirely precluded by the absence of conventional meanings. This leaves for the composer only the possibility of the emotive type of communication. He cannot use his materials as conventional signs to describe emotions or attitudes, but must resort to means that prove to be far more subtle and by no means less effective. His principal method involves the use of temporal, spatial, and dynamic characteristics of his materials as the basis for analogies resting on similarities between the tonal-rhythmic patterns of music and the emotive-conative patterns of his experience.

Musical Meaning as Intrinsic or Extrinsic

As we speak of communication in art the question naturally

---

[1] For a more detailed analysis of the topic see Karl Britton, *Communication*, pp. 244 ff. New York: Harcourt, Brace and Company, 1939.

arises: "What is it that is communicated?" If we could discover this in music could we not point to it as the meaning? Stated from this point of view the question: "What is the meaning of music?" is equivalent to asking: "What is communicated in music?" That music has a meaning in this sense is generally agreed; but opinions differ greatly as to just what this meaning is. The opposing views may be distinguished according to whether they hold that the meaning is extrinsic or intrinsic. In other words the question is whether music is a means of expressing or communicating realities or meanings of any kind that have their existence independent of their expression in music, or whether music is a means of expressing or communicating realities or meanings that have their existence only within the music itself.

The Autonomous Viewpoint

The theory that regards the meaning of music as intrinsic is called autonomous. According to this view the meaning of music is purely musical and as such it is to be found at all levels and in all aspects of the musical experience: in material, form, content, subject matter, expression, composition, performance, and listening. In carrying out the analysis of meaning in this sense, which I shall ordinarily refer to simply as *musical meaning,* we find there is both an intellectual and an affective side to its perception. The acid test of any rational explanation of a musical meaning is to play the passage in question and to see if the intellectual analysis checks with the felt quality.

The materials of music, the individual tones, are full of musical meanings, direct and indirect, intellectual and intuitive. The meanings of tones are identified in terms of the intrinsic qualities of tones: *pitch, loudness, quality,* and *duration.* Thus the individual tone has as a meaning a pitch, a loudness, a quality, and a duration component, each of which is labeled with an appropriate name. These are meanings which are perceived both intellectually and intuitively. Furthermore, each tone has an affective quality which we attribute to it as a meaning, and for which we often, but not always, have a name. Such meanings are rather emotive than intellectual, and can be varied over a wide range of subtly differentiated meanings by ever so slight a change in any one or all, or any combination of, the intrinsic qualities, orders, or dimensions of tone. Here I think we have the key to the solution of the problem of the affective power of music; for if, at this level, the composer or performer can control so sensitively the emotive pattern of our experience, how infinitely great are his resources at the higher levels of musical complication! But I am getting ahead of the discussion.

So far we have considered the meanings of tones more or less in isolation. A further type of musical meaning accrues to individual tones by reason of their use in a musical context. For example, a single tone has a certain felt quality or meaning which we may identify in nontechnical terms as "stationary" or "static"; the musical term for such a feeling is *tonic*. (Strike the tone D on the piano.) However, as all musicians know, the felt quality of that same tone may be changed by introducing it into a scale pattern as the second degree. It now has a different felt quality (although acoustically it is the same tone), which we recognize by calling it by a different name—*supertonic*. (Play the descending scale of C major stopping on D.) If we introduce the tone D into a scale as the third degree, we again change its felt quality to that which we call *mediant*. (Play the descending B-flat major scale stopping on D.) What we have done in each case is to change the musical meaning of the tone. The felt qualities become the conventional meanings of the respective terms *tonic, supertonic, mediant*. If we analyze this meaning situation further, we can detect a certain intellectual activity in the experience which produces another meaning which we identify when we call the tone the first, second, or third degree of the scale. The felt quality is different from the intellectual identification. If we should carry the analysis still further, I think we should find that the felt qualities which we have identified in turn give rise to, or are attended by, additional affective qualities whose presence in the experience is suggested by the fact that insofar as we can give them names these names are of a subjective nature, such as *stolidity, restlessness, sweetness.* Regardless of whether or not my analysis is strictly accurate in all details, there can be little doubt as to the wealth of resources in meaning that the composer or performer has at his disposal, even at this very elementary level, for the control of the meaning-patterns in both their intellectual and emotive use.

If time permitted we could continue the analysis through the successively higher levels of musical complication in intervals, chords, motives, themes, melodies, and entire compositions. The study of these meanings is, in a sense, one of the main purposes of all our courses in theory, harmony, counterpoint, form and analysis, and orchestration. A knowledge of them is basic to all kinds of specifically musical activities whether in composition, performance, or listening.

Material, Form, and Content as Purely Musical

According to the autonomous theory the material, form, and content of music and the attendant intrinsic meanings are all strictly musical. The meanings involve both intellectual and emotional or affective perception. The basic raw materials of music are sounds, which may be defined from a physical viewpoint in terms of vibrations, or from a psychological viewpoint in terms of sensation. Meanings in music at this level have already been discussed. Form refers to the organization of the sensory materials into perceptual groups. The content is the thematic material as it is elaborated in the composition. When the sounds of music are put together in accordance with the principles of musical composition there arise musical meanings rich in intellectual and emotional significance.

Consider the opening bars of the Brahms first symphony. The materials are the tones. The form is the way these tones are organized. The content is the specifically musical idea which is to be distinguished from any reality existing apart from the specific musical structure as it is perceived. It is embodied in the musical material and form, but is not identical with it. It cannot be expressed in words for it is not a matter of discursive knowledge. It can only be grasped in perceptive intuition. It involves thinking and feeling in terms of tones.

Let us examine the music more in detail. The movement begins with the full orchestra (except for the E-flat horns which rest for three eighths) sounding the tone C in octaves. This C is sustained in some instruments and is repeated in eighth note values in others until the fourth beat when some of the instruments move to B-flat and G as dotted quarter notes. Now there arises a new meaning by virtue of the new combination of sounds. This in turn is modified as, on the sixth beat, some of the instruments take the C-sharp, and so on. Each tonal movement produces new meanings which are conditioned by what has gone before, by what is going on at a given moment, and by some feeling of anticipation of what is to come. The analysis of the composition, in itself an intellectual process, helps to bring out the musical meanings; it is the kind of thing that goes on in analysis in all the arts.

In short, the formal structure of music is full of meanings that are intellectually perceived and emotionally felt. Not that anyone listening could get all the meaning of the music at any one hearing—or perhaps ever for that matter. One could scarcely get all the meanings at a given point in the music at one time because even in a relatively simple situation the range of possible meaning is exceedingly wide. And as the music continues, the complexity becomes so great that it is beyond the capacity of the human mind to encompass it. But each time a person hears the composition he may attend to different relations and perceive new meanings. This is doubtless part of what makes the composition of continued interest to the listener.

Composition, Performance, and Listening as Autonomous

From the autonomous viewpoint, composition is the creation of specifically musical meanings, meanings that have no existence apart from their expression in the particular composition.

The composer may be motivated in the act of composition by a desire to express an emotion arising out of a nonmusical life-situation. Indeed, he may be successful in evoking, through his music, a similar emotion in an auditor; even so, this is irrelevant to the specifically musical expressiveness of the music, to the intrinstic meaning of the music. It is the function of the composer to create compositions that will evoke in the listener an awareness of significant musical meanings, meanings that are both intellectual and emotive in character. The intellectual meanings can be analyzed and described in musical-technical terms: but emotive meanings can only be hinted at discursively. Some attempts to describe the emotive meanings have been made in the field known as musical hermeneutics. One can get the musical meaning only by studying, playing, and listening to the music. This is undoubtedly why musicians, when talking shop, revert to their musical-technical vocabulary and refer to this musical effect (or meaning) as a "Neapolitan sixth," and to that as a "transition to the submediant minor," etc. But even this is something like getting the dictionary meaning of a word, because it only suggests the generic meaning of these expressions and misses the specific meaning inherent in the particular context.

Effective musical performance is dependent, in large measure, on the individual's grasp of the autonomous musical meaning. Unfortunately, many students of music depend too much on imitation; the results remind one of a child's delivery of a poem or an oration he has learned by rote, or of an inexperienced actor's "reciting" his lines.

Good listening to music, according to the autonomous viewpoint, involves the grasping of a comparatively large amount of the musical meaning of a composition. The average listener, whether a trained musician or not, probably attends chiefly to the affective qualities of the music since they are most readily accessible to all through perceptual intuition. The untrained musician misses the less obvious meanings, chiefly intellectual in character, the apprehension of which depends largely upon technical analysis. The important point here, according to the autonomous theory, is to note that the affective qualities referred to are intrinsic. The measure of the aesthetic value is to be found in the pleasurable aspects of the experience. Criticism involves a rational evaluation of the musical experience in terms of the interaction between the organism and the tonal-rhythmic structure.

The Heteronomous Viewpoint

The theory that regards the meaning of music as extrinsic is called heteronomous. According to this view the meaning of music is in itself nonmusical, a reality existing independent of the tonal-rhythmic pattern of music, but which is referred to, expressed, or communicated by it. The most plausible of several varieties of heteronomous doctrine maintains that the independent reality is the whole wide range of man's emotive-conative impulses; that music is the art *par excellence* for the expression of man's feelings, moods, emotions, and attitudes such as yearning, wishing, desiring, willing, and striving. The composer communicates these meanings by evoking through the tonal-rhythmic patterns of his music, if not the same, at least notably similar emotive-conative states in the listener. In other words the composer translates into sounds feelings that existed in him prior to, or apart from, the actual musical composition.

Before we attempt an evaluation of the relative merits of autonomous and heteronomous theories, let us consider briefly how extrinsic meanings may be expressed in music, or, stated in other words, how ideas of realities existing independently may, through music, be evoked in the listener. We have suggested earlier that the chief means is by use of analogy. The basis of most of the analogies used is the time-space concept of movement that permeates all musical experience. That the idea of space itself is closely related to that of movement is indicated by the fact that space is sometimes referred to as "the possibility of motion." The idea of movement in space also obviously implies a time element. Thus the ideas of time, space, and movement are closely interrelated. The psychology of music has shown that these ideas are intrinsic to our experience of music.

That these concepts, as they are applied to our musical experience, are not merely metaphorical can be readily shown. Extensity, a spatial concept, is to be found in the vibratory motion of the transmitting medium which constitutes the physical nature of tones. For purposes of analysis we may think of the individual particle of air as moving to and fro within a certain spatial orbit. As the intensity is increased the orbit described by the moving particle is increased in size; its amplitude is greater. Therefore when we speak of a loud tone as bigger than a soft tone we find that we are not using the term metaphorically but literally as referring to the actual reality. In fact, some textbooks still use the term *volume* for *loudness*. If time permitted we might find it interesting to explore the situation further, but perhaps enough has been said to illustrate the point.

That tones in succession should be observed as motion has not, so far as I know, been explained psychologically. However, the facts are well known and generally acknowledged. The whole musical-technical vocabulary used to describe changes occurring in any one of the intrinsic orders of tonal organization is full of words indicating movement, including many temporal and spatial terms. Melodies move up and down in going from tone to tone. In the visual and kinesthetic fields the movement involved is generally that of a thing or an object, whereas in the auditory field it is not. This difference has led to the notion that movement in music is a kind of "idealized" or "pure" movement. Although I cannot discuss the matter in greater detail now, I should like to suggest that, in my opinion, a more tangible physical basis could be found for our perception of movement in music with a closer investigation of the spatial characteristics of sounds. I shall cite only a single example of what I mean. I have already pointed out that a soft tone is smaller than a loud tone. If a soft tone is followed by a loud tone, similar in pitch, quality, and duration, the space occupied by the second tone is greater than that of the first; and the change from the smaller to the larger space involves movement in a very real sense. This movement would be comparable to that in the field of vision if a rubber balloon of a certain size were suddenly inflated to a perceptibly larger size. Or, if a single tone were gradually increased in intensity the increase in extensity would resemble the gradual inflation of a balloon.

At any rate, whether movement in music is real or illusional, it undoubtedly provides the basis for the expression by analogy of anything nonmusical that is itself characterized by movement in any way. This principle of movement, if we may call it that, has been exploited in various ways in different periods of musical history. Its clearest use is to be found in music with text. In the sixteenth century, for example, words of movement such as "ascending" and "descending" were often simply set to ascending or descending melodic movements. Numerous other words suggestive of spatial or temporal ideas of movement were represented in music by similar analogies—height, depth, speed, slowness, stepping, jumping, shortness, and length. This sort of procedure, which may be traced in considerable detail throughout the Baroque period, is especially prominent in the works of J. S. Bach, as has been amply demonstrated in the monumental volume of André Pirro, *L'Esthétique de J. S. Bach*.[2] The perception of the analogies between the music and text here is essentially an intellectual matter. Most of them would pass unnoticed unless they were called especially to the listener's attention.

Of course, other types of allusion to extrinsic meanings have been used than those based on movement. An extreme case is to be found in the Bach cantata "And Thou Shalt Love the Lord Thy God," in which as many as five different types of reference have been used simultaneously: (1) The fugal treatment refers to canonical law; (2) the chorale melody "These Are the Holy Ten Commandments," used as thematic material, alludes to the Ten Commandments; (3) the occurrence of

[2] Paris: Librairie Fischbacher, 1907.

the melody canonically in augmentation in the bass suggests the fundamental importance of the Ten Commandments in life; (4) the trumpet, used to state the theme, represents the majesty or even the voice of God; and (5) the tenfold repetition of the theme is a perhaps almost too subtle reference to the number 10. If the music is good, it cannot be because of these references to extrinsic meanings, it must almost rather be in spite of them; and yet one's enjoyment of the music may be enhanced by an awareness of them.

Of much greater importance in the problem of the meaning of music is the exploitation of the dynamic elements in music in the representation or expression of emotion. This type of expression in music depends upon similarities between the temporal and spatial patterns of movement in music as heard and the dynamic structure of the emotions as felt, and the transfer of perceptual qualities of experience from one sense modality to another, from hearing to feeling and *vice versa*. Thus we may say that the music sounds the way the emotions feel. The transfer from one sense modality to another does not seem so strange or mysterious on close examination as it does at first glance. Psychologists have pointed out that auditory sensation is intimately connected with tactile sensation. In fact it has been suggested that the organs of the inner ear developed phylogenetically from some more general type of tactile structure, so that one may not be too far wrong in regarding the sensation of sound as a very highly refined type of tactile response.

Although attempts at this type of representation of emotional content may be traced in the history of music from the sixteenth century on, its use became particularly prominent in the music of the Romantic era. Here, at the risk of oversimplifying a rather complex situation, we may say that in general the composer set himself to the task of expressing in music the entire gamut of man's emotions, moods, and conative impulses. Reverberations of this viewpoint are still prevalent in contemporary writings on musical aesthetics. That music can, within limits, accomplish such an objective, is beyond doubt. This has been demonstrated on countless occasions in all kinds of functional music and in all types of music with texts.   But the question still remains in all such music and in pure instrumental music as to whether or not this kind of expression represents the primary meaning of the music.

Before turning to a consideration of this question, I should like to comment briefly on the activities of composition, performance, and listening, from the heteronomous viewpoint. Composition, according to this theory, is the translation of so-called "life-feelings" into tone; performance is primarily a matter of the performer's attempting to understand these meanings and to interpret them through his performance so as to evoke similar feelings in the listener; and listening is a process of attending to the music so as to permit the evocation of emotive-conative states similar to those of the composer prior to his translation of them into tone.

Partial Reconciliation of Opposing Viewpoints

The truth of the situation is to be found in a partial reconciliation of the two extreme viewpoints on the basis that intrinsic, autonomous musical meanings are direct and primary, and afford the principal criteria of musical value; and that extrinsic, heteronomous meanings are indirect and secondary, and can afford only subordinate criteria of musical value.   Intrinsic musical meanings are direct and primary because they tend to be at the center of attention in the highest type of composition, performance, and listening.   Extrinsic musical meanings are indirect and secondary because they tend to be in the background of attention in the highest type of composition, performance, and listening.   In this interpretation of the situation, I believe adequate answers can be found to most, if not all, significant questions concerning the meaning of music.

In closing, I should like to point out that the interpretation of the problem of meaning in music which I have sketched in barest outline provides for the functioning of a wide range of conceptual and perceptual meaning in the musical experience of the individual as he operates in the process or event which

I have identified as a particular instance of music. Let us consider an extreme case to illustrate how knowledge of facts in themselves nonmusical may work to enrich meaningfully the musical experience. Last week I attended an organ recital at which the organist made a few comments about each composition before he played it. Of a *Fantasia in F minor* by Mozart he said that it was originally written for a mechanical instrument and that it was transcribed for organ. As I listened to the performance of the piece I found meanings in the music that arose from my knowledge of the facts mentioned about it. To some extent the experience became more meaningful. This may be a poor example, but it suggests something of how matters in themselves extrinsic to the music as such may color the experience and add to the richness of its meaning. This bit of meaning, though obviously indirect and secondary in my experience, contributed something to it. The example also illustrates how the perceiving self contributes to the meaning of every musical experience and suggests how extensive the potential range of meaning is. And yet, in all instances, intrinsic meanings are primary; extrinsic, secondary.

One point which I should like especially to emphasize is that the peculiar expressive quality which we ordinarily attribute to the music is an essential meaningful element in music. Most aestheticians seem to be referring to this when they speak of the beauty of the work of art. Psychologically it is a quality of the experience evoked within the organism by the objective stimulus. It is the part of music which musician and layman can most readily follow in listening, and yet which they have the most difficulty in identifying discursively. One may simply say the music is more or less expressive according to the quality he perceives. Another may resort to adjectives related to space-time-movement concepts: vigorous, forceful, graceful, elegant, flowing, sparkling, scintillating, full, heavy, thin, and the like. Still another may use terms of a more pronounced emotional character: tragic, gay, sweet, sentimental, exalted, earthy, morbid, sad, happy, and so on. Still another may speak in terms of more violent passion: love, hate, anger, ravishment, ecstasy, grief, misery, etc.   If anyone should be interested in following out the possibilities, I should suggest that he examine *Roget's Thesaurus* in which he will find hundreds of pages of lists of English words and phrases, an amazing number of which can be meaningfully applied to the description of music.   Those terms which we can apply without diverting our attention from the music to nonmusical affairs of life point to essential meaningful elements in music, and are intrinsic meanings.   Those terms which do indicate a diversion of the attention from the music to nonmusical interests point to meanings which, if they are musical at all, are indirect and secondary. Insofar as they are relevant, that is, insofar as they do not turn the experience into an experience of an entirely different sort, one not aesthetic, but religious, practical, or what not, they may broaden and enrich the musical experience.   If one is able to keep clearly in mind the distinction between intrinsic and extrinsic meaning, he should be able to find his way about in the many knotty problems of the meaning of music.

Music and Life

When a composer writes over a note or a phrase in the score the word *espressivo,* indicating that it is to be played with expression, just what does this mean from the point of view of performance?   Ordinarily it means that the performer is to produce a tone rich in overtones, he is to pay particular attention to the intensity of the tone, he is expected to make unusually sensitive adjustments in the phrasing, but more than anything else, if the instrument permits, it means that he is to use a vibrato.   To put it bluntly, to play a tone *espressivo* in general means to play it *vibrato.*   This simple device may have a profound meaning.   In order to suggest something of what I refer to I should like to analyze the situation in some detail.   I begin by saying it is expressive of life; it means life. How is this possible? you ask.   By way of analogy, an analogy based on movement.   How do we detect life except by evidences of movement?   I once found an opossum in my garage.

When I first saw it I thought it was feigning death because it made no movement. But as I poked it I found it was stiff and cold—dead. We may carry the analysis into as much detail as may be desired, but perhaps what I have said is enough to show how the slight movement of the tone characteristic of the vibrato is felt as life. We say the tone has life; without the vibrato it may be described meaningfully as "lifeless," "flat," or "dead." It should not be necessary to point out that pieces in fast tempo and with plenty of notes are called "lively." This is a metaphor, based on an analogy of movement, but it is very intimate in our inmost emotional feeling, for the bodily states most characteristic of our internal feeling of life are likewise shot through with movement. When we awaken from a deep sleep we may not be able to tell for an instant whether we are alive or dead. But as we "come to our senses" and manage to start moving around, we are able to decide that we are alive. I mean this seriously, for in both a superficial and a profound sense our conception of life depends on an awareness of movement. Therefore it should not be surprising that music, with all its infinite resources of movement, should be an extremely vital art.

THE LIBRARY OF CONGRESS

THE LOUIS CHARLES ELSON MEMORIAL FUND

THE COMMONWEALTH OF ART

A LECTURE DELIVERED BY

CURT SACHS

Visiting Professor of Music, New York University
Consultant, New York Public Library

IN

THE WHITTALL PAVILION

OF THE LIBRARY OF CONGRESS

APRIL 25, 1949

Washington, D. C.

1950

THE COMMONWEALTH OF ART

AESTHETICS is defined by Webster as "the branch of philosophy dealing with the beautiful"; by the Oxford Dictionary as "belonging to the appreciation of the beautiful"; by the American College Dictionary as "the science which deduces from nature and taste the rules and principles of art." Or else, we might simply call it an attitude towards art, based on knowledge and orderly thinking.

However we define it, there is something tragic about aesthetics. However we define it, we expect this discipline to trace the hidden laws under which the ever-present and ever-changing conditions of man create an ever-new art. And we hope for a unified conception from on high, in which all styles and even all individual masters would appear as different but necessary parts of a meaningful and well-organized whole.

Alas, we hope in vain. So far, the systems of aesthetical thinking, from the times of Confucius and Plato down to the twentieth century, have been disconcertingly controversial. They disapprove of at least a good half of all the works that art has created to this day, on the ground that these works disagree with the principles of good and sterling art. For they gauge art by uniform standards; against what they pretend, they build their theories on the drifting quicksand of their own tastes, conditioned as the tastes are by their personalities, generations, surroundings, nationalities, and even outright political opinions—much as are the artists of whom they speak.

Such an attitude is normative; it gives laws where it should find them and would be extremely dangerous in its narrow-minded arrogance, were it not that the creative artist does what he is compelled to do and laughs at the self-styled Solon.

An esthetic approach that shies from being normative must of necessity draw its conclusions, less from the author's experience, taste, and subsequent thinking than from the facts provided by thousands of years of art creation. This does not mean that the philosopher should yield to the historian. It rather implies that aesthetics should come from the fusion of philosophical and historical thinking. The philosopher must learn to forget about his individual taste and experience and realize that, on the contrary, the decisive fact is the overwhelming variety of tastes, from the Older Stone Age to our present day, documented in the innumerable works that the historian has uncovered and interpreted.

In preparing such a fusion of thought, I speak of the Commonwealth of Art, not of just one individual art.[1]

This title is not meant to cover the many doubtful attempts at combining different arts in a common effort. It also shall not cover the doubtful cooperation of several arts, such as playing phonograph records in museums as an additional auditive stimulus to visitors prepared for visual experiences; or such as, the other way around, offering impressive murals as an additional stimulus to musical audiences. Nor shall it cover the just as doubtful or at best quite personal transfers from art to art that we know as color hearing and vowel seeing and that psychology describes as synesthesias.

The Commonwealth of Art is rather meant as a problem of history: as a discussion of whether, why, and how the individual histories of painting, music, sculpting, poetry, dancing, and building, when put above each other, are almost congruent, progressing to the left and the right and forwards and backwards with their sister arts. And it is also meant as a problem of philosophy: as a discussion why, beyond the appeal

---

[1] Curt Sachs, *The Commonwealth of Art,* New York, W. W. Norton, 1946.

to different senses, the various arts meet in a common spirit which does not unveil itself completely unless we treat the arts as one.

Such discussions rest necessarily on a comparison of the histories of various arts, indeed, of the arts themselves. Is such comparison admissible, and if so, is it possible? Is there a common factor and *tertium comparationis* in creations as different as a church building, a symphony, a stage performance, a dance, a novel, a landscape painting? Would not any such comparison of necessity be superficial, arbitrary, or at best metaphorical?

This it would be indeed unless the comparer went back to the one elementary fact: that the psychophysical complex that we call art has incomparable as well as comparable components. In the main, the work of art has three components: its meaning—emotional or otherwise—is one; the material, with its specific conditions, is another; and the third is the technical act that conveys meaning to matter.

Two of these components—material and working technics—are the individual and exclusive property of only one of the arts: the architect creates in stone and steel, the musician in tones, the dancer in his body, the poet in words, the painter in colors. And he who wants to compare can certainly not straightway cross from bricks to words or gestures, to colors or tones. But the meaning and soul that the artist infuses into his work are beyond technique and material, beyond all writing, carving, and building, beyond melodic intervals, verse meters, and tints. It is an eloquent message from man to man and has therefore its law in man himself—in man as he feels and is at a certain moment of history and in a certain social or national habitat. Much in the same way as our gestures, words, and eyes unite in expressing the same emotion of our self, to whatever different fields of physiology they may belong, the arts reflect man's will and reaction however different they may appear to the senses.   And since they emanate from the same center, they can, indeed they must, be compared.

Emerson's *Essay on History* [2] says in a similar spirit: "To the senses what more unlike than an ode of Pindar, a marble Centaur, the Peristyle of the Parthenon and the last actions of Phocion?   Yet do these various external expressions proceed from one national mind. . . .   What is to be inferred from these facts but this: that in a certain state of thought is the common origin of very diverse works?   It is the spirit and not the fact that is identical. . . .   The roots of all things are in man."

It should be understood, however, that the "expression" in art that Emerson mentions and that I myself refer to, is never spontaneous; the master who paints a nightmare does not shake while he is doing so, nor does the composer of a funeral march lament and cry.   Art shapes emotions only after a long process of filtering and sublimation.

The medium that filters and sublimates might be described as the artist's personal, national, or generational attitude.

Artists' attitudes, ever different and ever changing, dodge definition and neat classification.   They are as motley, manifold, inscrutable as man himself.   Still, there is a rather reliable method that grants a rough orientation.   It consists in describing the extremes of attitude on either side or, to put it in a simile, in establishing both the freezing and the boiling point in order to gauge the numberless shades of temperature somewhere between them at their proper places.   It would not be a bad idea to catch at this simile and call the two extremes in artists' attitudes "cold" and "hot" instead of using one of those philosophical terminologies which ask for a long winded explanation (like "classical" and "nonclassical" or even my own dualism "ethos" and "pathos").

But even terms as comparatively unequivocal as "cold" and "hot" can hardly be defined beyond mistake and uncertainty. Instead of trying to define them, we had better study the scope

---

[2] Ralph Waldo Emerson, *Essays,* New York, A. L. Burt, s. a., pp. 12–14.

of cold and warmer attitudes and the different qualities that they impart to style.

Hot artists stress emotion, passion, frenzy, ecstasy, while colder masters hate the display of emotion and ignore or temper down all vehement passion. Not long before 400 B. C., Socrates marked the end of such a frigid age when he forced some sculptors in Athens to admit that statues, as the effigies of living humans, ought after all to show a few of the emotions that every human face betrays. It marked the beginning of another hot age when, around 1600, an Italian coined a novel word, *lo stile rappresentativo,* to label an unprecedented musical language that depicted deepest feeling and made the audiences cry from compassion and sadness.

Either one, the cold as well as the hot attitude entail a number of qualities, which confront their opposites in a similar dualism.

On the colder side, the human approach is more reserved and the artist withdraws from personal expression. He himself does not wish to impose his dreams and sufferings upon the beholder; and he also refrains from rendering himself to the personal, individual concerns of his models. In this attitude, he might go all the way to the frigidity of the soulless gods of the Periclean age.

Such flight from the unique and the personal must lead on the cooler side to the interest in types, that is in abstractions which emphasize restful permanence against the ever-changing uniqueness of the merely personal. One finds the examples in the one thousand years of Doric temples, in the immutable patterns of the *commedia dell'arte,* or in the depersonalized Lutheran chorale.

In the strife for types and permanence, the cooler artists drop not only the personal, but also the accidental. They stick to all traits immanent and inherent, which must not be changed by anything derived from without, not by atmospheric conditions or light and shadow, and not even by man's age:

[9]
29

Periclean statues show ageless gods; and the Oriental painter refuses to bestow shadows on his figures.

One consequence is that the cooler artist, more than the hotter one, desires beauty. I hesitate to use the word, because it is entirely beyond definition and so hopelessly worn out that it hardly stands any serious handling. And yet we must confront the trend that it covers, the trend to eliminating all individual flaws until the type is pure in its perfection. It seems to be this perfection that the senses perceive as beauty.

Perfection of the typical is achieved by an art that we call idealistic. It is an act of idealism when the painter Lomazzo demands in 1584 "that portraits should exalt the dignity and greatness of their models and suppress the natural imperfections of their subjects." It is idealism when Jacques-Louis David, the leading French painter around 1800, exclaims: "What matters truth if the poses are noble?"

I hardly need emphasize that the element of form in its own right has an overwhelming importance in the strife for types, objective aloofness, and all-valid laws. These laws are so much more all-valid as they have their roots in mathematical ratios. Thus Christopher Wren, the builder of St. Paul's in London, could say that in art "always the true test is natural or geometrical beauty"; the painter Charles Lebrun, chief decorator of the palace of Versailles, demanded that painting "be founded upon a demonstrable science," namely, geometry; and Father Mersenne, the greatest musicologist of the seventeenth century, who distrusted imagination, sensuous perception, and any judgment based on them, averred again and again that music was a mere part of mathematics.

Turning to the other, hot extreme of our scale, we see the impersonal replaced by a personal attitude. The artist makes common cause with his models. He represents himself, as Berlioz did when he wrote his *Symphonie phantastique* to introduce his audience to the torments and the obsessing *idée fixe* that he suffered from an as yet unrequited love for an English actress. Or else, the artist yields himself to his models, as Wagner did when he cried because at the end of "Lohengrin" Elsa had to die.

In so emotional, personal an attitude, the artist is much more interested in the individual than in the typical, in the unique than in the permanent, and hence in moving, transitory stages rather than in frozen statics. Under this impact, a "warm" portrait reflects not only a definite person instead of just a god or a king, but also a person at a definite age, indeed, at a definite moment and in a definite mood under definite atmospheric conditions. A phenomenon like shadow is no longer accidental but on the contrary essential. In the Baroque, even a building is meant to get additional life from the ever-changing shadows that mould its outlines and surfaces and stress the suggestion of three-dimensional space.

What these masters produce can be extremely beautiful. But their beauty is not the kind that stems from the elimination of individual flaws and the perfection of typical patterns. And it is a beauty ruthlessly sacrificed when it threatens convincing truth. As Hogarth said: "Were I to paint the character of Charon, I would thus distinguish his make from that of a common man's; and in spite of the word low, venture to give him a broad pair of shoulders, and spindle shanks, whether I had the authority of an ancient statue, or basso relievo, for it or not."

To the idealists or, as Hogarth called them, the nature menders, he opposed a strict naturalism. Nature-mending, to him and to his fellow-naturalists in every country and century, is untrue, is a lie; its patterns are soulless, and so is its very beauty; and the thing "in itself" that Plato and Kant exalt is nonexistent. Man cannot live or be understood without his proper environment, be it factual or spiritual. He cannot live and must not be depicted without the three-dimensional space

[11]

in which he breathes and moves. Nor, the naturalistic poets add, does he live outside the social situation that conditions his thoughts and his actions. Let it be ugly, evil, malodorant—at least it is true; and honest truth is better than mendacious beauty.

Structure, though never absent, plays a minor role in such an attitude. The artist of the hotter camp resents the emphasis on form as an interference with the illusion of life. For nature hardly ever arranges its creations in geometrical patterns. To him, all obtrusive form seems intentional, artificial, and untrue, delaying all movement and destroying the informality of nature. The Frenchman Noverre, one of the greatest ballet masters of all time, wrote in 1760 against the conventional choreographers and scolded them for clinging to strictly symmetrical arrays which would never allow five nymphs on the right and seven on the left side. "But," he asks, "was not the result cold exercise instead of spirited action?" And in this sentence we have the direct connection of the concept of symmetrical form with our very word cold.

It must be understood that this manifold dualism is chiefly a matter of method to deepen our insight and to guide our judgment. It does not imply that all the qualities on the left and the right of the versus sign must necessarily meet in every single work of art. This is not, and never will be, the case. The hotter phase of the high Renaissance, for instance, can hardly be called naturalistic, and architecture will even in naturalistic periods seldom swerve from static symmetry. This is the reason why no two styles are ever identical, even if they move in the same direction. And it also explains why, as a rule, no style is actually just cold or hot: by far the majority of styles live somewhere between the extremes, in regions that we might classify as cool or tepid or warm.

But even so modified a conception of style, though indispensable for methodical purposes, can be dangerous from the viewpoint of historical evaluation. It still suggests that in a certain period all works of art be shaped in the same spirit and in similar forms, and that they reach a new style with different forms and a different spirit through a "transitional" style. This is not tenable. There are no transitional styles, for the very simple reason that there are no lasting styles either. Every style moves on, develops, waxes, fades, and differs today from what it was yesterday and will be tomorrow. Therefore, we should insist that a style is not cool or hot, but moves in a cool or a hot direction.

This continuous flow, however, should not be seen as a straight forward-movement like that of a steamship at sea, but rather like the consistent, purposeful zigzag-veering that we know as the course of a sailboat. Art—every art—moves alternately to the warmer and to the cooler side; it changes direction when coolness threatens to stiffen in academic frigidity, and again when warmth threatens to dissolve all art in an overheated chaos. Did we not quite recently, in the 1920's, witness such sudden veering in all the arts from a noisy naturalism and expressionism to a somewhat coolish neoclassicism, with an overemphasis on craft and form and an underemphasis on emotion?

In those centuries of western history which our eye encompasses, one such phase lasts roughly a generation or a third of a century, seldom less, but sometime more. For this reason I speak of "generational reversals." It should be understood, however, that this does not imply that a man's whole style is determined by the date of his birth. The year in which he is born determines his first style only; the second and third of the customary three styles that critical analysis grants the great masters are unmistakably the styles of further generations; unwittingly, the masters obey rather than command; they obey, not the example of younger men, but the mysterious trends of changing times.

Veering from one direction to the opposite direction in the span of approximately a third of a century cannot account for the whole complicated course that art has steered in the four or more thousand years spread out before our eyes. The mere existence of style-concepts as generally accepted as Hellenistic, Romanesque, Gothic, Renaissance, and Baroque proves that periods much longer than a third of a century and even longer than a full hundred years can have a character decisively different from those of the centuries before and after. All of them show the imprints of alternatively cooler and hotter generations: the Renaissance, to mention one, forces before our eyes the alternation of a still, serene beginning down to the 1460's, the restless, emotional, dramatic end of the century, the classicistic reaction of the early sixteenth with Raphael at the helm, and the hotter middle of the century with Michelangelo as the representative power.

But is there not a similar alternation from style to style above the generational reversals? Indeed: Hellenism with the stress on Corinthian elegance, on movement, on passion is hotter than the preceding style of Greece; Flamboyant Gothic with the violence of its anti-harmonic surge upward, the all-side projection of its parts and particles, and the redundant profusion of its decorative details, is hotter than the thirteenth century; Baroque is hotter than the Renaissance, both in its popular concept of unbalanced exaggeration and in its actual facets, in naturalism, integration, and dramatic conception. This twofold alternation, in generational reversals as well as in larger style periods, can perhaps be grasped in a simile: we undergo a ceaseless alternation of warmer days and cooler nights, but also, in a much wider span, a ceaseless alternation of warmer summers and cooler winters. And as a rule, a cool summer night is still essentially warmer than a winter day, though nights are supposed to be cooler than days. This would explain or at least make acceptable that the cooler phase in a generational reversal is often warmer than the hotter phases in some other, basically colder style.

It even seems that we must visualize the existence of still larger cycles superimposed on these styles, indeed that every two of them are the phases cold and hot of some bigger cycle. Romanesque and Gothic unite in the complex of the High Middle Ages; Renaissance and Baroque join in what—as a makeshift—I dare to call the Greater Renaissance; the subsequent shorter periods, the Sentimental Age and Storm and Stress, Classicism and Romanticism, Naturalism and Impressionism, are all inseparable and join in what I called the Greater Romanticism. Again, the Greater Romanticism and the Greater Renaissance stand as the "Later Ages" strictly against the Middle Ages. They are characterized by an outspoken individualism and the three-dimensional concepts of perspective (in the visual arts) and chordal harmony (in music), where the Middle Ages had been collectivistic and basically two-dimensional. And what we witness today is not evolution, but very definitely a revolution, a ruthless breaking away from every trend and goal of the Later Ages between the early Renaissance and the dying Romanticism.

All the arts share in these reversals, styles, and cycles. None of them actually lags behind the others: Gothic music is coincident in time with Gothic architecture, and Baroque poetry coincides with Baroque painting. But there is clearly a different accent on the various arts in different phases of a style. Even without the impacts of general trends, the arts have different natural temperatures.

Building is by nature cooler than music: it is so impersonal that nonprofessionals are hardly interested in the names of architects; Chartres cathedral rests as anonymous as Rockefeller Center. Architecture is moored in the soil, therefore preponderantly static, and in its stationary nature more than any other art structural and even symmetrical; it is meant to serve innumerable generations with ever-changing tastes; and though it can convey emotion, it is but slightly emotional in itself.

Music appears to be in a quite different situation: it is so personal that music lovers are interested in biography much more than we historians like them to be. Progressing in time it is basically dynamic; it is emotional almost by definition; and no other art would tolerate forms as free as the phantasy, the rhapsody, and the toccata.

Sculpture has its place not far from architecture; even the most dynamic masters, like Michelangelo and Rodin, pay a heavy tribute to its static, statuesque laws. Painting and poetry keep to the side of music: the painters are free to snare transitory phases of motion and to describe the momentary appearance of objects under the impact of shadow, light, and air. Epic and dramatic poetry rely on action, change, development; and lyrical verses compete with music and pictures in catching the delicate shades of the soul. And both the arts of painting and poesy are almost as emotional as music is.

As a consequence of such difference in natural temperature, it is only logical that every art has a different reaction to impulses from either the cold or the hot side. A cold art would still be cool when the temperature goes up, and a hot art would still be warm when the wind blows icy.

But even this is not yet the whole truth. History shows that, like flowers and animals, the cooler arts thrive best in cooler periods, and the warmer arts, in warmer periods. We have quite a few weighty examples at hand. The best known is the history of the arts in the nineteenth century. The climate of romanticism, naturalism, impressionism was very, very warm. Consequently, it provided a rarely paralleled galaxy of great and greatest composers, painters, poets—from Beethoven to Debussy, from Turner to Hodler, from Goethe to Ibsen. But architecture was wintering. Instead of creating styles of its own, it lapsed from a Roman Revival into a Greek Revival, from a Gothic Revival into a Renaissance Revival, and finally into the unspeakable depravation that the English call Edwardian, the Germans Wilhelminian, and the French *le style Emile Loubet.*

A parallel example is the powerful climax of the Middle Ages in the fourteenth century. The musicians find in it an unprecedented bloom of composition with entirely novel ideas, sounds, and techniques and with epochal masters of the size of Philippe de Vitry, Machault, and Landino. Literature had its heyday with Dante, Petrarch, and Boccaccio; with Juan Ruiz and Eustache Deschamps; with Gower and Chaucer. And the painters boast of Giotto's novel naturalism, the Sienese lyricism, and the youthful loveliness of Wilhelm of Cologne. But architecture fails us; the builders led to the last, exaggerated phase of the Gothic style, which the French have called Flamboyant, and the English, Perpendicular. They present us with evolution, not, as the painters and poets, with full-fledged revolution.

Quite similar was the situation in ancient Greece from Alexander's century to the Roman conquest.

The other way around, one should mention the curious case of the Renaissance in Italy. Around 1425, the new movement started with Brunelleschi's buildings in Florence and led into the Baroque in the days of Palladio and Vignola. In between, we find architectural geniuses of the size of Alberti, Bramante, and Michelangelo: architecture was the leading art despite the eminent work of sculptors and painters. And it led Italian art so far into the cooler regions of expression that the country was unable to produce any musician of note: during a full hundred and fifty years, it imported composers from the north, from Burgundy, Flanders, Brabant, and Holland. Not before the 1560's did Italian musicians emerge and terminate the world domination of the Netherlands.

Our three examples come from different kinds of phases. Two are hot: the nineteenth and the fourteenth century. They conclude two large cycles, the Later and the Middle Ages. One is cooler: the fifteenth century. It introduces the Renaissance and, with the Renaissance, the whole cycle of the Later Ages. And there seems a further law of evolution to consider.

This law would be well illustrated by the art of children (though any reference to their behavior is not altogether flawless in historical research). What our boys and girls endeavor to draw is inspired by knowledge rather than by visual perception of things. They outline sums of details, not integrated wholes—a head on a neck on a torso on two legs on two feet, but not a unified, organic man as he appears to the eyes; or trees and a stream and a house and a little dog, but not an actual landscape. The man they draw would at best be "being," but neither acting nor feeling; the sun, a circle with radiating beams around it, might perch in the sky; but it would not light the scene or make the objects cast their shadows. Children's art is on the side of essence, station, coolness. Only later do we learn to observe, to draw what we actually see, and to become interested in appearance, coherence, action, emotion.

In a similar way, it seems to be a common law that styles and larger cycles begin with a cooler phase. The archaic styles of Sumer, Egypt, Greece, and the Middle Ages are cool, insulating, stationary, and hence preponderantly architectural. There is little in the other arts to match the pyramids of Gizeh, the Doric temple, and the cathedral of Pisa. But aged, matured civilizations differ: the colorful art of the eighteenth Egyptian dynasty is warm, dynamic, attempting at group formation, and preponderantly pictorial (we do not know about their music); the late Minoan in Crete is similar; and the same is true of later Grecian art.

And therewith, it seems, we have found a final law: all styles and cycles, whatever their lengths, develop from static to dynamic goals, from coolness to warmth, from essence to appearance, from the lead of architecture to the lead of music.

Here are a few of the aesthetical facts that the history of art discloses. I shall not try to derive their lawful and consistent rhythm from politics, social conditions, biological changes in man, or whatever the causality fiends hold in readiness. We have yet no insight into the hidden forces that control the march of art.

But though we do not know these forces, we know that the march of art is a steady alternation of opposite trends, comparable to our own marching in steady alternation of the left and the right foot and in a continual shift of balance. Whoever takes sides in this regular alternation confuses the issue. Only those who see that the right foot has the same duties and rights as the left foot can hope to understand the life of art.

THE LIBRARY OF CONGRESS

THE LOUIS CHARLES ELSON MEMORIAL FUND

MUSIC AS THE LANGUAGE OF EMOTION

A LECTURE DELIVERED BY

CARROLL C. PRATT

Professor of Psychology, Princeton University

IN

THE WHITTALL PAVILION

OF THE LIBRARY OF CONGRESS

DECEMBER 21, 1950

Washington, D. C., 1952

MUSIC AS THE LANGUAGE
OF EMOTION

ALL FORMS of art are thought of as involving some kind or degree of emotion either through direct arousal or through indirect representation. In this regard music is often assigned first place. "Music stands quite alone," said Schopenhauer in his penetrating treatise on art. "It is cut off from all the other arts. It does not express a particular and definite joy, sorrow, anguish, delight, or mood of peace, but joy, sorrow, anguish, delight, peace of mind *themselves,* in the abstract, in their essential nature, without accessories, and therefore without their customary motives. Yet it enables us to grasp and share them in their full quintessence."

It is not an easy matter to explain what it means psychologically to say that music is the language of emotion. The problem is no easier if the same question is raised, as it has been ever since the days of Greek philosophy, about emotion in relation to any other form of art. The Aristotelian concept of *Katharsis* in connection with the drama has been taken to mean the purging of emotion by the engrossment of the spectator in the events portrayed on the stage. The context in which *Katharsis* is treated makes it impossible to know, however, whether Aristotle meant to imply that the emotion is actually aroused, or whether it is only represented or known by inference, or whether perhaps it is merely grasped intellectually as the sort of experience that real people would have if they were involved in the drama. In the tomes written since Aristotle, confusion has only become worse confounded, so that today the various answers to the question as to how emotion is related to art, and especially to music, are all more or less unsatisfactory.

The difficulty of the question can best be appreciated by noting briefly what a few of the better known answers have run up against from the point of view of modern psychology. These answers are not necessarily wrong, but neither are they quite right, for they make assumptions about the operation and location of emotion which are either dubious or leave the question unsettled.

EMBODIMENT OF EMOTION

Music may be a language of emotion by way of the embodiment in external tonal form of the qualities which define mood and feeling. Literature on aesthetics is full of references to art as the objectification of the subjective, the projection by the artist of his inner life into the durable media of sound and color. If such phrases are understood as figures of speech, no objection can be taken to them. Aesthetics is not yet a science, whatever else it may be; and writers in this field may be allowed the license of picturesque words. If taken literally, however, the notion that music can embody or contain an emotion is psychological nonsense. Emotions can only be located inside the individual who has them. They do not lie around outside the living organism, in spite of the curious introspection of the invalid who, in reply to the question as to whether she was in pain, said that there was certainly a pain somewhere in the room, but she was not sure whether it was hers or not.

In recent years the famous James-Lange theory of emotion has been vigorously attacked for reasons which are of no direct concern to the present topic; but no one has expressed any doubt about the theory's basic tenet that felt emotions are closely bound up with bodily or organic processes. The fact that the theory states the obvious in no way detracts from the brilliance and originality of William James in giving it precise formulation. Where are emotions? Clearly the only possible answer is that emotions have their locus within the bodily structure.

They cannot exist in some medium outside the individual. It is therefore impossible for any form of art to *embody* an emotion, unless such a phrase is intended to be merely figurative in meaning. Emotions are an awareness of bodily disturbances. These disturbances or changes, as James said, "are so indefinitely numerous and subtle that the entire organism may be called a sounding-board, which every change of consciousness, however slight, may make reverberate." Music may be a sounding-board for the *representation* of emotion, but an emotion which is thus portrayed is no real emotion at all, and so cannot furnish an answer to the question as to the manner in which real emotions find their way into music. Art as the embodiment of emotion is merely a manner of speaking.

AROUSAL OF EMOTION

The problem would be solved at once if it could be demonstrated that music aroused real emotions in the listener. *Solvitur audiendo.* The difficulty is that the solution is not found by listening to music, for many lovers of the art which Schopenhauer placed on the lonely high pedestal insist that in listening to music they do not themselves experience real emotion. The music in some elusive manner has an emotional significance, but the experience is said to be in no way comparable to the real emotions of everyday life. The more sophisticated the listener, the more emphatic he is likely to become in his assertion that he himself is not filled with joy or sadness by the sounds of great music, although he may be equally emphatic in his conviction that such moods are somehow related to the music which he has heard. The music may be joyful. It may be sad. But in neither case does he, the listener, experience joy or sadness. He likes the music. He admires the skill of the performers and the genius of the composer. But he himself is not bowed down with grief nor lifted up with joy.

It must be admitted that the theory of arousal of real emotion does indeed apply to some listeners. Studies designed to dis-

cover the effects of music on listeners show that a few individuals do actually experience what seem to be real emotions.
They feel elated, depressed, melancholy, excited and in other
various ways deeply moved by what they hear. In extreme
cases they have a genuine emotional bath in a flood of sound.
These have been called subjective listeners. They listen with
their viscera. But these individuals constitute a minority
among the lovers of music. To them the theory of emotional
arousal seems to apply, but the same theory leaves out of
account entirely the large number of music lovers who are
keenly sensitive to the emotional qualities of music but who
deny the subjective origin of such qualities.

Except for those individuals whose visceral sounding-board
is set into actual vibration by music, it is reasonably certain that
musical experience ordinarily stops some considerable distance
this side of real bodily emotion, otherwise a strange psychological incompatibility would at times be set into operation.
The lover of music who has high regard, say, for the slow movement of the *Eroica,* listens with rapt pleasure to a performance
by a fine orchestra under an inspired conductor. He agrees
with those critics who call that particular movement, especially
the fugal passage, the most intense and poignant expression
of grief in any form of art. Now, if the effect on him were one
of real and powerful grief, it would be difficult to understand
how at the same time he could enjoy the experience. The
dilemma is easily and quickly resolved. He *does* enjoy the
experience, but he does *not* suffer real grief. The sadness of
the music is genuine and is there for him who has ears to hear,
but there is no sadness of the viscera.

If an emotion is to be real, the organs of the body, and in
particular the viscera, must be made to vibrate. For most
listeners music makes an appeal to the mind, not to the body.
The good lover of music can sit through the second act of
Tristan and Isolde without a blush, without the slightest trace
of embarrassment. He may derive keen pleasure from the last

movement of Tchaikovsky's *VIth,* whereas if his body were involved he might find that movement an ordeal to be sweated out to the last dying gasps of the bass viols. The rage of many of the passages in Beethoven's scherzos is spiritual, not visceral; and the melancholy of Mozart is the quintessence of all sadness, but in the abstract, without any bodily concomitants or motives.

The moods of music, or the *tertiary qualities,* as they are sometimes called, unquestionably play an important even if elusive role in judgments of aesthetic excellence. But if this role or criterion were based on the arousal of real emotion, then music or any other form of art would occupy a lowly position far down on a scale of values. The death of a friend or relative, a game of poker, business success or failure: such events stir up the adrenals as no work of art could ever hope or want to do. The view that music arouses real emotion can therefore be put to one side, not so much because it is wrong, but rather because in fits only a small and relatively unimportant group of listeners.

THE SUBTLER EMOTIONS

"These are the moral, intellectual and aesthetic feelings," said James at the end of his chapter on the emotions. "Concords of sounds, of colors, of lines, logical consistencies, teleological fitnesses, affect us with a pleasure that seems ingrained in the very form of the representation itself, and to borrow nothing from any reverberation surging up from the parts below the brain." It is obvious that from the point of view of his own theory James was bothered by what he called the subtler emotions. He was right in suspecting that they involve very little if any visceral action, and was therefore also right in his conclusion that strictly speaking they do not belong within the range of emotional experience that his theory sought to encompass. His descriptions of the subtler emotions reveal the same penetrating insight and skill that are found in all of his writings, but unfortunately in this instance he did nothing to advance the problem. It may even be said that he added further verbal confusion, for he dropped the problem with the suggestion that the subtler feelings may be thought of as *intellectual* or *aesthetic* emotions.

Aesthetic experience certainly involves pleasure and displeasure, and it may be that these feelings, for aught that modern psychology can offer on the subject, are mixed up with the same mechanisms as those which underly emotion. Majority opinion, however, tends to doubt the connection, as did James himself. The aesthetic judgment, suffused as it is with pleasure or displeasure, is calm and somewhat detached from its object as compared with the impulse to quick or violent action which emotion tends to stir up. When Chopin was pleased with a new piece of music, his comment was apt to be "Rien ne me choque." If his viscera were involved in that judgment, they were manifestly under superlative control. An exquisite proof or a neat argument produces pleasure and satisfaction, but nothing like the intense joy from the news that a child, whose life had been despaired of, has been saved by the use of penicillin. In any event, whatever may be the ultimate finding about the physiological relation between feeling and emotion, the problem is not helped at all by referring to the subtler experiences in art as aesthetic emotions. One might just as well refer to domestic, national, religious, social, educational, professional, economic, military, political, and legal emotions, and so on *ad infinitum,* or at least to the end of the dictionary, without thereby doing more than pile up words.

THE THEORY OF EMPATHY

It is clear from even this brief survey that aesthetic theory, in trying to deal with the relation between art and emotion, is confronted with a problem which is not nearly so simple as it might appear. Objects of art, whether regarded as independent physical events or as dependent perceptual data, cannot themselves embody emotion. The emotions do not exist "out there" in visual or auditory forms. Neither as a rule do they exist as full-blown visceral events, except in the case of a few individuals whose appreciation of art is extremely subjective. If they are located neither in the object nor in the person, where can they be found?

One of the best-known answers to this question is in the theory of *Einfühlung* or empathy. Objects of art do not of course contain emotions, but they seem to embody an emotional quality because of the projection into them of moods and incipient emotions which actually have their origin within the individual. Emotions or tertiary qualities are not the property of perceived objects. They are aroused or subexcited, however, at the moment when the objects are perceived, and by a process of associative projection are then seen by the individual as though they actually belonged to the object. The gracefulness of a line, for example, is not an attribute of visual perception, but is a projection into the visual form of smooth and agreeable eye-movements, just as conversely the awkwardness of a line is the projection of unpleasant and jagged eye-movements. The sprightliness of music is not in the sounds but in the bright and lively muscle-flutters in the body of the listener. Nor is the melancholy mood of music in the tonal structure but in the drooping structure of the listener.

The theory of empathy has been drawn upon to account for many phenomena in visual and auditory perception which are not directly related to aesthetics. The perceptual field is replete with qualities which are difficult to explain in terms of the usual sensory dimensions. Shapes and patterns that are jagged, smooth-flowing, agitated, calm, enticing, drooping, sluggish, towering, or what not, present difficulties to any system of psychology that confines its units of description to the mere extensity, intensity, and protensity of sensory quality. It is here that empathy seems to offer welcome assistance. If in the perception of these shapes various muscular responses are present, the latter may be the source of the qualities that seem so closely bound up with the shapes. A certain visual or auditory form produces, let us say, a soothing effect on the observer. If the observer calls the form itself soothing, it is a sort of figure of speech which is explained by the fact that he has projected his own feeling into the perceptual field. A good deal of impressive evidence has lent strong support to the theory of empathy as originally formulated by Theodore Lipps some fifty years ago. Recent studies, however, tend to cast doubt upon the theory, except in its application to very special and isolated cases. The same doubt would therefore extend to the use of the theory in aesthetics.

In 1912 Wertheimer made an important study of perceived visual movement. Before that time it was assumed that visual movement is a product of visual quality plus concomitant adjustment of muscles of the eye. Rapid differences in external location are accompanied by an ocular muscular sweep, and the two together give an impression of movement in the visual field. The phenomenon may be considered a case of empathy at a simple level. Wertheimer showed, however, that if a line in one location is shown sixty-thousandths of a second after another line in a different location, the observer sees a quick movement between the two. But the eye cannot begin to move in sixty-thousandths of a second. Therefore the perceived movement must have been wholly visual, for the eye muscles made no contribution. In another experiment, Wertheimer exposed very briefly one spot, followed sixty-thousandths of a second later by several spots exposed out on the periphery. The observer saw one spot swiftly moving out in all directions. Obviously a movement of that kind would be impossible for the eye muscles. The conclusion was inescapable: visual movement is a property of the visual field itself, and although it may at times be supplemented by eye movement, it can exist in its own right without any empathic projection of ocular kinaesthesis. The kind of movement studied by Wertheimer is identical with the movement perceived in moving pictures. Stills are shown in rapid succession, too rapid for the eye to follow. The phenomenon with which everyone is familiar in the movies is therefore a perfect illustration of pure visual movement which can be explained without reference to eye muscles or to empathy.

Similar doubts regarding the role of empathy have been raised in connection with lines and shapes which are called graceful or awkward. Studies of eye-movement show that the eye sweeps over the visual field in much the same way, no matter what shapes or items are present. For jagged lines and for smooth lines the movements are indistinguishable. It must therefore follow that the quality which distinguishes a graceful from an awkward line must reside within the visual material itself. Any appeal to the theory of empathy is quite unnecessary. It is not only unnecessary. It would not help much even if the appeal were made, for the doctrine of empathy does not really explain aesthetic and tertiary qualities. It merely pushes the problem over into another area.

If tertiary qualities cannot exist in their own right in the visual and auditory areas, if they need assistance from organic and kinaesthetic modalities in order to make themselves palpable to the eye or ear, how does it happen that these qualities can exist in their own right in the area of bodily perception? The kinaesthetic and organic modalities are sense departments, just as are the visual and auditory modalities. A theory which denies tertiary qualities to visual and auditory patterns but at the same time accepts without question their existence in the bodily senses can hardly settle the question. It merely poses the same question in another domain.

The theory of empathy encounters even greater difficulties at the higher levels of aesthetic appreciation, although demonstrable proof of its inadequacy is found more easily at the simpler level of the tertiary qualities just described. Lipps and his followers have considered *Einfühlung* the essential element of aesthetic appreciation in all forms of art. If taken literally this view imposes upon the artist a serious if not fatal limitation—a limitation which fortunately every great artist has magnificently ignored. Empathy means that the greatness of a work of art is directly proportional to the amount of greatness which can be projected into it by the person who sees or hears it. A ballet can be no more beautiful than the incipient pantomimic responses of the audience, which must mean that every muscularly clumsy dolt would see in the dancing of Miss Tallchief merely a projection of his own unfortunate want of skill. Rakes and strumpets would hear wanton wiles in the music of the *B-minor Mass,* and prudes might fail to detect a trace of romance in the sounds of the *Liebestod.* Never could an artist soar to great heights unless his admirers had the same capacity. The tonal shouts of joy in the *IXth Symphony* would be inaudible to those of sad disposition, and the wistful melancholy of Mozart could only be heard by one person in ten thousand. Instead of the blessing that art has been to mankind, it would be no more than the portrayal of the commonplace, the representation of the average.

Some observations made by the writer a few years ago reveal plainly the difficulties in the theories of emotional arousal and of empathic projection. A group of 227 college students was given the task of assigning musical or aesthetic qualities, by the method of matching, to four recorded compositions: the introductory measures to Brahms' *First Symphony,* about 40 measures in the middle of Mendelssohn's overture to *A Midsummer Night's Dream,* the transitional passage between the third and fourth movements of Mozart's string *Quintet in G-minor,* and several measures from the third movement of Tchaikovsky's *VIth Symphony.* Experts in a department of music had agreed that the passage from Brahms could best be described as *stately,* the measures from Mendelssohn as *sprightly,* the transitional movement from Mozart as *wistful,* and the measures from Tchaikovsky as *vigorous.* These four adjectives were written on the blackboard, and the students were told to assign to each composition the adjective they considered most appropriate. The compositions were played through twice in random order, without of course indicating what compositions they were or how they were supposed to be described. If the students made their judgments by sheer chance, they would have been about 25 percent correct. If the judgments exceeded 25 percent by an appreciable margin, it would appear that something in the music was coercive or compelling in leading the students to select one adjective rather than another. The high uniformity in the results went beyond the most sanguine expectation. All of the compositions were judged more than 90 percent "correct" by the students, as can be seen in the following table:

TABLE I

PERCENTAGE OF CASES IN WHICH THE ADJECTIVES IN THE HORIZONTAL COLUMN WERE JUDGED APPROPRIATE TO COMPOSITIONS BY THE COMPOSERS LISTED IN THE VEᴌTICAL COLUMN

[Total number of cases 227]

	Stately	Sprightly	Wistful	Vigorous
Brahms....................	91. 20	0	3. 08	5. 72
Mendelssohn...............	0	98. 67	0	1. 33
Mozart....................	3. 09	0	96. 91	0
Tchaikovsky...............	5. 72	1. 77	0	92. 51

None of the theories designed to account for music as a language of emotion makes it clear how these results can be explained. The compositions cannot be said to *embody* emotion. That view is definitely ruled out. Nor is it reasonable to assume that real emotions were aroused in the listeners. The students looked somewhat bored by the experiment, or at best mildly amused. The theory of empathy also makes it necessary to assume that the students had at least incipient subjective moods which by a process of projection led to the selection of

[15]

the proper adjective, a possibility which is again hardly likely. Did these young men have a feeling of stateliness within them while they were listening to Brahms? They certainly did not look sprightly during the playing of Mendelssohn. Did Mozart make them feel wistful? A few of them may have felt a bit wistful, and then experienced a quick shift to a more vigorous internal state when the full orchestra and big chords of Tchaikovsky came at them. It is of course conceivable that the students were ascribing their own emotional experiences to the music. The method gives no guarantee against such a pathetic fallacy. It strains credulity, however, to believe that such a large group of undergraduates would experience such homogeneity of feeling at precisely the right moments. No. These young people were not reporting upon their own sprightly feelings, their wistful moods, or their stately affections. They were selecting from the list presented to them those words which best described the auditory structures of the music to which they were listening.

II

The last sentence in the preceding section gives a hint as to the way out of the dilemma regarding the place of emotion in musical experience. The students in the experiment just noted were describing the tonal characteristics, the tertiary qualities of the music, but were having no traffic whatever with real emotion either in themselves or in the music. The problem is solved by the simple but very important assertion that the music which they heard, and art in general, may be called a language of emotion only if that phrase is understood in a figurative sense. Real emotion does not enter into music at all.

This radical view is likely to be received at first with incredulity. Music not the language of emotion! What was Schopenhauer talking about? What have artists and philosophers and critics and psychologists been trying to explain by their elaborate theories?   What do the following adjectives, all of them and many more easily culled more or less at random from writings on music, refer to?

pensive	pompous	serene
wistful	passionate	enravishing
restless	agitated	stirring
mournful	soothing	dramatic
erotic	lanquid	placid
fervent	exciting	gladsome
alluring	seductive	martial
tender	somber	cheerful

The answer to these questions, although it involves a simple denial of the presence of any emotion anywhere in music, is not at all simple. Nor is it easy to explain. It lies at the very center of a verbal confusion which has plagued aesthetic theory from the beginning.

Music presents to the ear an array of auditory patterns which at the purely formal level are very similar to if not identical with the bodily patterns which are the basis of real emotion. The two kinds of patterns are with respect to their form practically the same, but the auditory patterns make music, whereas the organic and visceral patterns make emotion.   Just there lies the source of all the confusion, for the same words are used for both kinds of experience, as for example in the case of a word like "agitation."

What does it feel like to be agitated?   A description might include reference to such things as increased rate of breathing and heartbeat, unsteady organics in the region of the diaphragm, tapping of the feet or fingers, inability to keep still, etc. The same kind of disturbances and movements, at the level of form, are present in many passages of music.   Staccato notes, trills, strong accents, quavers, rapid accelerandos and crescendos, shakes, wide jumps in pitch, percussions and fortissimos— all such devices conduce to the creation of an auditory pattern which is appropriately described as agitated. Agitation is both an organic feel and an auditory perception, but in the former case it is an emotion and in the latter it is a tertiary sensory impression—two quite different psychological modes of experience, which nevertheless, because of the similarity in form between them, are called by the same name. The verbal confusion is largely responsible for the confusion in theory, because if a tonal passage is called agitated, the philosopher will want to know how agitation, by which he will mean an emotion, has made its way into music. Until recently it had apparently not occurred to anyone that emotion need not be present in the experience of agitation, provided the experience is in the auditory and not the organic domain.

A simple illustration of similarity of form between two different sense departments has been made familiar in the literature of *Gestalttheorie*. In the space below are two meaningless forms. The reader will be able to decide without any trouble which of the meaningless sounds, *uloomu* and *takete,* applies to which form.

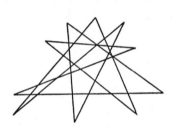 

The demonstration shows that impressions from different sense departments may be very similar with respect to form. Each of the sounds, *takete* and *uloomu,* fits perfectly one of the visual designs, but not the other. The impressions are different in content—one is visual and the other auditory—but similar in form. An even better example of identity of form across sense departments is furnished by rhythms. A rhythm can be visual, auditory, or tactual, and in each case the form may be made identical. A three-fourths rhythm or an iambic pentameter meter can be as easily recognized in one sense department as in another.

The great composer does indeed make of music an expressive language of emotion. Music is for him a means of giving objective and permanent form to his inner life. The miracle is accomplished by arranging sounds in such a way that the design is recognized by the listener as sprightly or languid or somber or majestic. The recognition may be only half conscious and ordinarily is not made explicit by the use of words, unless the listener happens to be a critic whose task is to describe what the music sounds like. The critic will struggle with words and will have recourse to a vocabulary that baffles the philosopher, for the words seem to imply that the music has embodied or aroused various emotions.

In the life-history of the composer himself there must of course have been real moods and emotions which laid the basis of the temperament which his artistic genius was capable of translating into sounds. Art reveals the temperament of the artist. The great works of Bach came from a noble and lofty nature, whether or not his contemporaries were able to perceive it in his everyday life. Beethoven struggled with tremendous inner forces, but also achieved moments of heavenly serenity. Mozart may have seemed a commonplace sort of fellow to those who knew him, but somewhere down deep within him humor and pathos dwelt together, untouched by any worldly vulgarity, whereas in Tchaikovsky and Wagner the outer and inner worlds were more blatantly mixed. Music more than any other art discloses both the surface and the depths of the artist. One reason for this luminous character of music is the absence in the perception of tone of the ordinary meanings and objects that clutter almost all other kinds of awareness.

Music is an artificial construction in the sense that the material out of which it is made is found nowhere in nature.

Musical sounds and the instruments for their production are man-made. The sounds do not symbolize or stand for objects of any kind. A strain of music cannot in and of itself represent a tree or a wild rose or the afternoon of a faun. To be sure, almost any meaning can be fastened to music by the use of words, titles, and program notes, and such associations may stick fast enough to make it possible by means of tones to indicate the town pump, the Democratic Party, or almost anything one likes. Pure music, however, is meaningless, a circumstance which gives it an appeal and capacity that are unique. In all other arts the tertiary qualities, the unspoken moods of the inner life, have to be represented by words and signs and symbols. In music these moods and qualities are conveyed at once to the mind of the listener without the intervention of any disturbing thoughts or objects, except those that may flit through consciousness by way of wandering associations.

Poetry, on the other hand, although ideally an auditory art, is one in which sound is apt to be subordinated to sense. A prosaic illustration of the minor role of sound in the perception of words as contrasted with tones is furnished by the ordinary word-association test. The reader may try the test on himself or on a group of friends, and he will find that the demonstration rarely fails. The task is simply to respond with the first word that comes to mind when a list of words, such as the following, is read or recited:

TABLE   DOG   MAN   KING   DOLLAR

The chances are that "chair" will be associated with "table," "cat" with "dog", "woman" with "man", "queen" with "king", and "cent" with "dollar"—or if not just those particular words, certainly words that are associated with the stimulus-words by way of meanings or related objects. Now there is nothing in the principle of associationism which states that connections between words are necessarily brought about by their meaning. Association by sound is presumably as valid a principle as association by meaning, yet only in very rare cases in the word-association test does anyone respond with a rhyme instead of a meaning. It practically never occurs to anyone to say "fable" for "table", "log" for "dog," "pan" for "man," "ring" for "king," or "collar" for "dollar." If the test is given to a large group of people, a wide variety of different words may turn up without a single instance of a rhyme. Even if the people are asked to give unusual and out-of-way associations, they may think long and hard without coming up with a rhyme. It may be a good sign that they do not, for there is some evidence that if in such a test a person gives too many associations by sound he has begun to lose control of his logical faculties. Be that as it may, the results of such a test show that psychologically the element of sound in the spoken word is almost negligible. It serves merely as a quick clue to meaning. Meaning, not sound, is the important thing. The poet, as compared with the composer, has an initial disadvantage if he wishes to impress upon the mind of his hearers the excellence of his auditory design.

Since the tertiary qualities of music are inextricably bound up with the sounds themselves—indeed it may be said that musical mood and musical sound are one and the same thing— the appeal of music is direct and universal. Nothing needs to be learned or translated. Schopenhauer was profoundly right when he said that the "emotions" of music are given in the abstract, in their full quintessence, without the disturbing distractions of ordinary associations. The sadness of music is not the sadness produced by a particular event, but universal sadness, without accessories or motives or consequences.

Other arts, like abstract painting, may try to imitate music, but the material with which they have to deal suffers in comparison with musical sound. The ordinary layman when confronted with abstract visual design is made puzzled and unhappy by the lack of meaning. The vulgar but irresistible "What is that?" is an obstacle the painter may never fully overcome. Visual material seems to require a context of meaning, whereas musical sound does not.

If the language of music is universal, it must presumably be understood at all times and in all places. It would be a strange commentary on human nature, and also an embarrassing argument against the present theory, if the grief in the slow movement of the *Eroica* sounded like a paean of joy, let us say to the Koreans. Felt grief is very much the same everywhere, and the bodily basis of joy must be the same for a New Yorker as for a Hottentot. The aesthetic qualities of music are the direct counterpart in tone of the bodily reverberations involved in real emotion, from which it must follow that the identification of those qualities would not go far wrong in different parts of the globe.

Reasonable and self-evident as this hypothesis may be, it would be extremely difficult to give it a fair and reliable test. The first requirement would be to find a group of subjects entirely unacquainted with Western music. Such a group in these days is not easy to come by. In almost all remote places of the world, radio and records have made the local inhabitants familiar with Bach and Beethoven and Tin Pan Alley, just as to some extent an earlier generation in the same regions had learned to sing gospel songs along with their native chants.

Another difficulty is bound up with the very nature of tonal structure, or rather, with the manner in which the ear apprehends tonal designs of any complexity. The ear is a selective instrument. What is "out there" as far as the sounds themselves are concerned is often selectively rearranged in such a way as to obscure certain parts and favor others. Although listening to the same sounds, two people may not hear the same things. If the music is strange or novel, some time may be required to detect the tertiary qualities which the composer has woven into his tonal texture. The appeal of the music may still be direct and powerful, but the interpretation may not coincide with the composer's intention until selective exploration has exhausted various possibilities of tonal rearrangement. Failure on the part of a Korean to assign the proper adjectives to joyful and to mournful music would not prove that those qualities were lacking in the compositions, unless after several attempts his oriental ear still made no better than a chance discrimination.

If the reader wants a striking demonstration of the selective nature of the ear, let him play over to himself or to friends the music printed below. The task is not to identify the mood of the music, but rather, what should be much easier, to pick out a well-known melody concealed somewhere within the tonal design. It can be said with almost complete assurance that nearly everyone in this country has heard the melody again and again. No note has been altered. What is the melody?

Very rarely does anyone hear the familiar melody the first time the piece is played, no matter how keen his musical ear. Indeed there is some evidence that the more musical the person, the more difficulty he has in finding the melody. If the reader wishes to try himself out, he should skip the next paragraph until he has given himself the test.

The melody starts in the tenor on the half-note *f,* proceeds from there to the two eighth-notes in the bass, then to the two eighth-notes in the tenor, then in the next measure to the quarter-note in the tenor, then the quarter-note in the soprano, and then the eighth-note and dotted quarter in the alto. From that point on the melody can be easily located.

This demonstration is intended to show the susceptibility of tonal material to organization by the ear of the listener. The notes that make up the melody have not been altered in any way. They have merely been surrounded by different harmony and embedded in the minor rather than in the customary major mode. This alteration in tonal context produces such a novel effect that even the trained musician usually finds it impossible at first to hear the well-known sequence of notes. So it might be with the members of any group, unaccustomed to Western music, if they were asked to identify the mood of what they heard. Failure would not prove that the mood was not there. It might mean rather that some momentarily more salient characteristic of the music obscured the mood.

III

The present view regarding the relation between art and emotion has made use of some of the principles of *Gestalttheorie.* Sensory *forms* have important characteristics which are not adequately described by the usual psychological dimensions. They are soothing or exciting or somber, *etc.* These tertiary qualities will eventually find their explanation in the physiological mechanisms of perception. Certain it is that in the meantime they cannot be properly understood by assuming that the emotional qualities of organic sensory material are projected into the sensory forms of audition, as the theory of empathy demands. Each sense department has its own unique material.

The material of the bodily senses is the stuff of emotion. The forms of tonal material, especially when designed by great artists, are so similar to those of the bodily senses that they are best described by using the same words that are also used to describe emotions. Tonal forms therefore seem to have emotional qualities, but these qualities must not be confused with real emotions. The latter exist only in the bodily senses.

Emotions are dynamic, not static. They go on in time and are filled with all kinds of movement. The origin of the word "emotion" illustrates the importance of movement in the subjective experiences to which the word finally became attached. In old English the word was frequently applied to external events: the emotions, meaning the movements, of the troops; an accidental emotion in the center of gravity; a flash of lightning that caused a great emotion in the air; *etc.* Only later was the word used exclusively for disturbances and movements within the human body. The German word *Gemütsbewegung* reveals with equal clarity the manner in which language took over a combination of words that places stress on the role of movement in the experience of emotion.

Music is also dynamic. It goes on in time and is filled with all kinds of movement. Descriptions of music, again selected more or less at random, abound in the use of words that refer to movement.

soar	ascend	surge
mount	rise	sink
bound	fall	quiver
climb	spring	throb
descend	shoot	flutter

It is appropriate and graphic to call music a language of emotion if that phrase is not taken to mean the arousal of real emotions in the listener. For most people music fortunately has no such capacity. Even if it had, the emotional response could be regarded as no more than an interesting but not particularly important byproduct. For the great majority of people the intrinsic character of the tonal design itself, rather than any bodily concomitants, is the supreme and unrivalled glory of music. The ears of those who love music are filled with the *form* but not with the material of emotion. In this sense music is the language of emotion, and is unequalled in this regard by any other art. *Music sounds the way emotions feel.*

THE LIBRARY OF CONGRESS

THE LOUIS CHARLES ELSON MEMORIAL FUND

MUSIC INTO WORDS

A LECTURE DELIVERED BY

JACQUES BARZUN

Professor of History, Columbia University

IN

THE WHITTALL PAVILION

OF THE LIBRARY OF CONGRESS

OCTOBER 23, 1951

Washington : 1953

MUSIC INTO WORDS

The world, the mind, is an endless miscellany.
—William Hazlitt (1829)

I

THE INVITATION to deliver one of the Elson lectures under the auspices of the Library of Congress must come to anyone as a great honor, and so it was to me. But I must candidly add that I found myself regarding it as providential besides, an opportunity ideally contrived to suit my own purposes. For the occasion would put at my mercy, for an hour or so, just the kind of audience I had long wished for, an audience interested in music and yet equally interested—or else it would not be here—in discourse about music.   I wanted such an audience in order to try out upon it some ideas about the relation of music and words that I had so far been able to test only piecemeal, in private conversation, where the irrelevant, skeptical, and—shall I say—uncalled-for interruptions of my guest or host interfered with full exposition.

Now in the usual kind of audience one is likely to find a mixture of amateurs, who derive their artistic pleasure almost exclusively from listening to music, and of "literary people" to whom music is worse than a closed book; for they can open a book but they cannot penetrate music. This fact defines my problem, which is also indicated by the title "music into words." The problem is, Are there genuine connections between music and words, or only accidental associations, some of them tolerable but most of them forced or farfetched? Is it possible to describe music in ordinary prose, or is technical jargon indispensable? And if description is allowed—perhaps "translation" would be the fitter term—does its possibility imply that music conveys a meaning outside itself, like the arts of literature and painting?

You can see that on the answer to these questions a good many of our activities depend for their justification—the whole status and value of music criticism for instance. You may not care much about music criticism; you may be willing to let it perish unwept. But you are something of a music critic every time you open your mouth about a concert you have just heard. Can it be that your words are meaningless, that you are saying just nothing with great vehemence? Again, the teaching of music is inseparable from comment, appreciation, and interpretation of styles. Are all the words of all the patient souls who push young talents through the mill just so much gibberish? We are inclined to say so even as we go on gibbering. We have been told so often that the adagio of the Moonlight Sonata is not "dreamy" and certainly not moonlight; that there is nothing "stark" about any of Bach's two-part inventions; and that pieces with a title like *Des pas sur la neige* are music in spite of their silly, reprehensible allusions. Snow is snow and music is music; the one is a physical, tangible thing, and hence there is a word for it; the other is immaterial, elusive, absolute, and hence no words can reach it.

From this it follows that only the names of the notes (which are interchangeable parts of no intrinsic significance) can legitimately be used in discussion, and hence discourse about music must remain technical. As such it can only interest professionals, and it is limited to some few salient points within a piece. A bar-by-bar technical analysis of a large work would be unendurable even to professionals—in short, great works of music are unquestionably great but their greatness is as it were unspeakable.

All this, I need hardly say, is the prevailing view. It has an astringent quality which was no doubt needed when the looseness of gushing "appreciation" became general fifty years ago. But on reflection this self-denial about words appears really as a rather crude remedy, which I suspect is now more often used as an instrument of intellectual pride than in any good cause. Indeed it resembles nothing so much as the cant of the old-fashioned scientist and secularist who loved to shock naive believers in Genesis by facing them with some bit of high school geology or astronomy. At any rate as regards music today, I think we have reached a point where we are in honor bound to avoid the naiveté of both parties: we know of old that a piece of music tells us nothing about snow. So it is childish to keep reminding the world that inarticulate sounds are not articulate. The formidable question remains, why the great musicians, the great critics, *and the great public* keep talking about music as if their words meant something.

The historical truth behind this question was deeply impressed upon me recently when I was engaged in selecting, translating, and editing for the general reader a collection of prose pieces about music.[1] Having to exclude technical discussions, I nevertheless found that I had on hand an abundance of stories, sketches, essays, confessions, letters, and anecdotes, which taken together gave an excellent idea of what music is for, what it is like, how it lives and moves in the lives of those attuned to it.

And when I looked at my cast of characters as a whole, I saw that it included the great composers from Monteverdi to Van Dieren; the great writers from Cellini to Shaw; the great performers (who might also be writers and composers) from Bach to Busoni. It was then I formulated the conclusion that whatever affectation we might be mouthing today about music being undiscussable must be deemed local and temporary. It could not withstand the weight of testimony that

---

[1] Pleasures of Music. A reader's choice of great writing about music and musicians from Cellini to Bernard Shaw. Edited with an introduction by Jacques Barzun. New York, 1951.

had grown under my hand in support of the proposition that music can be talked about like any other art; and that perhaps it must be talked about if it is to give its devotees full measure in enjoyment and significance.

What was further remarkable as I considered my two hundred thousand words about music was that no author or composer in the total span of four centuries had even tried to make rational the connection between his words and the musical experience that he discussed. All seemed to take the connection as self-evident, which must be because these literary and musical artists lacked on that point the benefit of modern skeptical thought. But given the prevalence of this skepticism we cannot be so lordly, we are compelled by the current opinion to build up a step-by-step defence of the position unconsciously taken in the past by the great composers and critics. At the same time it would be foolish to neglect whatever may be found valid in the negative view, for our whole effort should tend towards something I consider the great desideratum in contemporary American culture, namely a comprehensive grammar of criticism for dealing with art.

II

To TAKE OFF from the negative view that music is untranslatable, we must first separate the upholders of it into sheep and goats, that is to say, into musical people, who are usually gentle and much alike but limited in vocabulary—like sheep; and literary people, who feel vaguely put upon by music, and whose intellectual hides are tough—like goats. Both groups maintain that music cannot be talked about properly or usefully, but their grounds for thinking so are exactly opposite. The literary person proclaims that "he knows nothing" about music, and yet he may own a record collection and listen with enjoyment. He infers that he is tongue-tied because of his ignorance of technicalities and he concludes that the only possible criticism of music is technical. His argument amounts to saying: "I am a man of words; if words could be used about music I should be able to produce them; I can't, hence music is an experience absolutely self-contained."

To this reasoning the first rejoinder is that the "literary" listener has perhaps not sufficiently reflected about such musical experience as he has. How can a man "know nothing" about sensations he has undergone willingly, repeatedly, and pleasurably for a whole year, for ten years, for a lifetime? Obviously he is confusing the conventions of a trade with the essentials of human knowledge. He is suffering from the twentieth-century disease which is to suppose that knowledge and professionalism are synonymous; by which principle it is clear that primitive man could never learn to build bridges since there were as yet no schools of engineering.

Turn now to the professional or the accomplished amateur musician. He swims among sonatas like a fish in water, but contents himself with but a single pair of critical terms beyond the strictly technical: to him any musical work is either "a swell piece" or "pretty lousy." Immersed as he is in performance and in judging performance, he has no need to go whoring after more language. Music for him is quite truthfully a self-contained experience. He can share it with his fellows by an almost bodily communication of sympathy. He is moreover so busy practicing or composing or coaching others—not to speak of putting up music stands and dog-earing scores—that he rarely has time to straighten out his impressions. If he ever does so, his temper is bound to be hostile toward anything "literary." The violinist senses that the Razoumowsky Quartets do not pertain to the Napoleonic Wars as does Tolstoy's *War and Peace*. He assumes that he knows all there is to know about music, and concludes that it is an art diametrically opposed to the so-called "representative arts" of literature and painting. If challenged, he clinches his case by pointing out that each word in the language has a distinct meaning known to all, whereas single notes or chords mean nothing, and thus may mean anything.

It is here that the counter argument must take hold and destroy, once for all, the platitudes offered about words. It is not true that words have intrinsic meanings; it is not true that meanings reside in words. Turn to the dictionary and look up a common noun: the first striking fact about it is that it has eight, ten, a dozen, or a score of meanings. If someone were to break into this room shouting "Chair!" it would be impossible to tell whether he was asking for a seat or calling upon the chairman. He might be a mad professor who had been deprived of his post—for in a University (as you know) a chair is a post . . . which is why it cannot be sat on. In an eighteenth-century novel a chair is a vehicle, and in a twentieth-century drawing room a chair is almost anything that is not a rug or a lamp. This last fact is very important, for it reminds us how wrong it is to say that a word automatically puts us in mind of an object. On hearing the word "chair" and being told further that it means a seat, anyone will visualize something different; a thousand people will picture thousands of dissimilar objects. "Chair" is really an empty sound which we can fill with meaning only with the help of many other words and of much other knowledge which is not and which never can be put into words.

This is universally true of workaday life, where we can seldom understand the snatches of conversation overheard on the street, the quick undertones exchanged within a strange family, or the easy allusions of other men talking shop. In short, there is nothing mechanical about verbal meanings, not even the practical meanings of daily life. All communication in words remains an art, no matter how habitual, and like every art it is made up of more elements than can ever be enumerated. Tone of voice, gesture, and facial expression, choice and placement of words, omission and superfluity of sounds, plus the indefinite sphere of relevancies that we call context, all play their role in the transmission of any one meaning, not excepting the most trivial.

Obvious though all this may be, it can stand being underscored again and again because discourse about art and criticism usually forgets it. Speech is so common that we seldom analyze its mysteries, and as a result comparisons among the arts are strangely distorted. For the sake of simplicity the stuff of each art is assigned some flat, blunt attributes that supposedly exclude one another: words stand for things and ideas; paint reproduces the visible world of nature; music is pure form; architecture is machinery for living—singly or in groups; poetry, dance, and music are time arts, the plastic and graphic arts are concerned with space . . . —none of these aphorisms is without suggestiveness and importance, but not one of them is wholly true. And the terms of each are in some sense transferable to the rest. Thus, on the basis of what has been so far rehearsed about the character of verbal meanings, one can say that the two forms of sound called speech and music are alike in requiring a multitude of qualities and modifiers before they can make a significant impression on a human mind. Just as you cannot produce a solitary middle C and expect a listener to be greatly affected one way or another, so you cannot utter the single word "chair" and hope for much of a response.

And even now the comparison still remains a little unfair to words, for the parallel has been drawn between the high art of music and the merely workaday use of speech. If we pass from daily talk to literature proper, the force of all that has been shown is augmented manifold. Augmented and also complicated by the presence of the new element which we recognize as artistry, though it is impossible to define and difficult to isolate. The borderline between the utilitarian and the literary uses of speech is not intrinsic and fixed, as we might casually suppose; it is circumstantial and shifting, and this variability is reproduced in all of the so-called fine arts, including music. A bugle sounding taps in camp says "go to bed" just as clearly as the vesper bell says "come to church." This is by context and convention, exactly as in articulate speech. But in an opera those same musical sounds would be quite transfigured and charged with new meanings. Again, certain pieces of music, for instance a jig or a Virginia reel, though they utter no distinct message, are nevertheless little else than invitations to the dance. The appeal to mind or spirit is slight, whereas the pull upon the legs is powerful. Yet a dance movement in a Bach suite or the finale of Beethoven's Seventh Symphony uses the same conventional rhythms and figures with wholly different effect.

It is therefore not the presence or absence of conventional forms and phrases that distinguishes art from messages of utility, or that distinguishes the art of music from any other. All we can say is that art differs from workaday communication in that it transcends the literal—not excludes it or denies it, for it often contains it—but it goes beyond. If this is so, then another imaginary barrier between music and the other arts disappears: no art denotes or gives out information. We can test this generality by considering in its light a passage of literature, say the scene in Shakespeare where Hamlet finds Yorick's skull and says: "I knew him, Horatio; a fellow of infinite jest, of most excellent fancy. He hath borne me on his back a thousand times. And now how abhorrèd in my imagination it is! My gorge rises at it. Here hung those lips that I have kissed I know not how oft . . ." etc. Clearly these words are not to *inform* us that Hamlet knew Yorick. They do not answer the question that a lawyer might put: did you or did you not know and associate with one Yorick, deceased? Their purpose is quite other, namely to impress us with certain realities of death and thus to heighten the shock with which we shall soon see Ophelia's burial procession. Nor is this all. The words, while disclosing yet another aspect of Hamlet's character, suggest his constant harking back to the old days when his father reigned; moreover, the facts presented fit and sustain the brooding atmosphere of the whole play, so that the effect—as it is the purpose—of those simple words is to reverberate endlessly.

If, contrariwise, Hamlet came on and said: "Death really does dreadful things to the nicest, jolliest people," the gist of his remarks would be exactly what it is in the scene as we have it, but the impression made would be nil. The *meaning* that only art conveys would be blotted out. As a working part of that meaning, altogether unlike "information," notice the small but effective shift from Hamlet's "he" and "him," denoting the Yorick he remembers, to: "how abhorrèd in my imagination *it* is." *It* is at once Hamlet's recollection and Yorick turned to earth. This, if I may say so, is the secret of literature; the adjective "literary" means: doing this sort of thing with words; it does not mean using words to denote physical objects.

For conceivably Shakespeare could have used many other objects, invented other details, to serve his same purpose in the same way. Hence we should never mistake the literal ballast of the sentences for the meaning of the piece. The play—any play—is not about the ideas, people, or cocktail glasses that it juggles with; in a strict sense literature is not *about* anything, it *is*—precisely like music. And precisely like music, like any art, literature offers a presentment having significance. What kind of significance will be suggested in a moment; at this point it is enough to conclude from all we have said that the things signified are not the things named.

If it should be objected that a poetic drama such as *Hamlet* is not a fair test (even though the passage chosen was common prose) I would remind the objector of a scene in *Madame Bovary*, a prose work notoriously designed to exhibit the prosaic in life. Well, in *Madame Bovary* Flaubert makes one of the principal love scenes take place in a cab that keeps driving aimlessly round and round the provincial city; the incident is in keeping with the rest of the story, but it is safe to say that anyone who believes in the literal circuit of that vehicle knows nothing about love, cabs, or literature.

Here, of course, one must beware of falling into the trap of symbolic interpretation: the cab does not "stand for" anything. Such an explanation would only be literalism at the second remove, duller still than the simple-minded sort. Let someone suggest that Flaubert's cab means the wild drive of the passions, or the vicious circle of sensuality, and the very thought makes one groan. Why? Because it is limiting and mechanical; it sets us to solving riddles instead of grasping meanings. Allegories are frigid for this very reason, that they seem to offer significance only to dilute it into information. Similarly, works of literature that communicate by means of broad generalities about love, death, fate or revenge are invariably tedious and, paradoxically, false. We cease to believe in propositions which in other contexts we should readily accept. And this in turn explains why it is fatal for an author to go directly after the eternal verities. He can state them, but the statement won't be art; for let me repeat at the risk of being tedious myself, literature does not reside in propositions; though it may say a great deal, it tells nothing; it thereby resembles music: it is a music of meanings.

If this assertion is true we should expect that great works of literature, in spite of being verbally explicit, would give rise to widely different interpretations. This is exactly what we find. No two critics agree about the meaning of any given masterpiece, and the greater the work the greater the disagreement. This remains true after the most laborious reading of the text and the most honest attention to previous commentaries. From this one can infer what must be the unspoken differences that co-exist in the thousands of minds which have read *Hamlet* or *The Divine Comedy*. We get a glimpse of this chaos of opinion when we discover what an earlier century thought of a work that we think we know well: it seems like a wholly other treatment of the same subject—the movie we gape at after reading the novel.[2]

You have no doubt jumped ahead of me in applying this generality to our continuing parallel between the art of words and the art of music: the well-worn argument that denies clear meaning to a piece of music because no two listeners give the same account of it is an argument that works equally well against clear meaning in literature. Yet, it will be said, no one will ever confuse what happens in *Hamlet* with what happens in *King Lear,* whereas your musical program hunter will hear the waves of the ocean in a piece which another takes for the Rape of the Sabine Women. Quite so, but this contrast is only superficially correct. The plots of Shakespeare's dramas are not likely to be confused because they are the skeleton, not the significance of the piece; whereas what the programmatizer hopes to tell us with his ocean or his Sabines is the significance, the upshot, the net effect. If we want in music the true parallel of plot we must look for the form of the work and its key relationships, a skeleton about which there will be no confusion either, assuming an educated listener.

Returning now to the significance of the given piece of music, we may grant that the inventor of programs is almost certain to fail; he fails, that is, to convince us that the piece is the same thing as, or a true copy of, a storm on the ocean. Being now profound students of literature we know why he fails. He fails because he has tried to equate a work of art with a proposition or with the name of a thing or an idea. And we rebel against this either because we know such an equation to be impossible or, in less conscious moments, because we have a pet name or proposition of our own, which clashes with the other; this conflict itself helping to prove the impossibility.

Thus when Sir Laurence Olivier produced his motion picture version of *Hamlet* he prefaced it with a short explanation—

---

[2] Note that within living memory Mozart has turned from a gay, superficial composer to a profound and tragic one.

a few programmatic words—that defined the forthcoming action as "the tragedy of a man who could not make up his mind." My feelings were immediately up in arms against this hoary misinterpretation of a play in which the hero makes up his mind quickly, repeatedly, and brilliantly. But the play would not be more accurately described by maintaining the opposite of Olivier's view—which happens also to be Goethe's view and Coleridge's. Rather we must give up these attempts at summarizing, or at least acknowledge that they are nothing but shorthand reminders, and careless shorthand at that. Is Tolstoy's *War and Peace* a novel about Napoleon—no, certainly not; and yet . . . well, yes and no. Is *Don Giovanni* an opera about a Spanish libertine? Does the Ninth Symphony celebrate the brotherhood of man? Is Velasquez' "Surrender at Breda" a historical painting? Yes and no; yes and no; yes and no. The "yes" answer is correct in the same sense as the statement that the earth is one of the planets. It *is* one of the planets, but to an earth dweller it does not feel like one: there is so much more to say, a myriad qualities to add, which swamp the mere definition.

The analogy is one to which the critic of the arts must keep coming back: a great work resembles an animated world that is perceived and inhabited by the beholder. It is various, extensive, treacherous, perfectly still and yet in constant motion. Like the moon seen from a vehicle, it follows one about while looking down with indifference. The masterpiece mirrors the mind of one man and of all men; it annoys, delights, instructs, and sometimes preaches, though it contradicts itself and other revelations equally true; it shapes the conduct of multitudes who have never so much as heard of it, and it is often powerless to improve the behavior of those who study and believe its message. It was created out of nothing, but pieces of other worlds lie embedded in it like meteorites; it is the cause of endless unimaginable creations after itself, yet its own existence is so precarious that its survival often suggests miraculous intervention through the agency of fools and thieves. It seems to have neither purpose nor utility, though it commands veneration, it bestows money and prestige, and it arouses a hunger that some find insatiable.

This and much else is the fluid phenomenon named Art, which we try to decant into our little individual flasks of consciousness with the aid of words. The attempt must seem hopeless until we remember that it is quite like another task which we have no option but to perform—the task of organizing the experience of living. We begin this second task as soon as we learn to talk, and the volume of words which comes out thereafter shows how necessary we feel discourse to be, even about familiar acts. But the words by which we capture the flux of life were not given mankind ready-made. Hard as it is to believe, the best words, like the worst clichés, had to be invented; they were once strange and fresh; and the entire charting of our perceptions, from stomachache to religious ecstasy, had to be made bit by bit like a geodetic survey. The coverage is by now so extensive that we forget its historical growth, its slow progress towards sharper and sharper analysis. We come to believe that every experience for which we have a word, be it heartburn, hypocrisy, or ambivalence, was a plain fact from the beginning. Nothing could be further from the truth. Each piece of reality had to be carved out from all its neighboring parts, had to be named, and the name elaborately explained until it became a commonplace. I mentioned "ambivalence" to give an example of recent carving and naming: in many places the word and the fact would not be as readily understood as the word and the fact of hypocrisy, while these in turn would in primitive circles be less intelligible than heartburn.

The point of these commonplace truths is that if we agree to see art as a source of meaning, something like the carving and naming of experience has to take place. Something *like* it, rather than something identical with it, for we have not yet considered the way art and life are related, nor the kinds of words that can apply to each. And before we can be critics we must be clear about these relations. Life, art, discourse—an eternal triangle in which it is difficult to avoid mistaking parts, as we discovered in dealing with literature: we mistake words for things and knowledge for information. We can err in the same way about life and suppose that it is made up, simply, of all the things named in the dictionary. The truth is, the experience of life is not by any means exhaustively rendered by words. We have, for example, the word "anger," but each angry man, each bout of anger, is in some respects unlike any other. The common words by which to mark those differences soon run out. We feel about *our* anger, or that of our friends, or about any vivid example of an enemy's anger, an inexpressible immediacy and richness that overflows the poor word. What do we do about that? We turn to art. We refer to Achilles' rage, to the furies, to Othello, or to any other creations that we have "experienced" as if they embodied those fireworks of feeling erupting from the abstract core of human anger. But it is not because Shakespeare copies, it is because he discriminates and distils that we go to him for an extension of awareness. He—or any artist—enlarges the scope of our perceptions without throwing us back into the total stream. For one thing, the choice of a single medium, such as words, or paint, brings clarification. Through it the artist gives us not life but equivalent sensations sorted out. There is no anger in the stage Othello nor in ourselves watching him. I should in fact be willing to define art in relation to life as "equivalent sensation"; it being understood that in a work of art the sensations are purposefully organized.

But contrary to a prevalent notion it is not the organizing that is fundamental, or else we could take no pleasure in fragments of ancient sculpture. The fundamental thing is that the fragment speaks to us. In color and texture it is as unlike flesh as can be, but the equivalence intended by the human fashioner still holds for a human observer.

In other words, the several arts compel the different materials at hand to serve the curious purpose of producing sensations that we recognize as commentaries on our existence. By habit or convention some of these materials seem to be "closer" than others to the original impressions of life, but this is merely habit or convention. "Closer" has no meaning here. Stone is not closer to flesh than word is to thing. Just think of the immense diversity of words used in different languages for the same things, the great diversity of styles used in the graphic arts for the creation of lifelikeness, and the enormously rapid change in musical taste without much change in the effect produced on human beings. The means of artistic communication are infinite, and a tapestry is as lifelike as a ballet. If I were asked to illustrate the situation of the arts in relation to life, I should create a sort of seven-layer cake, with a large ineffable fruit in the exact centre. From this a single strong flavor irradiates the whole confection. Each layer is one of the arts, and it tastes different by virtue of the different filler within; but all draw a common sweetness and nutritious force from the central fruit. We can eat our slice and have it too, for it grows back magically—art is inexhaustible. But the fruit is to most of us out of reach; much of the time we taste it through art alone, which in the broad sense that includes language is the conveyer, distiller and organizer of life par excellence.

III

IT WOULD BE EASY but highhanded to argue that since this is true of the arts and since music is an art, music must also present an equivalence of life. Many would continue to doubt the validity of the reasoning, or at least would puzzle over the connection. "Does he really mean to say," they would ask themselves, "that music embodies anger, or manifests hypocrisy? Why, I thought he admitted that music doesn't tell us anything. Of course, he did say that literature doesn't tell us anything either: it's all very confusing." I am glad you remembered literature because what was asserted of it was that it speaks to us *by virtue* of not being literal. So does music, as I hope an example will make clear. In the introduction to the first movement of Beethoven's Ninth Symphony, we are given sensations contrived in such a way that the ear—the thinking ear, that is—remains uncertain of the tonality, the direction, the fulfillment of the sounds. This is protracted until the tutti comes crashing down upon us in D Minor and all doubts are at an end. This is a favorite effect of Beethoven's, another instance being the transition from the Scherzo to the finale of the Fifth.

Now, why is it "an effect"—an affecting thing? Why do we respond to it, and respond to it, I should imagine, all alike even though it may cause annoyance to some and pleasure to others? The impression as a whole has no name, and no good would be served by calling it Resolution of Uncertainty. Any such term is limiting, literal, and—you may properly add—unmusical. Just so: music is a medium through which certain unnamable experiences of life are exquisitely conveyed through equivalent sensations for the ear. As Mr. Roger Sessions has admirably put it: "Emotion is specific, individual, and conscious; music goes deeper than this, to the energies which animate our psychic life. . . . It reproduces for us the most intimate essence, the tempo, and the energy of our spiritual being; our tranquillity and our restlessness, our animation and our discouragement . . .—all, in fact, of the fine shades . . . of our inner life." [3]

I would qualify this statement in only one way, by pointing out that although music is not like, nor about, namable emotions, being neither literal nor abstract, it has a way of interweaving itself with some of our perceptions that do have names, and so tempts us to tag the music with the experience of which we are reminded. This accounts for the programmatizing, the naming of pieces large and small, and the in-

---

[3] "The Message of the Composer," in *The Intent of the Artist*, edited by A. Centeno (Princeton, 1941), pp. 123–4.

evitable amateur comments about passages that are like sunset on the Matterhorn or the kiss of an archangel. Notice that these analogies are usually with the rare and the fanciful, precisely because they are not readily namable in spite of their vividness and intimacy. If you should ask, "what is the kiss of an archangel like?" you would probably be told, "It's just like the close of the Siegfried Idyll."

The fact that music begins to speak to us at the point where words stop accounts also for something rather more important and certainly more aboriginal—the fact that articulate and inarticulate sounds can combine to form one meaning, the fact that songs can be composed and understood. If a good judge can say that one setting of given words is better than another, it is not merely because one tune is better adapted to the conventional accent of those words but also because it wraps itself more snugly around their significance. We appreciate this in reverse when we remark that the Star-Spangled Banner is a tune somewhat wanting in martial fire and ill-adapted to the patriotic feeling of the words. When we know that its traditional form was that of a convivial song "To Anacreon in Heaven," we recognize its fitness to that theme and discover that the awkward wandering of the notes turns from blemish to expressiveness.

Music's same power to present the sensations missing from the verbal signs of an experience explains why as a general rule the text of the best songs and operas is inferior in its kind to the musical setting. A great poem is complete in itself and needs no additions from another art. Great music is complete in itself, and only a disagreeable overlap of intentions can result from its being harnessed to great literature. Fortunately, many musicians have shown a certain indifference to poetic expression and thus have expended their powers on verse that was literal and required to be made into art. We then enjoy both the independent beauty of the music and the pleasure of its adaptation to a rudimentary conception in words.

This rudimentary conception is still with us, of course, in instrumental music, to which we must return as the true test of our entire theory. For music has taken rank among the high arts by virtue of its relatively recent emergence as a presentment that can stand by itself: all its claims to absoluteness and disconnection from life rest on the fact that intelligent people will sit silent and motionless for twenty minutes while upwards of a hundred men blow and scrape "meaningless" notes. But consider this strange institution. In order to find one's way in this supposed desert of significance, it appears advisable to distinguish "suspensions" of sound, "resolutions," cadences (or fallings), appoggiaturas (or leanings), sequences (something like raised eyebrows), broken chords and what not other inarticulate suggestions of bodily experience. Again, the movements are called gay, fast, walking, dying, joking, or retarded—all in defiance of plain fact, since nothing moves or dies, is suspended or resolved. Stranger still, there is often a madman, sandwiched between the performing and the listening lunatics, who is delegated to lead and interpret the meaningless sounds by means of a pantomime which is said to be as necessary as it is expensive.

When the noise and gestures have subsided, the audience are heard to say whether the new piece has merit or whether the old one was played right. Obviously they are comparing the flood of sensations with a preexisting pattern in their minds or memories, a pattern to which they readily ascribe a value akin to revelation as well as the power of producing pleasure. The sensations offered are extraordinarily complex and the receiving mind must be extraordinarily acute, for it sometimes happens that all the notes of a familiar piece are played in the right order at the right speed, and yet good judges declare they could hardly recognize the work. It lacked force or coherence or was subtly bereft of its accustomed virtue. This fairly usual experience surely goes to prove that music communicates something beyond the relation of its audible parts.

It conveys a meaning which some people catch and others not; a meaning which is not *in* the notes, since these can be played correctly and yet meaninglessly; a meaning which is not universally intelligible, since listeners vary in their judgment of composers, of works, of performances; a meaning which like verbal meaning depends on a mass of previous knowledge and feeling.

This last truth is not merely one of common observation, it has also been the subject of experiment. The classic statement of the results is that of Dr. Philip Vernon, a British musician and psychologist, who twenty years ago subjected the Cambridge Musical Society to a series of tests proving conclusively that to consider music a purely auditory experience is contrary to fact. His report should be read and pondered by every amateur or professional listener who believes that, whatever vulgar souls may do, his own pleasure in the art is the contemplation of pure form. The facts are so enlightening, and so amusing besides, that I have reprinted Dr. Vernon's article in the anthology to which I referred earlier. The honest reader cannot fail to recognize how much that is commonly deemed non-musical goes into intelligent listening.

The reason for this paradox is that on his side, the artist-composer, even while he attends to the demands of his material or to his formal design, consciously or unconsciously endows the familiar elements with qualities that also correspond to his grasp of life as a whole. The order in which he puts things, the things he repeats and the things he avoids; the suggestions, emphases, and climaxes; the pace of his thought and the intensity of his will; the stops, the false starts, the crashes, and the silences—everything he does or leaves undone—is a signal to the listening mind that recalls to it the qualities of life. The composer has probably no intention of being autobiographical; he may indeed be a dramatist composing the wordless biography of some imaginary being, like Mozart depicting Figaro or the Queen of the Night; but the concourse of sounds is as surely the equivalent of a lived experience as are the lines of an expressive face or the gestures of an inspired actor.

The conclusion is inescapable that musical meaning relates to the existence of the creature that man is, not solely because music delights man, and not solely because he assigns to it a value beyond mere delight, but because it requires from him a special attention to particulars within and without his own mind. He must, as we say, understand the idiom, that is, he must record and relate the multitude of sensations aroused in him, and so make them into food for his soul.

IV

It follows readily enough that what the artist has put together, the critic can take apart and restate in the foreign tongue of prose discourse. In doing this, he is really doing no more than accounting to himself and to others for what he has undergone. The critic may, for example, ask himself how it is that some works using all the devices of modulation, cadence, anticipation, etc., according to rule are nonetheless unbearably dull; whereas others are not only agreeable but great? One composer, we say, has good or great ideas, another has not. But this is to repeat the fact without explaining it. The ideas we refer to are obviously something else than clever tricks for linking the common elements of the medium, though this cleverness is not to be despised when, as we also say, there is a *point* to it. And the point is always something larger than devices and the linking of devices; for we can recognize the presence of genuine ideas at both extremes of technical knowledge: Bach is not a great composer because he was adept at counterpoint, but because he had a purpose in using it. Gluck is a great composer despite his clumsiness of technique—if art that is successful can ever be called clumsy. Both equally served an intention that we can recover and rejoice in. When we receive a communication we value, it is idle to carp at the means employed, art being the first and truest pragmatism.

But criticism immediately asks how a diversity of means can achieve similar results. This remains a complete mystery unless we admit the proposition to which our long argument has been leading, namely, that the "point" of speech or music or art is to summon up and shape the stuff of human experience. Anything we understand, we understand in the light of human experience, actual or potential. We must bring our little share of wisdom and remembered life with us, and pour it into the given mould, or else remain deaf and dumb to messages the most heavenly; since, as we know, neither words, nor paint, nor music nor science can take up and unload at our feet the full cargo of even the smallest portion of reality.

For "potential experience" we have the word Imagination, and it is this faculty that the artist possesses in great strength and uses to spur our own. By a combination of instinct and design he so orders the elements of his art that the interplay of resulting sensations produces a decipherable code to new meanings. Our attention is arrested and sustained. The stream of impressions holds us because it refers to our past and future being, to our conscious or submerged memories, to our anxieties and our purposes; it arouses and satisfies our expectations on all planes, from rhythmic sympathy with our heartbeat to flattering our ego by subtlety. When I say that the work of art, the musical masterpiece, does all this, I mean that in any given instance it may do some or all of these things. At first, the very great work may appear to do none of them: it defies our expectations and unpleasantly disturbs our heartbeat. Our ego is flouted and our anxieties increased. We leave the concert hall muttering. But history has taught us that we should expose ourselves repeatedly to such icy showers of seemingly *non*-equivalent sensations until one of two things happens: either we reject the new alien world for good, or we adopt it by adapting to it. In gifted or determined devotees of art, adaptation comes easily, of course, but most of us need help, and even the gifted ones occasionally find themselves face to face with art that looks impossible to assimilate. It is to help digestion by resolving doubts and dispelling mysteries that criticism exists. The traditional belief that criticism is intended to separate the good from the bad seems to be a confusion between means and ends. It may at times be necessary to point out the bad, but only as a corollary to defining the character of a piece by imputing to it an intention that is bad, or an intention that is good but poorly executed. Again, those who maintain that criticism judges and gives grades for the sake of the artist's next performance mistake criticisms for teaching. Even the teacher might be said not so much to pass judgment as to show the pupil, like a critic, what the pupil's own work does and fails to do.

The role of critic is, in a word, to act as go-between, as midwife, between the artist's conception and the beholder's recognition of it in the created thing. The critic says: "Where you see chaos, or possibly where you see nothing at all, there exists nevertheless a valuable entity. It has such and such features. Look at this, and again look at that. If you will but subject yourself to its influence once again, noting the truly salient parts, I will try to point out their connection and their meaning. I will, in the fullest sense of the term, identify the object for you, so that you will never again misconceive its place and purport, nor mistake it for another or for a dead thing."

Obviously, an undertaking so ambitious is never perfect or complete, which is why there can hardly be too much criticism—despite one's frequent feeling that there are too many critics. The remedy to this excess is to improve the quality of criticism by making stringent demands on those who criticize. In music particularly we should be very exacting, and also very receptive, because music criticism is still in its infancy. Indeed we may pray that its puniness is not a sign of stunted growth, due to the impediments of prejudice and false belief that it has encountered and that I have been enumerating. Their removal is prerequisite to critical performance because otherwise the common goal of all critics is hidden from the musician by his own self-righteousness: he denies the possibility expressed in the title of our discussion. And yet, still, notwithstanding, the critic of music must, like the critic of literature, translate one kind of experience into another. To do so he must use words, for they are the most general medium of communication. And he is entitled to translate music into words because all the arts concern themselves with one central subject matter, which is the stream of impressions, named and unnamed, that human beings call their life.

If he is himself at home in life, in music, and in words, the critic may rely on his readers' keeping in mind the difference between life and art and between words and music. His remarks will naturally replace literalism with significance, and will automatically show that meaning is always above and beyond the thing said. The stupidest man is brighter than any device of speech because he always finds more in it than a device. Establish that same happy relation between the naive listener and music in general and you have got rid forever of the bugbear of "programmatic" interpretation.

Remains the question of vocabulary. What words are appropriate to lead the listener into the neighborhood of musical understanding and give him the push that will make him land in the very center of direct perception? A full answer would amount to a manual of critical practice. Here I can only sketch out a few general principles, most of them implicit in all that you have heard. First, the criticism of music, like that of the other arts, must be written for the layman; an educated layman if possible, but a layman and not a professor. The educated reader may be expected to pick up some rudiments of terminology; that is all he knows and all he needs to know. Technical terms are used in criticism simply to point to a part of the work. Just as in a painting we draw attention to a "patch of cobalt blue in the middle distance," so we may refer in a piece of music to the cadence, the tutti, the arpeggios, or the second subject. Beyond this the critic attention to a "patch of cobalt blue in the middle distance," must reserve his profundities for the learned journals, exactly as the literary scholar reserves his discussion of acatalectic meters and double syllepsis. All these matters have importance for the trade, not for the public.

Having singled out the parts that he considers noteworthy, the critic then explains what makes them so. Here he uses ordinary words and the range of possible phraseology is infinite. No one can predict what type of commentary will enlighten a particular mind, though it is safe to say that a critic ought to be aware of current doctrines and superstitions, whether or not he takes one of these as a text for his sermon. He should ideally begin where the unaided listener left off—in bewilderment if the work was new and difficult but well spoken of; in horror if it was new and badly spoken of. The critic begins in some familiar key and modulates to his own prearranged full close.

In the course of this exercise nothing is a priori excluded. Provided they are themselves intelligible at sight, the facts of history, biography, psychology, poetry, architecture, or of any art or science may be equally relevant. Analogies may be drawn from the workshop or the boudoir, provided always that anything said really makes a point, that the point is anchored to some precise part of the given musical experience, and that interest attaches to the remark or thesis for people who care about art and life.

This is a tall order and the record shows that it cannot be carried out without recourse to a device I have just mentioned—analogy. The justification for this need not be argued again, for you are (I hope) convinced that in this world things may be alike, though no more than alike. We may say of any group of things: A is to B as C is to D. The statement of a bold critic long ago that the overture to *Figaro* was like champagne, means the sensation in my palate when I drink the celebrated wine resembles the sensation in my ears when I listen to the celebrated overture. The analogy might of course be boiled down to the single adjective "sparkling," but words of this convenient sort tend to lose their sharpness by overuse. They do not discriminate sufficiently deep and break down under the strain of building up more elaborate analyses. Hence the obligation for critics to keep inventing metaphors and employing their very strangeness to force attention upon what is deemed the critical point.

Analogy is of course not without danger. It can impart an indelible character to the work or the passage it seeks to illuminate. Much nineteenth-century music suffers from having a certain kind of poetical character thus stamped upon it. The Moonlight Sonata, the Pathétique, the Appassionata, have almost become trite through their label, as if the suggestiveness of the music were imprisoned beneath. Perhaps the most striking example is that of Berlioz's *Fantastic Symphony,* in which five movements differing markedly in atmosphere are heard and spoken of as if all were demonic like the last; the result being that the adagio, one of the loveliest of pastoral movements, hardly penetrates the mind-hardened eardrum. Such misconceptions are perhaps inevitable; they do result from criticism, and better criticism is the only antidote. The mishap only reinforces the need for the best criticism we can produce—informed, sensitive, and above all explicit; criticism fit to reconcile the tone-deaf and raise the spirits of the frightened Philistine, as well as enchant those who do not need it.

The existence of such criticism matters not only to artists and amateurs but to society at large. In a civilization as old and changeful as ours there is a constant movement between art and social thought. Ideas, attitudes, models for the physique and for the mind, come from the hand of the artist and are popularized by critics. New forms arise as the old

[25]

filter downwards. This is what Shelley meant when he called poets "the unacknowledged legislators of the world." And music's effect is surely as strong as poetry's, acting as it does on the nerves and the very bowels of mankind. But because the art is wonderfully complex in its higher reaches, its action is more uncertain and diffuse. It takes the critic speaking the speech of the literate man to arouse in that man the desire for music new and strange, and to ease the road to pleasure through that desire.

The goal for the critic to keep steadily in view is that of significance. It is meaning that makes sensations cohere, meaning that rewards and justifies the groping eye, ear, mind. In this first half century we have assimilated, among other things, primitive sculpture and non-objective art; in the previous century, a band of geniuses conquered inanimate nature itself as a realm of art—the literal God of thunder had long departed and nature was mute; but now the mountain echoes began to speak ethics and esthetics and to inspire masterpieces in their own image. There is no reason why in the next half century the meaning of music should not become just as well understood as that of the eternal hills. If the critics seek the way, this civilizing effort will not prove a superhuman task, despite the relative backwardness of discourse about music. The language of criticism by which we assimilate and assess literature was not found ready-made. It had to be invented, phrase by phrase and term by term. And so it must be for music. Once made and tested by public use, the critic's grammar and vocabulary are available to all for their several purposes. Music will then no longer be a thing apart, jealously or scornfully cut off from the total sphere of pleasure and significance. At that time the problem that has occupied us will no longer be a stumbling-block. Every literate being will feel as free to translate music into words as he now is to translate love, religion, the joy of living, or the spectacle of nature. It will then be a platitude rather than a heresy to say with Hazlitt: "We listen to the notes of a thrush with delight from the circumstance not only of sound, but of seasons, of solitude, the recollections of a country life, and of our own."

And lastly, under that dispensation, the false division with which we had to start, of sheep and goats using the words "literary" and "musical" as terms of faint abuse or misplaced pride—that division will abolish itself, and all persons with artistic feelers of whatever kind will share equally the blessings of a common tongue.

THE LIBRARY OF CONGRESS

THE LOUIS CHARLES ELSON MEMORIAL FUND

WORDS AND MUSIC

A LECTURE DELIVERED BY

ARCHIBALD T. DAVISON

Professor of Music, Harvard University

IN

THE WHITTALL PAVILION

OF THE LIBRARY OF CONGRESS

DECEMBER 10, 1953

Washington : 1954

WORDS AND MUSIC

THE MOST direct conveyance of the meaning and the sentiment contained in words is through speech delivered with appropriate inflection; but when words are imaginatively propulsive—and only then is it likely that save in exceptional cases they will prove incitements to the composer—the step from speech to song is a relatively short one. A text will supply meanings and a physical framework for the support of the music. Music, in its turn, will transfigure plain meanings and clothe the verbal substance with a kind of incandescence that words by themselves cannot achieve. These two appear to have been destined for one another from the beginning and their generally happy union is sanctified by long usage. If fancifully viewed this collaboration may, indeed, be compared with almost any human partnership; the basic difference between life and art in this case being that in the former, freedom of choice prevails, while in the world of art the composer selects the partners, writes the contract, and dictates the nature of the relationship.

Inasmuch as it is the composer who decrees the union, it will be his responsibility to deal equitably with both members, determining the relative amount of emphasis to be laid on words or music as the situation may require. There will be occasions when it will be advisable to relegate the text to a subordinate position, while at other times the words, because of their significance, will demand precedence over the music. Although his interest will, naturally, be focused on his own contribution, the composer must not, as so many appear to do, regard the text merely as a convenient clotheshorse, a display rack over which he may effectively drape his music; the text must be for him the animating source of his whole creation and he must be constantly intent on mirroring every shade of meaning and emotion resident in the words. Devotees of the clotheshorse theory of text treatment have been numerous among Italian composers; the French, on the other hand, have traditionally been considerate of the rights of words. Although in its highest manifestations the joining of words with music represents a union so complete that one is hardly conscious of the partners as separate entities, each is, notwithstanding, autonomous, endowed with its own powers of expression, and possessing its own prerogatives. What I shall be calling "the rights of words" and "the rights of music" are important issues, and not a little of the excellence of any vocal work depends upon the extent to which those rights, in due proportion, are regarded.

Not all poets, certainly, have trusted the composer where the rights of words are concerned. Alfred Housman strongly objected to the setting of his poems by any composer, and that attitude is understandable because an author may justifiably wish to avoid the pain of seeing his work committed to what seems to him to be unsympathetic musical hands. But Vaughan Williams put music to verses from "A Shropshire Lad" in a song cycle which makes us grateful that Housman did not realize his ambition. That setting, incidentally, represents one case in which the music even adds stature to the poetry.

It would be reassuring to believe that Housman's unwillingness to confide his poetry to musical interpretation arose not so much from a high respect for his own verse as from the realization that to join words and music under any circumstances is to bring together two elements so different in nature that a perfect union may prove all but impossible. If, as is so often said, a marked dissimilarity in character tends to draw two individuals into a harmonious relationship, then that may account in part for the general accord which exists between words and music when combined to serve a single purpose. Combarieu [1] goes so far as to declare that the natural difference between poetry and music is the chief reason

---

[1] Jules Combarieu, *Les Rapports de la musique et de la poésie considérées au point de vue de l'expression* (Paris: Ancienne Librairie Germer Baillière et cie, 1894), p. 284.

for their union. Whether or not this is true, words and music certainly are fundamentally unlike in their natures, and without embarking on a lengthy excursion into the field of aesthetics, or of falling Laocoön-like into the clutches of the serpents of semantics, I want to refer briefly to those particular differences which have significance for this lecture. After that we may proceed to discover how these differences have sometimes been reconciled in the interests of artistic concord and to consider some of the sacrifices which each partner has been called upon to make.

To begin with, we have two quite separate types of ideas and meanings, those of music springing from the imagination; and those of words originating in the intellect; under no circumstances may these two types be considered to be identical in nature. The most familiar misunderstanding of this principle occurs in the field of church music when the worshiper, palpitating emotionally after the performance of some anthem, will assert that music such as this could not fail to make him a better man. He is most conscious of the music because the music, belonging primarily to the senses, will have had a much more immediate effect on him than the words whose impact will be slower because they must be acted on by the intellect. Actually, it is only the words—provided they embody some dynamic ethical idea—that may be counted on to be spiritually beneficial, to make him, perhaps, a better man. The music, to be sure, may not be destructive of the religious mood, but it may just as possibly project within the worshiper those vague emotional stirrings which have no direct connection with what is called "religious feeling." The confusion is as understandable as it is common. Because both words and music are presented simultaneously, and because the meanings of the text are precise while those of the music are elusive, it is easy to conceive of the musical idea as absorbed in that of the words with a resulting identity of meaning.

I think we would agree that a large proportion of the ideas expressed in words logically combined are intelligible to those familiar with the particular language employed. The ideas expressed in music, on the other hand, are quite indefinite and have as many meanings as there are ears to hear them, and these will be the meanings ascribed to them by the listener; but the composer's meaning may, and probably will be, entirely different. If the composition is what we call "abstract" or "pure" music, as distinct from "program" music, we may assume that the idea presented is beauty, and that alone. In program music, however, the composer's task is to illuminate the ideas set forth in a picture or a story, and those ideas will not be subject to such a variety of interpretations as in the case of abstract music. The vocal composer is, in one sense, a "program" composer inasmuch as the primary source of his music is a text whose ideas are not his own. But beyond the idea lies the expression of it. Feeble ideas communicated either through words or music are never to be respected, but they may, nonetheless, be persuasively set forth.

Take the case of words, for instance. The composer in selecting his text may display a fine literary sense or he may be susceptible to stimulation by language not distinguished for its beauty of expression, and although we consider the ideal relationship to represent a parity of excellence, as it did in the Elizabethan age, the practical truth is—much as we might wish it otherwise—that literary quality is not the first requirement of a good text but rather its adaptability to a musical setting and its appeal to the composer. A number of the texts selected by Monteverdi, Bach, Mozart, Rameau, and Schubert are no match in quality for the music that accompanies them. We are familiar, on the other hand, with examples of fine literature subjected to an unimaginative musical treatment that is sometimes little more than commonplace. In the partnership of words and music it is the latter which must be of unexceptionable quality, for great music may make us forget literary inadequacy and can even appear occasionally to transfigure a text of indifferent literary worth; but poor music either ruins a good text or further debases a bad one.

We take it for granted that the composer finds some strong appeal to his imagination in the text he chooses, but on the basis of his selection we are sometimes prompted to wonder just what it was that set his imagination going. What was the force that stirred up a creative ferment within him? Why do some composers deal primarily with the products of their own imagination while others, including composers of vocal music, place their reliance on second-hand ideas, preferring to seek inspiration in a world outside themselves? And what of those schizoid imaginations which operate freely in either field? These are questions which, I believe, have not been fully answered and they may, indeed, be quite unanswerable.

When I inquire concerning a composer's response to a text, I am not thinking first of the text so poetic in nature that it could hardly fail to invite the collaboration of music; I have in mind, rather, the text that is so factual and so prosaic in character that it would seem to defy the musical imagination to lift it out of its sphere of literalness; words before which we can visualize music standing with vacant countenance:

> Eli Sykes, in the town of Batley
> Killed his sweetheart, Hannah Brooke.

or

> The brown girl had a knife in her hand
> It was both keen and sharp
> And twixt the long ribs and the short
> She pricked fair Eleanor's heart.

These are folksong verses and folksong is, of course, a law unto itself, its texts being often no more than an excuse for making music; strings of proper names or sanguinary verses like the ones just read. Most composers, certainly, would blanch before the prospect of devising music to fit these words, but even in the field of art music one comes on examples of seemingly unproductive texts. There is Handel with "And great was the company of the preachers" and "Whatever is is right," and those incomparable examples from the literature of the English anthem: "Behold, two blind men sitting," "How dreadful is this place," and "Arise and sit down, O Jerusalem." If texts like these seem aggressively unfriendly to musical ideas, there are some which lie quite at the other extreme; texts which have undoubtedly stimulated the imaginations of many composers but which, in spite of that, have had comparatively few settings. Because these texts are so completely self-sufficient or so superb as literature, conscientious composers have generally drawn back from them, feeling that no music, however exalted, could fittingly partner them. The words "O death, where is thy sting? O grave, where is thy victory?" did not deter Brahms and he, probably as much as any composer could, dealt imaginatively with them; but even Brahms added nothing to what was already there.

There are many composers whose music impresses us as standing in close relationship to the text and whose handling of voices is skillful. There are others, however, to whose musical ideas one would seldom take exception but whose way with voices leaves something to be desired. The ideas with which Beethoven clothed his texts were generally unexceptionable and it certainly was not a deficiency in either ideas or imagination that was Beethoven's undoing as a choral writer. On the contrary, it would seem that his imagination soared so high that it prevented him from making his ideas fully articulate within the narrow limits of human voices. But if the lofty flight of Beethoven's imagination sometimes led him to write music that is vocally impractical, that, surely, is to be preferred to the exercise of little or no imagination even when buttressed by a highly developed technique in choral scoring. The Victorians admirably fulfill this prescription. They were endowed with great expertness in chorestration—if I may be allowed to invent a word; they wrote reams of music to all sorts of texts, many of them of fine literary quality; but the total aesthetic horsepower was quite insufficient to move the sheer bulk of the output.

The routine treatment of words to which the Victorians were so much addicted is generally ascribed to a lack of imagination, and while that may be true of the Victorians it does not apply to all cases in which words fail to receive their due. An apparent absence of eloquence may result from a composer's too frequent contact with the same text, and the Mass is a luminous example of this. We can only assume that sixteenth-century composers approached the composition of the Mass with the intention of providing music representative of their highest capacity. Yet how often, even in the work of the greatest, do these ambitions seem to be unfulfilled. We feel, chiefly, that the composer has not written music consistently expressive of the full meaning and spirit of the text.

But just as the definition of a radical depends on who does the defining, so the characterization of some music of an earlier day as "inexpressive" depends on one's point of view. Now there is a period when words and music unite but seem to progress separately; to walk side by side, but to remain strangers nonetheless. The Compostela style of the twelfth century, the organum of the thirteenth, and not a little of the complex music of the fourteenth and early fifteenth centuries might be so described. Especially do many of the isorhythmic pieces of the late Middle Ages appear to us to be utterly inexpressive and without the slightest artistic interest. Was the composer mainly concerned with the necessarily elaborate contrivance of music or with an eloquent setting of the text? Could an isorhythmic motet possibly have made any impact as beauty on the listeners of an earlier day? I can see no reason to believe that medieval composers, writing in what appears to us to be a restricted musical language but which to them must have represented at least a communicable medium, should not have found the music expressive of the texts they were setting. Furthermore, that language was an art language familiar to the listener of that day, and it is hardly credible that he would have patiently endured a long composition which invoked his admiration only because it was skillfully devised. His ear, accustomed to what sounds to us like the labyrinthian complications of pure technique, may well have found this music as lucid and communicating as is to us a Bach cantata or a Schubert Mass.

I take it that music first attained expressiveness, as we understand that word, in the period of the *musica reservata*. Out of the numerous and diverse definitions of that term we may, at least, draw the inference that it had to do in some way with a sympathetic music rendering of the words. In the music of Josquin, for instance, there are many examples of a close parallelism between words and music; the word "high" will be characterized by music higher in pitch than that which has just preceded it, and the word "low" will be treated accordingly. This naïve procedure finds its normal continuance in numerous examples of descriptive writing: Jannequin with his imitations of birds or a group of ladies engaged in animated conversation; Cesti, Purcell, Lully, and Jeremiah Clarke with their "trembling" or "shivering" choruses; Handel with his dwarf menagerie in *Israel in Egypt;* Haydn with his hum of the bagpipe's drone in the *Seasons;* and any number of other instances. Particularly stimulating in Josquin are those places where only the implications of the text are suggested in the music: the resort to familiar style to emphasize a phrase of deep religious significance such as "tu redemisti nos"; or, in the "Ave Maria," where, to mark the contrast between the Virgin and the lowly suppliant, a soaring passage on "Mater Dei" is followed by a simple chordal phrase with the soprano descending at the words "memento mei."

A striking example also occurs in the motet "Ave Christe" where at the words "spes infirmorum" the static and repetitive substance of the music is depressingly suggestive of the invalid immobilized in his wheel chair. By his genius for transferring to music what has been called "the inner nerve of the text," Josquin, more than any other composer, opened the door to expressiveness in our modern sense, and all perceptive joiners of words and music since his day have capitalized on his achievement. One has only to recall Byrd's "Justorum Animae," Gombert's "Super Flumina Babylonis," Morales' "Emendemus in melius," Gesualdo's "Io pur respiro," Morley's "Fire, Fire, My Heart," or Vaughan Williams' "O Vos Omnes," to trace a direct line of descent from Josquin. Works like these display the extent to which an imaginative treatment of words may result in music of great expressiveness, and it is more than a coincidence that all the pieces I have named are in unaccompanied style.

Ideal as is the *a cappella* style, it nonetheless has its limitations. Any attempt to extend an unaccompanied work to major proportions is beset by three obstacles: first, the fallibility of the human voice which, if overtried, will eventually weary and depart from the path of tonal rectitude; second, the inescapably monochrome character of voices however skillfully combined; and third, the absence from choral writing of those resources which are the exclusive property of the instrumental ensemble. Among these difficulties none is more persistent than singleness of color, and choral music bears constant witness to the composer's artfulness in attempting to alleviate this condition. "The Seal-woman's Croon" by Granville Bantock represents a particularly ingenious effort in this direction. In this piece, which is wordless except for the solo part, the composer has subdivided his chorus into several groups approximating the orchestral families such as woodwind and strings, sometimes even imitating the technique of those instruments. However, a hearing of even so short a piece as this one demonstrates how brief is the novelty offered by such a procedure.

But what may be said of unaccompanied vocal music that employs no text? Plato, who believed that music without words represented a thoroughly low-caste form of art, would certainly have disapproved of it, and Zarlino, in his definition of music, ignores it altogether. "Music," he says, "is a compound of words, harmony and rhythm," [2] and this is confirmed by his seventh rule which states that "with any note whatever that is put for the beginning of the music, or after any pause whatever, the utterance of a syllable is absolutely necessary." [3]

Textless vocal music has its freedoms, to be sure, but its rewards may be briefly listed. As in the case of abstract instrumental writing, the composer of wordless music is at liberty to exploit his own ideas without reference to any secondhand source, and he has at his disposal the resource of vocal color just for its own sake. The singer, too, is relieved of the burden of enunciation and may concentrate, as so many singers love to do, on the beauty of the sounds he makes. But textless vocal music is disembodied music without essential mean-

---

[2] See the translation from Gioseffo Zarlino's *Tutte le Opere* (Vienna: 1589) by H. E. Wooldridge in his article "The Treatment of Words in Polyphonic Music," *Musical Antiquary* (January, 1910), p. 89.
[3] *Ibid.*, p. 91.

ing and if long continued is generally wisely supported by a highly varied orchestral accompaniment, as is the case with Ravel's *Daphnis and Chloë* and with Vaughan Williams' *Flos Campi*.

In these days there is little to commend the writing of an instrumental background that does little more than double the singers' notes. Such a device is not an accompaniment, it is insurance taken out where none should be necessary. The only valid reason, it seems to me, for uniting instruments with voices is to furnish where desirable those features which voices cannot supply: variety of color, dynamic extremes, wide range, percussive effects, agility in execution, and dramatic strokes; any and all of them to be used not as purely musical adjuncts but as reinforcements of the text. Instrumental preludes, postludes, and interludes, and especially the longer instrumental commentary are strong unifying elements. In the writing of these Wagner was particularly gifted, for often in the purely instrumental sections of his music dramas we feel that although no text is there, words lie just beyond our hearing.

Do the elaborate instrumental overlays furnished for their Masses by Haydn, Mozart, Liszt, and Rossini emphasize the significance of the words "sanctus" or "incarnatus" more strongly than do the purely choral settings of these same words by Byrd, Palestrina, or Lassus? It would not seem so. The Mass accompaniments of Haydn, for example, add an exterior musical interest that often stands in remote relationship to the text, and if we did not have Haydn's word for it we could feel that he dealt rather cavalierly with holy words like these. If Palestrina seems to us to be nearer the truth than Haydn, it may be because in *a cappella* style there is only the word and its immediate conveyance, the voice. Haydn, on the other hand, was capable of diluting the impact of the holy word by interposing between it and the listener a deal of musical beguilement, and not the least potent of his weapons was the orchestra.

Before taking up the more detailed aspects of the composer's treatment of words and voices I should like to touch on the matter of form in vocal music. The problem of form does not enter with anything like the same degree into the composition of a piece of abstract music as it does in the writing of a vocal composition. In a symphony or string quartet, the composer's ideas may be counted on to follow one another in a natural sequence, and this logical continuity leads normally to structural coherence; the primary ideas with which the vocal composer must deal are presented in the text and they will often be numerous, of contrasting natures, and will occur in close order. The words may maintain one idea throughout, in which case the music may preserve uninterruptedly a single mood; but when there are several ideas involving emotional changes and varied situations, the composer must faithfully incorporate these by suggestion in his music. In the end, his piece must have form of some kind and this is as true of the brief *a cappella* composition as of the more extended one with accompaniment. A complete agreement between text and music is of course assumed, but this, essential as it is, may simply result in a formless patchwork.

The true test of formal completeness in any vocal piece, long or short, consists in an examination of the music apart from the words. If, from the first note to the last, the music seems to have a destiny of its own, it will, from the point of view of structure, be satisfying. This means more than the setting of music *to* words, it is the setting of music *and* words, and one suspects that for the really vocally minded composer the form grows as naturally out of the music as the music develops from the words. Any form depends for its coherence on a certain amount of repetition. Brahms, for example, could invest even a long vocal work with a feeling of unity by returning, at the end, to material borrowed from the beginning, and the apotheosis of this principle is perhaps *Tristan and Isolde* in which Wagner, at the close, finally resolves the dissonance with which the prelude ends.

The larger categorical forms are generally unsuited to vocal music because the text with its variety of moods and ideas would make any strictness of form inappropriate. As might be supposed, however, Mendelssohn was quick to apply classical form to his choruses. In "He Watching Over Israel" from *Elijah* he has cast the movement in clear sonata form and justifies the choice, usually so inapt for vocal music, by writing a chorus which not only produces a sense of formal completeness that is quite unstrained but which also represents the ideal association between text and music, in that the latter exists only as an expositor of the words.

In the strophic setting the problem of form is immensely simplified, but the composer who chooses it must be sure, first, that the emotion which characterizes the text remains at a fairly steady level and then that his music is so persuasive that it will, in the case of a long poem, stand repetition without risk of monotony. Tovey thought well of the strophic setting for he writes: "No modern musical criterion is shallower than that which regards as lazy and primitive the setting of different stanzas of a poem to the same melody. Brahms regarded such strophic melody as a far higher achievement than *durchcomponirtes* declamation." [4]

There are, however, a goodly number of strophic settings which seem to me to deal unjustly with the text. Let us take Goethe's poem "Nur wer die Sehnsucht kennt," familiar to us as "None but the lonely heart," and try to discover how well the chosen form adapts itself to the meaning and emotion expressed in the words as they are interpreted by four composers. Although the basic idea of the poem remains unchanged, there is a crescendo of feeling, and even if there were not, loneliness is something that is not likely to remain static; it grows by what it feeds on; so that any composer who had ever experienced loneliness might be counted on to increase the musical tension.

The first two settings I have in mind are Zelter's and Beethoven's. Both are strophic arrangements, and each composer has retained his original music throughout; both settings are quite objective; one lives on an unchanging plane of loneliness. Beethoven, to be sure, injects a faint note of optimism by casting his music in triple meter, giving it somewhat the effect of a minuet in a mild state of depression. With respect to Schubert, however, there is an evident and a salutary emotional tightening after the first statement.

---

[4] Donald F. Tovey, *The Main Stream of Music and Other Essays, Collected, with an Introduction, by Hubert Foss* (New York: Oxford University Press, 1949), p. 212.

But it remained for Tschaikowsky to provide what is, in terms of music, practically a clinical survey of loneliness at successive stages of its development. No objective dissertation, this; the composer seizes the lapels of your coat, fixes you with his eye, and in the last measure persuades you that there is only one thoroughly lonely heart in the world, and that is his.

Form in vocal music, then, does not mean a scheme with clear divisions which may be graphically reproduced, though that is sometimes the case. The text will live in the music, but the text itself will play only a minor role in determining the form. It is the province of the music to give, quite by itself, an impression of orderliness and logic.

Up to this point I have been speaking of some of the broader issues which affect the union of words and music, and I have tried to emphasize the fact that I regard the partners primarily as two quite separate entities which the composer's magic may transform into one. Each is, nonetheless, absolute, and regardless of the standing of either as literature or as music, there is a limit to the liberties which may properly be taken with them. Both, as I have said before, will occasionally be called on to make concessions; sacrifices which are demanded by the general artistic interest. It is no light matter to distort either words or music out of its true nature, and the composer who does so should have good reason for his action. We forgive him, provided—and only provided—that in the end he produces a work of art. He has caused both words and music to suffer in their pride, but words have been the more abused.

Let us take an obvious case first: the literal dismemberment of a word, the wrenching of it apart syllable by syllable. In Verdi you find this:

La -- cry - - - mo - - - sa   (etc.)

and in Pergolesi, for the word "complaceam," this:

The Italians are noted for such ruthless behavior, but composers of other nations, who fell under the Italian influence, were also addicted to this device.   In Graun's *Der Tod Jesu,* for instance, you have:

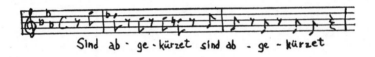

As one might suppose, parody is not far behind, and the Lord Chancellor in *Iolanthe* very neatly supplies it with:

> I took her for the proprietor
> Of a la—dies' se—mi—na—ry!

Another kind of word distortion consists in the spreading of a multiplicity of notes over a single vowel.   In the St. Martial style of the twelfth century one finds as many as thirty or forty notes of florid writing to a single syllable.   But what may be viewed as evidence of the presence of growing pains in the music of the Middle Ages must have adult meaning if it is to be valued in fully developed art music.   In the Renaissance, Roman Catholic composers from Dufay on cultivated the melismatic style in varying degree in their church music, but they were generally unwilling to lessen the impact of secular words by dwelling too long on them.   Most aspects of worldly love, for example, do not seem hospitable to decorative musical treatment.   A declaration of passion if swathed in vocal ornamentation may turn out to be musically impressive, but it certainly represents most inefficient love-making.

The instinct to beautify by decoration, however, has doubtless always existed in mankind, and it was bound eventually to be adopted by all types of music. Italian composers, in particular, turned their gift for melody writing in the direction of the *bel canto* aria, whose lyric properties depended materially on the resources of sheer vocalization, and to the virtuoso aria, in which words were callously slaughtered to make a vocal holiday. The text is generally devoid of any rational association with the music and lies submerged beneath a relentless tide of coloratura. A single instance is the passage in Rossini's *Semiramis* where the composer separates the words "doit" and "être," whose sense obviously depends on their connected delivery, by forty-one notes of melodic tracery. But the voice, like the violin, is most itself in moments of lyric expression, and in *bel canto* the singer can find what a singer always covets, the opportunity to give his voice its head free of the checkrein of enunciation. The humble choral singer, too, gratefully experiences the same sense of spaciousness and relaxation as with full voice and concerned with only a single vowel he delivers some resounding Handelian roulade.

The exact reverse of the process of word extension is the overlapping or telescoping of phrases, a practice common in contrapuntal choral writing. A few words may have to be omitted from a part in order to preserve the sense of the text in all the voices simultaneously; or a part may withdraw briefly from the texture. When this latter situation arises it must be met by the construction of a terminal phrase which in melody, rhythm, and words will be natural, complete, and seemingly uncontrived. Here, if ever, the rights of words are paramount and should be fully respected. In its persistent disregard of these rights I know of no composition to compare with Lassus' setting of the psalm "By the Waters of Babylon," cast in the form of an old-fashioned spelling lesson: S. U. su P. E. R. per super F. L. U. flu per flu su—per flu, etc.

Whatever idea lay behind this curious piece—and it has provoked much speculation—the result is certainly not one to invite a serious attitude toward a text that is so poignant. Crowding a contrapuntal page with words or syllables many times repeated results, as in this case, in a feverish, half-intelligible chattering, out of which the sense of the text is grasped with difficulty.

But if the meaning is severely taxed under these circumstances it suffers even more when several texts are used at the same time, as in the thirteenth-century motet. When applied to more fully developed music the jungle of words becomes impenetrable, and good sense has long since done away with this practice. One of the most interesting throwbacks to polytextual use is Haydn's employment not of four different texts, but of four sections of the same text sung simultaneously in the Credo of his *Missa Brevis*. This results in gratifying brevity on the one hand, and in verbal chaos on the other.

Separation, extension, and telescoping are usages whose influence may be said to be mainly local. They do not necessarily affect the setting of an entire text as rhyme and meter do. Rhyme is not an integral part of poetry; it is a device calculated to enhance the effect of poetry, and the virtues of rhyming are much more likely to appeal to the poet than to the musician who sets his verses. It would be going too far to say that rhyming puts the composer at a disadvantage, yet it is quite likely that the impressiveness and the sense of naturalness which obtain in the great musical settings of prose result in some measure from the absence of rhyme. Rhyme adds nothing to the ideas set forth in the words and it often shackles the composer severely in the matter of rhythm.

The sixteenth-century composer (and poet) Thomas Campion decried what he termed "the vulgar and unartificial custom of riming" [5] in English poetry, and long after his day another English poet, Robert Bridges, expressed his opinion on this matter as follows: "Rime has had a long reign, and still flourishes, and it is in English one of the chief metrical factors. Like a low-born upstart it has even sought to establish its kinship with the ancient family of rhythm by incorporating the aristocratic *h* and *y* into its name. As it distinguishes verses that have no other distinction, its disposition

---

[5] Peter Warlock, *The English Ayre* (London: Oxford University Press, 1926), p. 100.

determines stanza forms, &c.; and for this reason it usurps a prominence for which it is ill-suited." [6]

Bridges' reference to rhyme as one of the chief metrical factors in English may be illustrated by these lines from Christopher Marlowe:

> Come live with me and be my love,
> And we will all the pleasures prove
> That valleys, groves, hills, and fields,
> Woods, or steepy mountain yields. [7]

The persistent meter of this poetry if pursued over a reasonably long period—and especially in a homorhythmic setting—is likely to result in a monotony which strongly belies the exciting variety promised by the lover in Marlowe's lines. The first severe discipline imposed on words by meter in music was the intractably ternary system of the thirteenth century, known as modal rhythm; a scheme that is so artificial, so rigid, and so insensitive to correct text accentuation that its interpretation has been persistently questioned by modern scholars. If transcriptions of this music into our notation truthfully represent the intentions of medieval musicians, then it must be said that at no other point in music history have such drastic sacrifices been demanded of words.

With the passing of modal rhythm the problem became one of mensuration. Each line was, in a sense, a solo voice, having notes of a length appropriate to the natural accentual flow of the text, and, what is more important, a flow that was undisturbed by the presence of bar lines. In the Renaissance, rhymed verse set with evenly spaced pulses was often felt to be so categorical in its effect that a reaction against it was inevitable, and this was manifested in the work of the *Académie de Poésie et de Musique* founded in 1570. *Musique mesurée à l'antique* rejected the narrower concept of meter in favor of scansion in long and short feet according to the classical idea, and the familiar patterns were added to by ingenious combina-

---

[6] Robert Bridges, "A Letter to a Musician on English Prosody," *Musical Antiquary* (October, 1909), p. 25.

[7] Christopher Marlowe, "The Passionate Shepherd to His Love."

tions resulting in highly original rhythms. The composer Le Jeune
was a leader in this movement, and after his death there appeared in
the publication *Le Printemps* the statement that "the wonderful
effects produced by ancient music, as described in the fables of
Orpheus and Amphion, had been lost by the modern masters of
harmony," adding that Le Jeune was "the first to see that the
absence of rhythm accounted for this loss; that he had unearthed
this poor rhythm, and by uniting it to harmony, had given the soul
to the body." [8]

Composition according to the principles of *musique mesurée à
l'antique* is characterized by great rhythmic flexibility and vitality,
and it is easy to lament the brevity of a period which brought forth
such a wealth of delightful pieces in which words and music unite
so naturally. The seventeenth century, however, was primarily an
instrumental age, and instrumental music was subject to rhythms
in which barring had its place. In spite of the obstacle to correct
accentuation which regular barring presents, some composers, by
the exercise of conscientious care in adjusting their music to the
words, have succeeded in overcoming what has been called the
"tyranny of the bar line." It is this, we may suppose, that Milton
had in mind in his sonnet in praise of Henry Lawes when he spoke
of that composer's ability to "span words and music with just note
and accent."

Rossini—a composer whom I still love in spite of his offenses
against words—was no relative of Henry Lawes. In his "Stabat
Mater" he gives to each of the three words "ut te cum" four deliberate quarter notes; a manifest inequity inasmuch as two of these
words are much less important than the third. Care in the avoid-
ance of ineptitudes like this contributes not a little to the realization
of a kind of music which William Byrd once described as "framed
to the life of the words."

Modern composers and editors have tried many avenues of escape
from the tyranny of the bar line, but only Bernard van Dieren, I

---

[8] See the article on Le Jeune in *Grove's Dictionary of Music and Musicians,*
vol. 5, 1906 ed.

think, has gone so far as to dispense with all bar lines in his music. Sometimes employed as a more workable substitute is the polymetric system of scoring which calls for a variety of meters in each voice. How comparatively recent is this usage may be shown by a brief quotation belonging to the early years of this century: "No musical composer would think of writing a piece of music with one or two bars in 3/8 time, the next in 4/4 time, and another in 12/8, and so on, because this would result in musical chaos." [9]   The polymetric system is the only one which insures accentual agreement between words and music under all circumstances, and it is a heartening witness to our respect for the rights of words.

The sin committed against the text by misaccentuation is greatly surpassed in both extent and degree by text repetition, the most persistent of all the destroyers of textual integrity. The repeating of words and phrases is a long established practice in vocal music, and it may be pointed out that in a vast majority of cases initiative springs not from the needs of the text but from those of music; words are repeated simply as an excuse for spinning out the musical substance. Extensive text repetition is usually tolerable only when it is accompanied by constantly changing music which in variety and significance fully compensates for the monotony induced by hearing the same words reiterated again and again.

To this dictum folksong and other popular types are exceptions, for in them there may be not only text repetition but musical repetition as well, the reiterated words or syllables invariably set to the same music. Fa-la-la, hey-nonny-no, lanky-down-dilly—these make no pretense at meaning but they are fun to sing and are an irresistible provocation to go on singing. Often, to be sure, the words do make sense, as in the cumulative or house-that-Jack-built type of folksong in which the text of each verse is reviewed a number of times, each time with a new feature added. Thus, in the "Twelve Days of Christmas" the growing list of the lover's benefactions is recapitulated in reverse in each stanza until with the twelfth appearance of

---

[9] J. P. Dabney, *The Musical Basis of Verse* (New York: Longmans, Green, and Co., 1901), p. 53.

the partridge in his pear tree there has been enough music, presumably, and the gentleman has run out of money.

In the "Twelve Days of Christmas" the words are, at least, clearly heard, but in forms like the round and the catch the sense of the text is quickly lost in the complexities of imitation. Particularly shameless is the catch in which the words may be so ingeniously manipulated as to distort them into something that would make any decorous noun or verb blush in deepest embarrassment. The danger of monotony when a phrase is several times set to identical music is especially great in fugal writing where with each recurrence of the subject we are likely to hear the same bit of text, with the result that the impact of the words is progressively weakened. This is not serious if the words are, for example, "Jehovah's praise forever shall endure," but the continued recurrence of a phrase such as "Our children's children shall rehearse thy deeds in never-dying verse" eventually fills us with a positive loathing for the whole idea of filial devotion.

Now almost all the practices of which I have been speaking, although they may be justified under certain circumstances, do, notwithstanding, conflict with the rights of words, and many writers have protested the injustice done not only to words but to common sense as well by a treatment that reduces the text to a position of marked inferiority. Yet when we think of the harmonic part song or the pedestrian hymn we may justifiably ask ourselves whether some playing fast and loose with the text is not, after all, commend- able. In some cases, certainly, this tampering does minister to artistic completeness. Word extension, for example, is thoroughly convincing when the resulting musical elaboration seems to grow naturally out of the text rather than to be merely superimposed on it. Mozart was a great master of this detail. In somewhat the same way in which Bach, in his instrumental music, could write a decorative passage that is not abstract ornamentation but the apparently inevitable consequence of the long-held note which just precedes it, so Mozart could overlay a single word with a vocal luxuriance that is the word itself become music. The Benedictus from the C minor

Mass and the *terzettino* "Soave sia il vento" from *Così Fan Tutti* are first-rate examples of this.

In vocal style it is the function of music to enhance the significance of words, and this is practically always accomplished without loss to music itself; but on occasion music will step out of character. Never, probably, is music at so great a disadvantage or the parity between words and their accompaniment more drastically upset than in the field of humorous vocal literature. Here, if ever, words are quite enough; their purpose is to amuse, perhaps even to cause laughter, and in this distracted world one is tempted not to decry their presence too forcefully. But music, when allied to comic words, generally loses its self-respect. Everyone will laugh at the text but recognition of the music will be confined to an awareness of its appropriate behavior; separated from the text it will be in most cases of no artistic importance whatever. Such a statement applies, of course, only to music set to words which are comical rather than humorous in any subtle way; poems which ask the singer to imitate the more provocative sounds of nature; the barnyard repertory, the too realistic drinking song, the verse about the brass band. Included, as well, are such poems as parody advertisements of patent medicines and all other writings that appeal to one's sense of humor in its most childlike phase.

There are, naturally, stages which separate the better from the worse. Not all compositions which demand outright imitation in the music are without claim to recognition. Take, for example, those pieces which concern themselves with the cuckoo, a bird which bobs in and out of music literature with the regularity of his mechanical counterpart lurking behind the little doors of his clock, and who can assume enough dignity even to warrant his incorporation into the cantus of a Mass. Such a bird, surely, cannot be shrugged off as no more than the stuff of humor. But in many cases it is his music which is the really amusing feature. At best, any piece of humorous vocal music is aesthetically suspect. It may, on occasions, have its place; but if it is intended to be outright funny its music is bound to be no more than a servile companion to the words, and this is demeaning to music as an art. Fancy is not to be confused with humor. It may be said that one happy function of music is to make us smile occasionally, but I doubt whether it can ever make us laugh without sacrificing its true nature.

The composer alone is to be blamed for any injustice done to music by his fitting to it words of a humorous character. There are, however, circumstances under which he must be viewed as the plain victim of a lack of taste and even of decency exhibited by others who arbitrarily attach words to music which the composer did not intend to be vocal. Regardless of whether a melody is susceptible of being set to words, it is fair to assume that had the composer wished to accompany it with text he would so have ordered. But this is an opportunity not to be lost by the avid educator who hopes, by the addition of words, to fix an instrumental melody in the memory of youthful listeners. In the preface of a recent volume of these atrocities a noted conductor declares that once the music has been fixed in memory the "easy little jingles" will be forgotten. Unfortunately and even tragically, it is not the melody but the silly patter that invariably comes to mind. This is unavoidable because words mean something—though in these cases little enough, God knows—whereas instrumental music is only beauty without a convenient handle.

It is a melancholy experience to glance around a concert hall during the performance of a certain familiar orchestral work and to see numbers of persons soundlessly and resentfully moving their lips to that lethal bit of doggerel, "This is the symphony that Schubert wrote and never finished." The tendency, as in church, is to hear music and text as one, to invest music with the too easily understood meanings of words, and in the case of these so-called educational offerings to reduce the music to the sorry level of the text. Great music needs no crutch at any time. To debase the classics into commonness and cheapness by wedding them to literary trivia is a sin against art; and to poison at its source the natural stream of musical enjoyment by the use of these grotesque monstrosities is, among the many destructive obliquities of so-called music education, undoubtedly the most unforgivable.

If I am wrong about this, if the jingle method is really valid, then it immediately suggests the adoption of the device in reverse. Sunday schools should, perhaps, teach great moral precepts by means of jazzy reminders: "Blessed are the pure in heart" or "Thou shalt not steal" if presented in this way would never be forgotten once the music had evaporated, and a sterling contribution to the probity of future generations might thus be made.

Considering the limitations which beset the vocal, and particularly the choral, composer, how often must he envy the relative freedom of his instrumental colleague. The ideas with which the latter is concerned are entirely his own, he has at his disposal resources much more extensive, and he is not charged with the care of that varied wealth of detail, that prodigious amount of calculation, that falls on the writer of vocal and especially of choral music. The advantages of this freedom are, I think, generally recognized and they have occasionally been pointed out.

Thomas Morley expressed his respect for instrumental music when, in speaking of the composition of fantasies, he wrote: "In this may more art be showne than in any other musicke, because the composer is tied to nothing but that he may adde, diminish, and alter at his pleasure." [10] Michael Praetorius was of the same mind: "A capriccio or extemporized Fantasia results when one sets about elaborating a Fuga according to his own pleasure and fancy, yet does not linger on it for long but soon lights on another Fuga which may come into his mind. For just as in a regular Fuga no text may be underlaid, so here also one is not bound to words, may make much or little, may digress, add, subtract, turn and twist as he will." [11] And Chris-

---

[10] Thomas Morley, *A Plaine and Easie Introduction to Practicall Musicke* [Imprinted at London by Humfrey Lownes, dwelling on Bredstreet hill at the signe of the Star], 1608, p. 181.

[11] M. Praetorius, *Syntagma Musicum* (Wolfenbüttel, 1619; ed. E. Bernouilli, Leipzig: C. F. Kahnt Nachf., 1916), III, 33. (The passage quoted in the text was translated by Lloyd Hibberd.)

topher Simpson, referring to fancies for viols, mentions the presence of words as a distracting factor in composition: "In this sort of Musick the Composer (being not limited to words) doth imploy all his Art and Invention solely about the bringing in and carrying on of these Fuges, according to the Order and Method formerly shewed." [12]

But both Morley and Praetorius wrote quantities of music that is without hint of strained relations between the text and its setting. Of the three, Christopher Simpson seems to have been the most firmly convinced of the superiority of instrumental writing, for as far as I know he entered the field of vocal composition only once, and that briefly, to compose a single catch.

Words, then, supply a rational basis, a vehicle for voices, and a rhythmic underlay. Music in its turn capitalizes on these and adds its own particular grace, carrying the emotional and imaginative content of the text to a height to which words, by themselves, cannot attain. It may be that not an overwhelming number of these alliances were contracted in heaven, but, on the other hand, there are, surely, very few cases which could make us wish that words and music had never met.

---

[12] Christopher Simpson, *A Compendium of Practical Musick* (London: Printed by William Godbid for Henry Brome in Little Britain, 1667), pp. 141, 142.

THE LIBRARY OF CONGRESS

THE LOUIS CHARLES ELSON MEMORIAL FUND

SYMBOLISM IN THE MUSIC OF BACH

A LECTURE DELIVERED BY

KARL GEIRINGER

Professor of Music, Boston University

IN

THE WHITTALL PAVILION

OF THE LIBRARY OF CONGRESS

MAY 23, 1955

Washington : 1956

SYMBOLISM IN THE MUSIC
OF J. S. BACH

SYMBOLISM is as old as art itself. In primitive times men and women, groping with the mysteries of the world around them, devised methods of interpreting them by using symbols. The visible, the audible, the tangible were employed to substitute for the hidden, the immaterial, the spiritual, and out of this substitution religion and subsequently art were born.

Later, when a more advanced stage of civilization was reached, symbolism was losing some of its importance. The human mind learned to solve secrets of nature through the application of rational thinking, through observation and experimentation, and thus it was not forced constantly to have recourse to symbolic expression. However, a tremendous amount of symbolism was carried on through tradition from generation to generation. Even in modern times we are influenced by the symbolism adherent to certain colors, by symbolic connotations of certain numbers, shapes, and sounds handed down through the ages.

Through all times symbolism has permeated religion and art, and traces of it may be noticed in the great creative achievements of all generations.

This applies to a large extent to the music of J. S. Bach, which in many respects represents the glorious synthesis of artistic trends going back far into the Middle Ages. Symbolism plays a vital part in it, and we are only gradually learning to discern its different manifestations and to understand its importance to the composer.

His symbolism reveals itself in various ways, some of which we shall attempt to outline in this lecture. A borderline case which may be regarded as a primitive type of symbolism is pictorialism. This is an attempt to conjure through musical means visual impressions associated with the words to be set to music. Pictorialism was a device generally adopted in Baroque music, and Bach was all the more inclined to follow this trend of his time, as he had a natural bent for associating pictures with words. The "visual approach" to composition, as we might term it, came quite naturally to him and, we believe, we may discern in this attitude a family trait. Various Bachs showed gifts for painting. While this was particularly the case with the generations following Sebastian Bach, which produced three professional painters, we might point out that two contemporary kinsmen of Sebastian, Johann Ludwig and Nikolaus Ephraim, were apparently skilled painters, as they gave instruction in this art. More illuminating yet is the case of an uncle of Sebastian, Georg Christoph, a brother of Sebastian's father. This musician, a cantor at Schweinfurt, wrote a cantata on the words of Psalm 133, "Behold, how good and how pleasant it is for brethren to dwell together in unity," and he composed the work to celebrate his reunion with two younger brothers, Johann Christoph and Johann Ambrosius. The manuscript of the work has a very interesting title-page which in all likelihood was contributed by the composer. On it we see painted in water colors three objects which, as the composer explains, are meant to symbolize "the triple team of the Bach brothers and its flourishing, sweet and firm concord." Under the word "flourishing" we see a hand holding a three-leaf clover, under the word "sweet" a triangle with three rings, under the word "firm" a padlock with three chains. All these pictures came to Georg Christoph's mind when he thought of the concord of the three brothers which he celebrated through the composition of the cantata. Georg Christoph was apparently able to put down with brush and paints the pictures which he associated with the word "concord." Sebastian did not paint, but with similar inevitability pictures rose before his inner eye when he read a text, and this vision was one of the mainsprings of his musical inspiration.

When we look at his vocal works, countless examples present themselves for pictorialism in the most variegated aspects. In his *Coffee Cantata* a father tries to induce his stubborn daughter to give up drinking coffee by threatening to withhold various gifts, among them a modish crinoline. To illustrate the excessive width of this garment, the singer employs in his recitative the excessive skip of a ninth, an interval which the composer but rarely prescribes in a vocal solo.

Ex. 1

Ich will dir kein-en Fisch-bein Rock nach jetz'ger Wei - te schaf - fen.
You will not get a cri - no - line of mod- ish width with whale-bones.

In another secular cantata, *The Contest between Phoebus and Pan*, the foolish judge Midas expresses his admiration for Pan's inferior song. While Midas voices his opinion, the violins clearly forecast what is going to happen to the ill-advised critic; we hear the braying of a donkey, for Midas is destined to grow donkey's ears as a punishment for his misjudgment:

Ex. 2   Viol. I, II

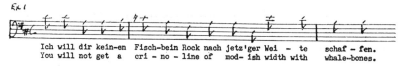

In Bach's *Orgelbüchlein* examples of pictorial symbolism are abundant. Famous is the twofold pictorialism in the chorale-prelude "Old Adam's Fall." Here the tragic fall from grace to sin is symbolized through a sequence of gruesome diminished sevenths, while simultaneously the writhing and wriggling theme in the alto describes the snake in paradise.

A typically baroque form of pictorialism is to be found in the *Gloria* of his *Magnificat*. The voices triumphantly rise twice to glorify God the Father and His Son. When the words "et Spiritui sancto" are intoned, the melodic line is inverted to symbolize the descent of the Holy Ghost.

In other cases Bach uses all the resources of his orchestra to convey the picture he has in mind. In Cantata 161, *Komm du süsse Todesstunde* (Come, Sweet Death, Thou Blessed Healer), the ecstatic recitative in which the singer expresses longing for deliverance from earthly fetters is accompanied by an orchestra which, through quickly repeated high flute notes, dark pizzicatos in the strings, and ponderous octave leaps in the basses, conjures the impression of tolling death-bells.

Not as easy to understand is the pictorialism in the exquisite aria "Am Abend da es kühle war" (At Even, Sweet Cool Hour of Rest) in the *St. Matthew Passion*. Here Bach depicts the atmosphere of the evening by painting just one detail of the situation; the slow note repetitions in the first violin seem to describe the mysterious whispering of the leaves when the faint evening breeze moves through them. The result is a tonal picture which we are inclined to term romantic, but its origin is not akin to that of romantic music, for Bach is not concerned in evoking a mood, as the romantic composer does; he lets us *see* the leaves of trees gently trembling under the evening breeze.

An example which is typical for the mixture of visual and audible elements in Bach's symbolism is to be found in a bass aria of the *St. Matthew Passion* which is but rarely heard. After Judas realizes the full horror of his betrayal, an aria on the words "Give me back my Lord, I pray ye" expresses his remorse. Throughout this aria a motive of the violins, which consists of a diagonally descending line and a horizontal one, conjures the picture of the Greek letter χ, which symbolizes both Christ and the Cross:

Ex. 3

The violin motive thus expresses the vision of Christ crucified which the repentant betrayer cannot shake off. Similar allusions to the Cross are quite frequent in Bach's music. German musicology uses the term "Chiasmus" to designate them.

That Bach expected the audience closely to follow his pictorial symbols is proved by a negative instance in the *St. Matthew Passion.* The composer adopts the method to accompany all the utterances of Jesus with the sounds of a string quartet which creates the effect of a halo. When Jesus on the Cross cries out in utter despair, "My God, why hast Thou forsaken me?" the suffering Saviour is momentarily reduced to a mere human being, and at this point the halo disappears.

Bach even attempted a pictorial symbol for abstract notions such as the passing of time. In Cantata 27, *Wer weiss wie nahe mir mein Ende* (Who Knows How Near Is My Last Hour), the orchestral accompaniment of the first chorus characterizes the flight of time by constantly recurring mysterious sounds imitating a pendulum clock.

While the examples of pictorialism we have outlined so far appeal mainly to the senses, another type of symbolism used with equal frequency by the composer is of an intellectual nature. Bach liked to employ certain musical forms to explain the true meaning of a text. Here again he adopted a principle known to other Baroque masters, and in so doing he was once more following the dictates of his own genius. For Bach everything connected with the Gospel was so vitally important that he felt driven to use any conceivable device in order to express it in all its details and significance. He considered his church music to be not so much a work of art as a part of the religious service, meant to teach the congregation, to elevate their souls, and to strengthen their faith. The religious message embodied in each of his sacred works had therefore to be conveyed with the utmost clarity. The form of the canon seemed to him admirably suited to clarify details of the religious lessons and he used it in manifold ways with a wealth of imagination which has rarely been equalled.

One of the most stunning examples of symbolic use of the canon occurs in the first chorus of his Cantata 80, *Ein' feste Burg* (A Mighty Fortress), based on the chorale tune of the same name. Bach writes a powerful fugue which is framed at the top and bottom by a canon based upon the immortal hymn. A stupendous symbol of the unshakable rule of God's law throughout the world from the highest to the lowest sphere is thus created, a symbol that the congregation at St. Thomas' church could not fail to understand.

Quite often the canon is used by Bach to illlustrate the *imitatio Christi;* so, for example, in Cantata 12, *Weinen Klagen* (Weeping, Crying). When the bass sings "I follow Jesus," a strict imitation of the vocal melody occurs in the strings, indicating man's desire to abide by the rule of God. Likewise in the *Orgelbüchlein* the chorale "In dulci jubilo" is given a canonic treatment which is clearly inspired by the words of the hymn *Trahe me post Te* (Draw Me After Thee).

The form of the canon is also well suited to symbolize uniformity. Thus in the B minor Mass the duet "Et in unum Dominum Jesum Christum filium Dei unigenitum" has an imitation in unison between the two singers to demonstrate the unity of Father and Son. On the other hand the similar statements of the two false witnesses against Jesus are portrayed in the *St. Matthew Passion* by a canon and this helps to create the picture of two men mechanically repeating each other's words.

Pictorialism and symbolic use of canonic devices are somewhat intermingled in Cantata 4, *Christ lag in Todesbanden* (Christ Lay in Death's Dark Prison). In Chorus 5 the text refers to one death swallowing the other, whereby a fight of devilish dragons devouring each other is envisioned. Bach closely follows this picture and writes a canon in which parts of equal significance seem to be entangled in mortal struggle until one after the other vanishes.

The idea of a canon conveying a symbolic meaning might seem unconvincing to musicians who see in Bach an eminent master so skilled in handling strict contrapuntal forms that they feel he used these just for art's sake. There is no doubt that Bach derived the joy of the expert craftsman from doing work of this kind, that it offered him true satisfaction to solve self-imposed technical problems, and that he never grew tired of experimenting with complicated forms. Nevertheless we are justified in assuming that many of the canons to be found in his works were due to his urge towards symbolic expression. Bach himself clearly indicated the working of his mind in his *Musical Offering*, that stupendous synthesis of canon technique which he submitted to King Frederick the Great of Prussia. When presenting a canon in augmentation he explained its symbolic meaning by the words "notulis crescentibus crescat fortuna Regis" ("May the fortune of the King grow with the length of the notes"); and to a spiral canon which ends one whole tone higher than it started, thus continuously modulating upwards, he added the remark "Ascendenteque modulatione ascendat Gloria Regis" ("And may the Glory of the King rise with the rising modulation").

Other traditional forms were used by Bach in a similar way. The Latin motet, which he did not cultivate as a separate form, symbolized for him the reverting to a venerable past. Thus in his *Magnificat* the section "Sicut locutus est ad patres nostros, Abrahae et semini eius" ("As it was told to our fathers, to Abraham, and to his progeny") is in the form of a brief motet without independent instrumental parts, and similarly in the Credo of the B minor Mass motet-like sections may be found which Bach inserted to emphasize the origin of the Christian creed in times long gone by.

It is significant that both pictorialism and form symbolism were more or less overlooked by 19th-century Bach scholars. The aesthetic evaluation of pictorialism had fundamentally changed since the Baroque era. For Bach's generation it was a method unhesitatingly employed by any composer and expected by his audience. Gradually, however, it lost more and more ground. After Haydn wrote his oratorio *The Seasons* he was attacked by critics for his aping of nature. Beethoven was so keenly aware of the change in aesthetic standards that he felt obliged to add the famous apology to the score of his Pastoral Symphony: "more an expression of feeling than painting." When a 19th-century scholar like Philipp Spitta came across an all too obvious instance of pictorialism in a Bach work, he felt almost embarrassed. Only at the turn of the century did music-lovers, mainly thanks to the pioneer work of men like André Pirro and Albert Schweitzer, begin to understand this side of Bach's art. As to the form symbolism, our eyes were opened to its significance by the basic research of the great German Bach scholar, Arnold Schering.

A different situation exists with regard to another type of symbolism cultivated by Bach. Again and again he had recourse to an esoteric use of Lutheran chorales. For a composer so deeply rooted in Protestant tradition, the treasury of Lutheran hymns formed the very foundation of his art. He not only included them in the most variegated arrangements in his vocal works; he also inserted the tunes themselves (without words or with a different text), whenever such an addition was likely to clarify the message he wanted to convey. These hymns were well known to any Protestant and thus Bach, when quoting them, could assume that his listeners would understand what he had in mind. If one of these venerable melodies was played by an instrument, the initiated were bound to associate with the tune the words familiar to them, and thus a work of sacred music could be imbued with deeper significance. Even long after Bach's death his method was always understood, as his music was mainly studied by Protestant scholars who by tradition were equipped to appreciate this aspect of his symbolism.

The symbolic use of the chorale may be found in all phases of Bach's creative growth. A striking example occurs in a chorus of the *Actus tragicus*, Cantata 106, *Gottes Zeit* (God's Own Time), written when Bach was in his early twenties. The singers are divided into two sections. The lower group, consisting of alto, tenor, and bass, intones the words from the Old Testament, "It is the covenant from the beginning, man thou must die"; here Bach writes a fugue using a theme of antiquated character, in which we find the "hard fall" of a descending diminished seventh. Against this sombre background the light sopranos, representing the New Testament, utter their yearning "O come, Lord Jesus, come," while the orchestra, consisting of recorders and viols, plays the tune of the chorale, "My cause is God's, and I am still, let Him do with me as He will." With this stirring tune the composer offers to mankind threatened by death the consolation of submission to the will of God.

In the first chorus of Cantata 9, *Es ist das Heil uns kommen her* (Salvation Sure Has Come to Man), Bach does not content himself with using as *cantus firmus* in the soprano the chorale which gave this cantata its title. He also alludes in the bass again and again to the Christmas chorale, "From Heaven above to earth I come," thus explaining that salvation came to us through the birth of Christ:

Instances of this kind might fill a whole book. I should like to mention only one more, as it displays a remarkable parallel to a great work of art preserved in this city. The National Gallery of Art owns Giovanni Battista Tiepolo's *Madonna of the Goldfinch*. According to George Ferguson, "the goldfinch is fond of eating thistles and thorns, and since all thorny plants have been accepted as an allusion to Christ's crown of thorns, the goldfinch has become an accepted symbol of the Passion of Christ. In this sense, it frequently appears with the Christ Child, showing the close connection between the Incarnation and the Passion." Similarly Bach's *Christmas Oratorio* uses the Passion chorale both at its beginning and end. The inclusion of this poignant tune in a work expressing joy over the birth of the Christ child is motivated by Bach's desire to imply that only through Jesus' sacrifice did His birth bring salvation to mankind.

Before we turn to the last aspect of Bach's symbolism, it should be pointed out that the methods we have so far described bear a striking resemblance to the precepts of 18th-century rhetoric. There cannot be any doubt that Bach was keenly interested in the art of oratory, and we have a significant testimonial to this effect from a personal friend of his, Magister Birnbaum, who taught rhetoric at Leipzig University. According to Scheibe's report, Birnbaum stated: "Bach so perfectly understood the resemblance which the performance of a musical piece has in common with rhetorical art that he was listened to with the utmost satisfaction and pleasure when he discoursed of the similarity and agreement between them; but we also wonder at the skillful use he made of this in his works."

It is quite possible that the study of manuals on rhetoric contributed to Bach's use of symbolism. In any case the Thomas Cantor adopted in his own work the aims laid down by rhetors: *docere, delectare, movere,* i. e., to instruct, to delight, and to move.

In recent times German musicologists, in particular Arnold Schmitz, have greatly stressed Bach's connection with the rhetorical technique of his era. They have even gone so far as to avoid the word "symbolism" and to attribute Bach's methods merely to the application of the so-called "rhetorical patterns." This seems to be primarily a question of terminology and does not really affect the foundation of Bach's artistic method as outlined here.

While the forms of symbolism discussed above were meant to appeal to discerning listeners, Bach pursued also a type of symbolism which was primarily intended for his own satisfaction. We have learned to discern traces of such symbolism thanks to the research carried out by the German scholars, Martin Jansen and Friedrich Smend. Bach acted like the builder of a medieval cathedral who devised multitudes of the most artistic statues placed high up on the edifice and invisible to most human eyes. The architect felt that for the glory of God he had to erect a building perfect in every detail, and similarly Bach devised intricate methods for deepening the content of his music and adding a new meaning. It is a significant feature of this type of symbolism that quite often it may be detected with the eye rather than with the ear. It centers around numbers which since time immemorial have played a significant part in the different liturgies. Number symbolism in the Bible was a favorite topic of the Church fathers, and especially St. Augustine and Gregory the Great laid down certain laws for the interpretation of numbers which remained valid for many centuries. In Bach's time there was still great interest in the symbolic use of figures and a book like Johann Jacob Schmidt's *Biblischer Mathematicus* (Biblical Mathematician) of 1736 may well have fascinated Bach as it fascinated many of his contemporaries.

It is also significant that in 1712 the philosopher Leibniz, who was descended from a line of Saxon organists, gave the following definition of music: "Musica est exercitium arithmeticae occultum nescientis se numerare animi." ("Music is a secret exercise in arithmetic of the soul, unaware of its act of counting.")

When we look at Bach's music from a numerical point of view, counting bars, notes, chords, entrances of themes, and so forth, we are quite staggered by the intricate web of mathematical elaboration we find wherever we make our investigations. Thus in his *Orgelbüchlein,* when he treats the chorale "These are the holy ten commandments," the motive of the counterpoint which he derives from the melody of the *cantus firmus,* appears exactly *ten* times.

When he subsequently arranged the same chorale in his *Clavierübung,* he wrote in one version a trio for two manuals and the pedal, and he subdivided it into *ten* sections. Moreover this prelude was given a two-part form, meant to symbolize the two tablets on which the ten commandments were written.

Turning to the *St. Matthew Passion* we find that whenever scenes occur in which the disciples are involved, their number is carefully indicated by the composer. During the vigil on the Mount of Olives the tenor representing Peter sings "I will watch with Jesus gladly" and the chorus adds the refrain "so all our sins have gone to sleep" ten times to refer to the remaining ten disciples. Bach emphasizes the fact that eleven men are involved, Judas having left on his errand of betrayal. Similarly the figure eleven is stressed in the duet with chorus following Christ's capture. Two soloists sing the duet, while the chorus interrupts with nine ejaculations. Thus again eleven disciples seem to raise their voices. There are also numerical features not as obvious as the examples given so far. When in the *St. John Passion* Pilate hands Jesus to the Jews to be judged by them, they reply: "It is not lawful for us to put any man to death." Bach's theme has here *five* weird chromatically ascending notes on the word "töten" (kill), thus referring to the *fifth* commandment the Jews have just mentioned. This theme is repeated *ten* times so as to make it quite clear that the composer actually refers to one of the ten commandments:

Ex. 5

tö . . . . ten

More intricate is another passage. In the *St. Matthew Passion* the description of the earthquake after the death of Jesus seems strangely inadequate. Why does Bach, who uses in this composition two orchestras and two choral groups, confine the music meant to portray the uproar of the elements to a mere continuo part? The answer may be given with the help of figure symbolism. The instrumental bass is clearly subdivided by the words of the text into three sections, which consist of 18, 68, and 104 notes respectively. On the other hand the earthquake is mentioned in Psalms 18, 68, and 104. Bach, so erudite a Bible scholar, wanted to refer to these Psalms when describing the earthquake.

When in the *St. Matthew Passion* Jesus at the Last Supper takes the cup and gives thanks, uttering the words, "Drink ye all of it, for this is my blood of the New Testament," the bass accompaniment to this deeply stirring tune consists of 116 notes; apparently Bach refers to Psalm 116, which is the only Psalm mentioning the cup of salvation. Its thirteenth verse reads: "I will take the cup of salvation, and call upon the name of the Lord."

Similarly, after Jesus refuses to answer the accusations of the false witnesses, a tenor voice states in an arioso, "My Jesus answers not." This arioso is accompanied by 39 chords, in reference to Psalm 39, "I was dumb, I opened not my mouth."

Those who might be inclined to consider such passages as merely accidental should be reminded that symbolic references to literary sources occur also quite frequently in paintings. In Giovanni Bellini's *Madonna of the Meadows,* preserved in the National Gallery of London, the Virgin is placed against the background of a cold, clear luminous landscape, with a white bird attacking a large serpent and with a ram placed next to a classical altar. Edgar Wind discovered here an allusion to a passage in Virgil's *Georgica,* where the poet explains that the best season for planting vines is a cold day of early spring "when the white bird, the foe of long snakes" is come. Virgil also mentions an altar prepared for a goat. "Thus," Mr. Wind writes, "the pictures in the background are not capriciously added but support the sacramental theme defined by the figure of the sleeping infant."

There is still another kind of figure symbolism which Bach apparently employed to a large extent. It was the common practice in his time to substitute numbers for letters of the alphabet, as shown in the following table:

A	1	K	10
B	2	L	11
C	3	M	12
D	4	N	13
E	5	O	14
F	6	P	15
G	7	Q	16
H	8	R	17
I, J	9	S	18

Bach seems to have liked these *lusus ingenii* (intellectual games), as they were called. His own name was particularly suited, as the word Bach corresponds to 14, which is $2+1+3+8$, and J. S. Bach to 41, which is $9+18+2+1+3+8$; and 41 is the inversion of 14. As a matter of fact these two numbers play a very important part in his musical thinking. It is interesting to read what Philipp Spitta wrote about Bach's earliest preserved clavier composition: "The piece betrays its youthful origin not only by the singular stiffness of the themes, but by the persistent clinging to the principal key through no less than fourteen consecutive entrances of the theme." The symbolic meaning of the fourteen entrances was not apparent to the scholar. When we now look at Bach's ultimate work, the organ chorale *Before Thy throne my God I stand,* which he dictated shortly before his death to his son-in-law, we find that he ornamented the hymn tune in the top voice in such a way as to have a first line comprising *fourteen* notes, while the whole melody consisted of *forty-one* notes, as if the composer wanted to express that Bach, J. S. Bach, was now preparing to enter the heavenly abode. It is hardly an accident that in another composition written during the later part of Bach's life the number 14 also plays an important part. In the *Musical Offering,* which is a personal tribute of the composer to King Frederick the Great of Prussia, the core of the work, a Trio Sonata for flute, violin and clavier, displays fourteen entrances of the theme. This work is now being mentioned for the second time in our lecture as it abounds in symbolic features.

The same figure fourteen is to be found in Bach's personal seal which shows fourteen jewels. When the composer was invited to join the "Mizlersche Societät" in Leipzig, a scholarly music organization, he hesitated at first, but changed his mind on hearing that Handel had accepted the invitation. Handel was the eleventh member; Bach, however, did not follow right after him but waited until he could join as the fourteenth member. At this occasion, according to the rules of the organization, an official portrait was painted of the Thomas Cantor. On this oil painting, by Elias Gottlieb Haussmann, Bach's garments are arranged in such a way that on the front and sleeves of his coat as well as on his vest exactly fourteen silver buttons are visible.

Whenever one takes the trouble to follow up in Bach's music other cues connected with the number alphabet, one gets remarkable results. Forty-three, for instance, symbolizes the word *Credo.* In the B minor Mass the word *Credo* appears forty-three times; moreover the music written to the words "credo in unum Deum Patrem omnipotentem" has one hundred twenty-nine bars, that is three times forty-three, to conform with the three repeats of the word "credo" prescribed by liturgy.

The list of examples might be extended indefinitely. I cannot claim to have covered all the types of symbolism employed by Bach who, like other composers of his time, was also inclined to give an esoteric significance to his choice of musical instruments. The trumpet stood for majesty and royal glory; the oboe d'amore was often employed as a symbol of brotherly love, the oboe da caccia frequently denoted a pastoral atmosphere. Moreover, various types of symbolism were frequently used by Bach simultaneously in a kind of symbolic counterpoint, as Schering aptly termed it. The examples mentioned should suffice, however, to prove the fascination that symbolism held for Bach. It satisfied his lucid, highly active mind; it enhanced the didactic character of his work; it allowed his fervent religious faith to reveal itself in variegated forms; and the very secrecy of some of his symbolisms appealed to his peculiar sense of humor.

The intellectual trains of thought leading to the use of symbolism in Bach's music should by no means be considered as opposed to, or even independent of, the creative act. Pictorialism, form symbolism, and chorale symbolism were so firmly rooted in Baroque man's consciousness that they acted as a powerful stimulus for the unfolding of Bach's creative imagination. Figure symbolism belongs to a different sphere, but even this type of symbolism was closely integrated into his compository work. We have for a long time been aware that in Bach the most variegated artistic and national heritage came to a superb fusion. This lecture has tried to point towards an important element in the spiritual and intellectual equipment of a personality which was as great as it was complex.

Bibliography

Das Erbe deutscher Musik, Reichsdenkmale, V. II. Leipzig, 1935.

Ferguson, George Wells. Signs & symbols in Christian art. New York, 1954. 346 p.

Geiringer, Karl. The Bach family. New York, 1954. 514 p.

Gurlitt, Wilibald. Johann Sebastian Bach. 3d ed. Kassel, 1949, 116 p.

Jansen, Martin. Bachs Zahlensymbolik, an seinen Passionen untersucht. *In:* Bach-Jahrbuch, 1937. p. 96–127.

Mies, Paul. Zur Frage des Mathematischen bei J. S. Bach. *In:* Bach-Jahrbuch, 1939. p. 43–49.

Pirro, André. L'esthétique de Jean-Sebastien Bach. Paris, 1907. 538 p.

Scheibe, Johann Adolph. Critischer Musikus. Leipzig, 1745. 24 p. 1., 1059, 24 p.

Schering, Arnold. Das Symbol in der Musik. Leipzig, 1941. 129 p.

Schmitz, Arnold. Die Bildlichkeit der wortgebundenen Musik Johann Sebastian Bachs. Mainz, 1950. 86 p.

Schweitzer, Albert. J. S. Bach. London, 1911; New York, 1950. (Translated by E. Newman.) 2 v.

Smend, Friedrich. J. S. Bach, Kirchen-Kantaten Berlin, 1947–49. 6 v.

Smend, Friedrich. Johann Sebastian Bach bei seinem Namen gerufen. Kassel, 1950. 36 p.

Spitta, Philipp. J. S. Bach. London, 1884–85. (Translated by Clara Bell and J. A. Fuller-Maitland.) 3 v.

Wind, Edgar. The eloquence of symbols. *In:* Burlington magazine, Dec., 1850. p. 349–50.

THE LIBRARY OF CONGRESS

THE LOUIS CHARLES ELSON MEMORIAL FUND

SOME SOCIOLOGICAL ASPECTS
OF MUSIC

A LECTURE DELIVERED BY

JAAP KUNST

Head Curator, Department of Cultural and Physical Anthropology
of the Royal Tropical Institute, Amsterdam

IN

THE WHITTALL PAVILION

OF THE LIBRARY OF CONGRESS

OCTOBER 27, 1955

Washington : 1958

SOME SOCIOLOGICAL ASPECTS
OF MUSIC

IF IN THE UNITED STATES or in western Europe a music lover
should decide to play a certain composition or have it played
for him, or if he should wish to learn to play any musical instrument
that takes his fancy, nothing will stop him, provided, of course, that
he is financially equal to it. Modern Westerners are inclined to
take this situation for granted and many even will think that this
liberty has always existed and will always exist. Now, this notion
is definitely incorrect. Restrictions exist even in the western world
of today. For instance, take Wagner's *Parsifal,* which was reserved
for the Bayreuth theatre by his widow, as long as the law permitted
it, or Strawinsky's *Ebony Concerto,* dedicated to and reserved by
its author for "Woody" Herman. Or, again, think of Béla Bar-
tók's concerto for viola which was written for the British viola virtuoso Primrose, with the restriction that only he was to perform it;
or think of Allegri's *Miserere,* which was jealously guarded from
the danger of being copied, to make sure that it would never be
heard outside the Sistine Chapel. However, young Mozart, who
had attended one performance, reproduced it by ear. About this,
Leopold Mozart—the father—wrote in a letter to his wife (April 14,
1770): "Du wirst . . . oft von dem berühmten *Miserere* . . .
gehört haben, welches so hoch geachtet ist, dass den *Musicis* der
Capellen unter der *excommunication* verboten ist eine Stimme
davon . . . zu copieren oder jemanden zu geben. Allein, wir
haben es schon. Der Wolfg: hat es schon aufgeschrieben . . .
Weil es eine der Geheimnisse von Rom ist, so wollen wir es night in
andere Hände lassen, *ut non incurremus mediate vel immediate in
censuram Ecclesiae.*" ("You have often heard of the famous
Miserere . . . which is so greatly prized that the performers in

the chapel are forbidden on pain of excommunication . . . to copy it or to give it to anyone. But we have it already. Wolfgang has written it down . . . As it is one of the secrets of Rome, we do not wish to let it fall into other hands, *ut non incurremus mediate vel immediate in censuram Ecclesiae."* Anderson tr.)

Outside of western civilization, however, the fact that certain compositions and musical instruments are exclusively meant for certain occasions, persons, or groups of persons, is quite normal. We may even assume that in primitive communities this was the usual situation. This phenomenon could have been called *musica reservata,* had it not been for the fact that this term is already used for an entirely different concept.[1] For that reason I had to content myself with a less characteristic and more longwinded title.

To systematize the various phenomena I intend to discuss, I shall file them under eleven headings:

I. Instruments or orchestras belonging to a certain caste or class;

II. Instruments or orchestras reserved for certain ceremonies or institutions;

III. Compositions belonging to certain personalities;

IV. Compositions reserved for certain ceremonies or institutions;

V. Instruments which should be played only by either males or females;

VI. Compositions which should be played only by either males or females;

VII. Compositions which should be performed only by a given individual;

VIII. Compositions which should be performed only by one given group (caste, tribe);

IX. Instruments and music which are confined to a given time or to a given season;

X. Instruments and music which are confined to a given place;

XI. Instruments which should be played only by the owner himself.

It is true, that the borderlines between the various categories, thus created, are not clearly defined and I have only done it this way for the sake of a clearer and simpler picture.

The examples I shall give you presently include some which do not fully represent the original situation. In many cases, a slackening of the tradition can be noted which increases in proportion with the levelling influence of western civilization. In this civilization, detached from nearly all magical and traditional sources, the original situation is completely lost.[2] That this is not always an improvement, that it can often be felt as a cultural loss, will be conceded by many. Others, to a greater extent *rerum novarum cupidi,* may perhaps contest this. It depends entirely on a person's mental attitude. The still existing musical restrictions in western civilization—apart from liturgic music—are usually not based on magic or tradition. As a rule, the underlying motives are economic ones. In the case of Bayreuth, quoted earlier, we may assume that motives of piety played a part, whereas the Strawinsky-Herman and Bartók-Primrose cases were based on feelings of friendship and admiration.

Of our first category, the one headed "Instruments and orchestras belonging to a certain caste or class," the kettle-drum is a typical example. The instrument is of Oriental, *i. e.,* Persian, origin and it is there—as, for that matter, in India also—usually mounted in pairs, with the difference of a fourth or a fifth between the instruments. In Arabia and Persia, as well as in Mogol Hindostan, these kettle-drums are found exclusively amongst the ruler's retinue.

The instrument came to the West through the Crusades. In this connection, Curt Sachs[3] quotes Joinville, brother in arms and historian of Louis the Holy (1214–1270), who writes about the Saracens in 1309: "La noise que il menoient de leur *nacaires* et de leurs cors sarrazinnoiz, estoit espoventable à escouter." ("The noise they made with their *nacaires* and with their Saracen horns was awful to hear.") The place can be found in the *Histoire de Saint Louis* by François Michel[4] and it shows that even at that time the French language had already formed the word *nacaire* from the Arab word for kettle-drum: *naqqara.*

In the West too, the kettle-drum long remained the instrument of the court and a royal prerogative for splendor and war, afterward becoming—through the mounted surroundings of the prince—the most favored instrument of the horsemen. The Hungarian and

German courts were famous for their kettle-drum playing during the middle of the 14th century. Only later was the instrument accepted in Western Europe. Not until the reign of Louis XIV were all cavalry companies of the *Maison du Roy,* except the musketeers, and all *Mestre de Camp* companies issued kettle-drums. In 1683 Sir James Turner says about the kettle-drum: "The Germans, Danes and Swedes permit none under a baron to have them, unless they are taken from the enemy in battle." In this connection we note that, until 1742, the kettle-drummers of the Saxon cavalry regiments did not wear uniforms, but electoral livery.

These and many other points of interest can be found in Curt Sachs' excellent *Handbuch der Musikinstrumentenkunde.*

At first, the metal straight trumpet, of Asiatic origin also, has the same social status as the kettle-drum. The two instruments belong to each other inseparably at the Arabian, Persian, and Indian courts. Apart from that, the trumpet is often a sacred instrument as well, both in the countries around the Mediterranean (the Hebrew *hasosra,* the Greek *salpinx,* the Roman *tuba*), as well as in the Far East (the Chinese *la-pa,* the Tibetan *kang,* the Indian and Hindu-Javanese *karana*).

The Crusades introduce the long and straight trumpet to the medieval West as a war and temple instrument. There, too, the trumpet remains at first the prerogative of the nobility and knighthood. Later it is adopted by the horsemen. Common people and foot-soldiers have to content themselves with horns. This was already so in ancient and medieval India, where the ordinary soldiers had to use the bent horn, the *sringa.* The social relation between trumpet and horn is expressed in the Italian proverb: *arrivare colle trombe e partire coi corni,* which means "arriving with a trumpet and leaving with horns,"—said of someone who arrives bragging and is then considerably cooled off.[5]

The high Javanese nobility too has its own ensembles, such as the gamelans *Munggang* and *Kodok ngorek* in the Central-Javanese *kratons,* the *gamelans Degung* in the *kabupatens* of the Sundanese Regents, the gamelans *sekati,* both at the courts of the four principalities as well as at the long since mediatized Cheribon Sultan's courts. As a matter of fact we could have put these orchestras—with the exception of the gamelan *Degung*—in our group II as well, because these orchestras are at the same time reserved for special occasions. For instance, the gamelan *Munggang* is played to add lustre to the arrival of high guests; to the former Saturday tournaments; to the nightly official repasts on the last five odd days of the month of fasting; to the first official meeting of a princely couple; to the *Garebegs;* to three large religious *kraton* celebrations; to the acting in state of the ruler; and formerly, to the arrival of a letter from one of the other Javanese rulers or from the Governor General.

The gamelan *Koḍok ngorek* is played on the occasion of the first official meeting of a princely couple. It is also played on the ruler's birthday; at the circumcision of a young prince; when during a *Garebeg* the *gunungans,* the sacred heaps of food, are brought in; during the highlights of a *wayang wong* performance; and in the olden days when, for popular entertainment, tigers were released in an arena after which they were speared when trying to escape, or during a fight between a tiger and a kerbau.[6]

Finally, the gamelan *sekati* is heard only during the *sekaten-*week, *i. e.,* the week in which the Javanese people commemorate the birth and death of the Prophet Mohammed, and on a few rare occasions, such as the 40th anniversary of the rule of His Princely Highness Paku Buwana X.[7]

The high esteem in which these age-old orchestras are held is apparent from the titles preceding their names: *Kangjeng Kjahi,* Venerable Sir. When any of these gamelans are to be played, they are assembled at a special traditional spot. (They could, therefore, have been discussed also in our group X.)

In Bali, which is still Hindu, the gamelans *Selunding,* which are found in a limited number in some villages of the *Bali-aga,* the original Balinese are performing a similar function.[8] These orchestras play only on special occasions, such as certain religious ceremonies, a visit of the Governor General, the breaking out of a contagious disease, and certain calamities at the hand of Fate. Such magic powers are attributed to these orchestras that they must never go through a door or gate. They have to be lifted over the walls surrounding all Balinese home properties. He who has touched a corpse and who consequently is considered *sebel,* impure, is barred from contact with the gamelan *Selunding* for the period of one month and seven days. The players—at least in the *Bali-aga* village of Bungaja—form a venerable corps of old men, who are pledged to remain with the gamelan until the *tabuh,* the playing mallet, falls from their powerless hands. A stranger or an uninitiated person is not permitted to touch the *Selunding.* Even the orchestra's guardians would think twice before sounding the instruments at unauthorized times. Dr. Korn [9] writes that one of the *Selunding* orchestras is particularly holy and is said to have descended directly from heaven.

Professor C. Hooykaas pointed out to me recently that the sub-rulers of the Malayan peninsula were not allowed to possess the complete Malaka orchestra, but that they had to see to it that their ensemble had at least one instrument less than that of their overlord.

D. H. Meyer's investigations have once again confirmed that in the Indonesian cultural world, the large wooden slit drums could only be possessed by certain chiefs and that only males were permitted to play them.[10]

It is not the Euro-Asiatic civilizations alone which furnish examples of special instruments reserved for specific social groups. This phenomenon is found also in Africa.

An extensive drum ensemble is a rigidly maintained prerogative of the chief of the (Wa)Tu(t)si, a Hamitic pastoral people in East Africa.[11] It is played in ever-changing rhythms on all state occasions. At the accession of a new ruler the drums are carried to the place in hammocks as if they were royal personages. They are the *Kalinga,* the most holy of them all; the *Chim'umugizi,* or he who makes the possessor of the throne rule; the *Mpats'ibihugu,* or he who is protecting the country; the *Ichy'umwe,* or the drum of the country of which the ruler is the uncontested master; the *Butare,* or strong as a rock; the *Gisaba rwanda,* or he who can be heard all over the country; the *Singkang'imilyanga,* or he who does not fill the subjects with fear, etc. Other drums remind the people of the daily routine: the *Ndamutsa* is sounded at 8 o'clock in the morning when the ruler is showing himself to the court and his subjects, in other words, during the event which in Versailles, at the time of Louis XIV, was called "le grand lever." The *Nchabagome* announces the sentencing of great criminals. The largest of all is the *Gihumurizu* or *Nyampundu* and it represents public rejoicing when the ruler graciously moves amongst his people. One drum is specially used for the tattoo. Another one, again, is used to announce that the ruler has retired. Still others mark the beginning of a war, the triumphant return from a war, the making of the "sacre du printemps." The drums are so closely connected with the life of the ruler, that the language contains expressions such as "during the peaceful drum of King" so and so; "a drum of peace and prosperity"; in which the word "drum" has replaced the word "government." In other expressions the word "drum" is used as the equivalent of the word kingdom, or even of the king himself.[12] (In our western world we could point to the same usage, as when we speak of "the Holy See," meaning the Pope or the Vatican as a theological or political power.) The excellent recordings made by the Denis Roosevelt expedition and, recently, by Hugh T. Tracey, convey a fair idea of the mighty sound of these drums.[13]

The position of the *tabl al-kabir*, the great drum, at the 14th century court of the Mughal Il-Khans in Bagdad, can be compared with the position of these royal Watutsi drums. It was the personal emblem of the Il-Khan and was always destroyed at his death. These monster drums, almost the height of a man, were sometimes carried on a chariot.[14]

According to Father Marcel Pauwels,[15] in Ruanda forged iron bells are made, to be worn as a mark of distinction by men who have killed an enemy or a lion; by women who have borne at least ten children; by cows which have given birth to a record number of calves, and by first-rate hunting dogs.[16]

As for adjacent Uganda, Dr. Wachsmann [17] says: "This *entaala* or *entamiivu* (*i. e.* an orchestra consisting of a 12-key xylophone and five drums) was the Kabaka's (the King's) privileged orchestra, which only a few important heads of clans and tribal chiefs were allowed to possess. . . . at the present time the Queen Mother and one other official of the court are known to keep an *entamiivu* complete with xylophone." [18]

After reading the first Dutch edition of this treatise, Dr. Hans Hickmann (Cairo) wrote to me: "I have noticed that the sociological ties in music, so eminently characteristic and so clearly existing, seem to be unknown of Ancient Egypt, presumably, because these things are completely buried in the Egyptian literature. This is to be regretted because it concerns here a historically demonstrable first proof in history, which also has the advantage of being recorded in writing. In this connection I think of the magico-religious use of the trumpet [19] which even in the modern state is considered a manly and royal instrument and which is manufactured in pairs. Further I refer to the ceremonial and magical instruments, each one of which has been dedicated to a deity, and also to the double function of each kind of instrument, namely as a religious ceremonial object, and as a sound-producing apparatus. In many cases this is quite striking. Finally I mention the custom of the ceremonial breaking of music instruments and the interment of lutes, lyres, harps and even clappers (a couple of clappers were found in a small sarcophagus, where they had been enshrined ceremonially), of bells and other sound devices, carefully wrapped in linen, like mummies." [20]

During the discussion of the sacred and "Herrenschicht" orchestras, we have, as you will have noted, moved from our first group to the group of the "instruments or orchestras, reserved for certain ceremonies or institutions."

New Guinea provides us with examples of a purely magico-religious nature, such as the "holy" flutes and the bull-roarers (*skabiek, sosom*). These instruments are or were played by men only and they served to imitate the voices of spirits, the former on the north coast, the latter at various places in the interior. The women of the tribe had to exercise care not to set eyes on the source of the sound whenever they heard it. Besides, they were supposed to provide an ample supply of good food (mainly sago cakes, preferably seasoned with succulent palm grubs), because the ghost was always hungry. It is almost needless to say that the spirit would choose the men's house as its place of residence. The food, hurriedly taken to the spirit's abode, was invariably found eaten to the last bit the following morning. In earlier times a woman who had seen such a musical instrument, or who had entertained doubts as to the spiritual appetite, would have been killed without mercy.[21] This knowledge undoubtedly strengthened her religious fervor.

It is no different with the *kende*, the oblong iron bells, sounded with a stick and belonging to the Kissi who live northeast of Sierra Leone and Liberia. They are initiation instruments, carefully guarded from the eyes of women. And of the men themselves, only a few specially chosen dignitaries, the *s'koa kengda*, are allowed to sound the *kende* during the initiation ceremonies at specified moments.[22]

Amongst the Kissi, too, the bullroarers, in these rites, play exactly the same part as the *sosom* amongst some Papuan tribes. About this, André Schaeffner says: "The men tell the women that this is a terrible thing, the Thing *toma*. The buzzing sound they can hear is the roar of a large ferocious animal, which has fallen down from heaven and which is now devouring their children in the sacred forest. If one of them sets eyes on the bullroarer, or if she meets a man carrying one, or if she simply finds out what produces this sound, she runs the risk of being killed." [23]

Edwin D. Neff discovered recently that amongst the Camayuras, a South American Indian tribe in the territory around the source of the Xingu, the flute stands in the same relation to the women. Only the men blow these very long flutes, which serve to promote the catching of fish. A woman setting eyes on one of these flutes is subject to group assault.[24]

The Chinese "scraping tiger," the *yu* or *ki'a*, is an instrument with an exclusively ritual function.[25] (Being inseparably bound to one definite spot, just as the gamelans *Hunggang, Kodok ngorek,* and *Sekati* in Java, it could also have been mentioned in our category X.)

. . . .

It is again the Javanese principalities which give us examples of our third category: "compositions belonging to certain personalities." The gamelan composition *Hundur-hundur kadjongan* was only played in the Solonese Kraton when, during a festivity, the ruler moved in state to another part of the palace and during the dance of the *chantang balung,* those officials whose task it was to find attractive and gracious wives for His Princely Highness.

Moreover, each of the four Central Javanese rulers had his private composition. For instance, the *ladrangan Srikaton* was the one belonging to Susuhunan Paku Buwana X. The *ketawang Barangganjur* belong to Sultan Hamangku Buwana VIII. The *ketawang Puspawarna* to His Highness Nangku Nagara VII. Nowadays these compositions are sometimes played in other places as well and they have nearly lost their "princely signature tune" quality.

Central Java also gives us a good example of our fourth category: "compositions reserved for certain ceremonies or institutions." It is the gamelan composition *Beḍaya ketawang* which is played exclusively to accompany the dance of the *beḍaya's,* one of the two specifically princely dancing groups (the other one being the group of the *serimpi's*). An atmosphere of venerability surrounds both the *beḍaya* dances—in any case this one—as well as the accompanying music. The dancers are supposed to be priestesses or envoys of the pre-Hindu Goddess of the South Sea (i. e. the Indian Ocean), *Ratu Kidul.* During the dance it is believed that she is present in the Kraton. About 1920, the *nyaga's* (musicians) and the Kraton inmates had still such a respect for the dance and the composition *Beḍaya ketawang* that rehearsals took place only on *Anggara kasih,* i. e. the Thursday coinciding with the Pasar-day *Kliwon,* which is once every 35 days. Furthermore, the dancers had to be absolutely pure and were dressed like brides. The humming of the holy melody was strictly forbidden (no one would have dreamt of doing it anyway), and if it were necessary to write the melody down, it was seen to it that at least one error was made. To produce a complete perfect notation would have been felt as evil presumptuousness in the face of higher powers.

A western counterpart of such an attitude towards a certain melody—although not so rigidly maintained—is, or at least was in 1913, embodied in the old Island of Terschelling song *Wat hoor ik hier in 't midden van de nacht.*[26]   This song, which is a paraphrase of a passage of the *Song of Songs* (Chapter 3, Verse 1–4), illustrates the coming of Jesus to the Soul-Virgin, in a free translation of an 11th-century *carmen* by the famous cardinal-bishop of Ostia, Petrus Damianus.   The present Terschelling people merely see it as a nightly visit of a lover to his girl.   However, the relation with the *carmen* mentioned seems certain on account of the content, the identical use of words and the peculiar rhyming scheme which, in both instances, show the same departure from the norm. Now, this song—and this also seems to testify to its spiritual origin— until recently was only sung at the conclusion of the large Terschelling festive summer wagon drive (which, originally a heathen midsummer festival, later turned into the Christian St. John's procession) and was timed so that the final strophe, which mentions the heavenly court, occurred at the moment the wagons were making their final run around the church.

The restriction that certain instruments "should be played only by either males or females"—our fifth group—is found all over the world.   Take the flute, for instance: among most peoples, past and present, playing the flute—almost any kind of flute—is regarded as a masculine prerogative, and, as we have stated above, sometimes prejudice has gone so far in this direction as to forbid a woman even to look at this instrument on pain of death.   Yet, on the other hand, for some inscrutable reason that rather rare variety, the central-hole flute, may be played, or at least is played, only by women.   I noted this myself among the Ngadanese and Nagess of midwestern Flores,[27] and Van der Tuuk records the same custom among the Toba-Batak.[28]   The same applies to the use of the panpipes in some regions, as, for instance, among the Nacao Indians in Venezuela and the Tinguians in North Luzon (Philippines).[29]

On the island of Nias, off the West coast of Sumatra, the *doli-doli,* a primitive xylophone, is only used when the rice is ripening and the fields are guarded (our group IX), and then by women only.[30]

The above mentioned Batak tribe also makes a distinction between the kind of mouth-harp played by girls and that reserved for

[11]

the use of the young men: among the ornaments suspended from the instrument meant for the men there is always a miniature bamboo spring clapper which is never found on the girls' harps.

Among the Bunum tribe on the island of Formosa, the musical bow is solely for the use of the male, the mouth-harp usually for the female. The flutes restricted to male use are played only on occasion of triumphal head-hunting, not for amusement.[31]

Regarding the flutes of the Venda of Northern Transvaal, Kirby states: They "are made in a special area, which is protected by special sacred ceremonies and taboos, by a specialist maker, and their sale is a monopoly. They are constructed in sets, and are always placed in charge of a selected individual. . . . The players are always males." [32]

The Central African *marimba* (*m'bila, timbila, balafon*) is a typically male instrument; the same may be said of the wooden slitdrum of Indonesian culture.[33]

In Surinam, women, the principal singers, never play drums. They believe that if they break the taboo their breasts will grow to the ground.[34]

On Manam Island (New Guinea) girls are called upon to sound a single death beat, but do not use drums at any other time.[34]

Among the Kissi, already mentioned, the *soo*, a rattle made from a gourd, is a woman's instrument in that it is made as well as played by women only, and furthermore is used, except sporadically in very special cases, exclusively for accompanying women's dances; [35] the Baganda (British East Africa) have castanets made of a particular kind of seeds which only girls are allowed to play,[36] while the Big Namba (Malekula, New Hebrides) consider the musical bow definitely a woman's instrument.[37]

To what extent this assignment of use of a given kind of instrument to one sex or the other is connected with the sex-suggestion inherent in some instruments, I do not know. Sometimes such a connection seems quite evident, as in the case of the flute, which is commonly regarded as a phallic symbol and to which naturally (one is reminded of certain equivocal expressions in many Western languages) male characteristics are ascribed, even though feminine.

But in other cases no such connection exists—or perhaps we should say exists any longer.

In Indonesia and elsewhere the drum is felt to be feminine. In those regions this instrument belongs to a group of concepts including darkness, an empty cavity, moisture, the maternal womb, the moon—ideas obviously related to the subconscious in true Freudian fashion. Yet for all that, the *beating* of the drum is not confined to one sex only. On the islands of Java and Bali the instrument is played by men exclusively, but in Timor and West Flores I saw it oftener, though not always, being played by women. It is quite possible that the cultural phase still manifesting itself on the Lesser Sunda Islands—and perhaps the same may be said of Borneo, where the Dyak priestesses often beat a narrow, high, one-headed drum (*ketobung belian*)—is an older one which clings more closely to the original view of things. The fact, as stated by Marius Schneider,[38] that drums were originally used to produce rain, accords with the above in that it is suggestive of one of the components of the group of concepts already mentioned, namely moisture.[39]

Our sixth category, "compositions which should be played only by either males or females," takes us again to the tropics.

In his analyses, Hübner [40] shows that the women of Lamuschmus in northern New Ireland, sing songs totally different from those sung by the males. These women's songs are examples of pentatonic singing, performed with "sehr zarter Tongebung" (*i. e.*, with a very soft tone), "ein etwas ans Wimmern gemahnender Gesang" (*i. e.*, reminiscent of whimpering), which according to this author is characteristic of the so called "Walzenbeilkultur" (a neolithic culture found also in New Guinea). In other women's songs he was struck by the "dunkelweiche Abdominalklang" (*i. e.*, the dark and tender abdominal sound). On the other hand, the male songs from Lamuschmus "stellen ein von starken motorischen Energien erfülltes, naturalistisches Geschehen dar, in den die Kräfte auf exponierten Hochton zusammengeballt werden um sich in 'strain'-artigen Abfall, zuweilen mit geradezu ausbruchshafter Gewalt, zu entladen" (*i. e.*, represent a naturalistic phenomenon filled with strong forces, in which the energy is concentrated on a high-pitched exposed tone that discharges itself in a 'strained' descent, often explosively dynamic), in other words, it concerns the same manner of singing I found amongst the Papuans in the Van Rees Mountains and which also characterizes the songs of some Australian tribes. Von Hornbostel called this melodic type "Treppenmelodik" [41] and I have named it "tiled" melodies." [42] Represented by Werner Danckert, the "Kulturkreis" ethnologists see these melodies as a characteristic expression of the totemistic cultures. Other examples can be found in the Congo area. They are magic songs, sung exclusively by women for the purpose of ensuring a favorable hunt for the males. A priceless example of this kind of singing is on a record published by the Paris "Boîte à Musique" (No. Part 5471/110).

. . . .

Of our seventh category: "compositions which should be performed only by one given individual," the literature shows some typical examples.

Amongst certain Eskimo tribes each man has his own song which is to be performed only by himself, this restriction being the strongest form of copyright one can imagine. Estreicher, in his treatise *La musique des Esquimaux-Caribous*,[43] says on the authority of Eskimo expert Jean Gabus: "si le compositeur d'un chant est considéré comme son unique possesseur, c'est parce que le chant est 'le porteur de son âme,' " (if the maker of a song is considered the sole possessor of that song, it is because it is "the carrier of his soul"). And he adds: "cette explication indique clairement que les Esquimaux-Caribous voient dans une mélodie l'expression individuelle de la personalité de son compositeur" (this explanation shows clearly that the Caribou Eskimos see in a melody the individual expression of the composer's personality). This is also the reason why such a melody disappears when the singer-owner dies. The song is never taken over by another unless it is of special benefit to family or tribe as a magic song. In that case the song is inherited by the next of kin.[44]

In the island of Biak, in Geelvink Bay, North New Guinea, a kind of copyright—at least for the tribe elders—is also recognized for certain songs.[45] And about the South African Basuto we read: "Each chief his his own tribal song or 'mukorotlo.' " [46]

About the *ecoc* (*echoich*) which is a conical end-blown flute of the Lango, a Bantu tribe, Driberg says: "Every man has his own whistle motif . . . which may be memorized by a few words, a catch or phrase of a private song . . . The motif may not be played by anyone else, and an infringement of this rule will certainly cause a violent quarrel, and may even lead to bloodshed. Nor is this surprising when it is remembered that a man blows his whistle motif in war and hunting to signify that he has obtained a kill, and that it is his method of revealing his presence or identity from a distance . . ." [47]

The right to an individual melody is also known amongst the North American Indians. Thus Apel's *Harvard Dictionary of Music* says: "The property idea regarding songs is common to many tribes and the individual owner of a song was often known to sell it to another member of the tribe. It could then be sung only by the purchaser." [48]

Helen H. Roberts, in her most recent publication on the songs of the Nootka Indians of western Vancouver Island, mentions examples of this kind: "Many songs," she says, "including practically all gambling songs . . . may be used by anyone, but many others, including all wealth-display songs, are the exclusive property of different chiefly families. As such, they come under the general class of intangible possessions or *topa-ti* which, along with tangible property . . . constitute the touchstones of social status . . . The song itself is a *topa-ti;* a dance may be a *topa-ti* or the two taken together; even an entire ceremonial, embracing four days of ceremonial practices, may be the *topa-ti* of a certain family." [49]

In a recent publication [50] another well-known American ethnomusicologist, Miss Frances Densmore, says: "It is difficult for a white person to understand the feeling of the Indian toward his individual song, probably received in a 'dream'. In another tribe an old Indian recorded a song, then bowed his head in apparent grief. The interpreter said: 'Niskigwun says he thinks he will not live long because he has given you his song.' "

Our 8th category—"compositions which should be performed only by one given group" or tribe—takes us to Australia. Regarding

the central tribes (Aranda and others) it is known that they sometimes confer a so-called "corroboree," *i. e.,* a ritual song and dance
festival, upon a friendly tribe as a token of goodwill and friendliness.
The corroboree thus transferred, plus the songs belonging to it, will
never again be performed by the donor tribe, but exclusively by
the receiving tribe.[51]   It happens too that a corroboree is learned
from another tribe against payment of, for instance, blankets or other
goods.[52]   In this fashion melodies sometimes travel for hundreds of
miles, their passing-on subject to payment each time.   The result is
that often songs are sung of which the words have no significance at
all to the performers.   In those cases the songs have come from a
different language-region.

We find the same situation in New Guinea, the Solomon Islands,
and the islands in the Torres Straits.   Father Schmidt,[53] Myers,[54]
Schmidt-Ernsthausen,[55] Guppy,[56] and Seligmann [57] refer to this.[58]
Father André Dupeyrat, in a commentary on Papuan songs he recorded in East New Guinea, also mentions a song of the Kittoro-
type which the tribe of the Roro (a coastal tribe opposite Yule
Island) had bought from the Rigo tribe, 130 miles to the east, because they wanted to sing this song themselves.

However, it is not amongst the primitive races only that we find
this phenomenon of certain musical forms and compositions being
confined to specific social groups.   According to Robert Lach [59]
Japan's entire musical heritage is (was?) divided into four categories.   The old classical hieratic music, which originated in China,
belongs exclusively to the *Gagaku,* the highest social level consisting
of courtiers and nobility.   The repertoire of the second social level,
the *Genin,* has a less artful kind of music which is always profane.
The third class, the *Inakabushi,* is the group of blind musicians, of
whom the most prominent, the Kengio subcast, are permitted to
wear white trousers.   This group, too, confines itself to popular
music, but of a kind different from that of the *Genin.*   And finally
there is a fourth cast, the *Geishas,* servants of the light Muse, inter-
preters of streetsongs and hit-tunes.   Each of the four social groups
mentioned has its own set of scales.

.   .   .   .

Of our 9th category: "instruments and music which are confined to a given time or to a given season," the examples are legion. For instance, the Central Javanese *patets*, melodic registers, each of which belongs to its specific time during the night of a *wayang* performance.[60] Another example is supplied by the registers used in the incantations of the ancient Aryan *soma* ritual, from which the *patet* division has possibly originated. From the Rig-Veda I quote: "in the morning ceremony one should employ a breast-tone like the roar of the tiger; at noon, a guttural tone like the monotonous quacking of the cha-krawana (a bird species); at night, the tone should ascend to the head so that it will sound like the voices of a peacock, goose and cuckoo."[61] The phenomenon is found also amongst the Indian *ragas*, melodic patterns, carefully selected for certain periods of day and year, to which they are characteristic.[62]

In the Ngada district in West Flores, according to Father Arndt,[63] the playing of the *foi dea*, the double flute, is permitted only during the ripening of the rice. The first playing of the year is always accompanied by a certain ritual. The village elders take their flutes to the *loka tua*, the sacred place where the palm wine is kept. They take a mouthful of this wine and then pronounce a prayer of gratitude. Then they proceed to the *vitu sipi* (the grinding stone), another holy place, formerly the place where the little rice-knives were sharpened. They seat themselves on the holy stone and start to play. After that they return to the village where they happily tell the people that the flute playing season has begun again and that everybody may now play to his heart's content.

In olden times in Zululand the *umtshingo* (kind of flute) was not to be played until the time of the *umkosi*, or annual festival of the Zulu king. This was held about Christmas time, and the entire Zulu people, including every one of rank and the entire army, assembled in court dress at the Royal Kraal. During this festival the king himself was "charmed" by the doctors, special songs were sung in praise of ancestors, new laws were proclaimed, and the people were formally given permission to partake of the new season's crops. The holding of the *umkosi* was the signal for all of the shepherds to make and play the *umtshingo* and also the *igemfe*, another wind instrument made from reed. The whole countryside would be filled with joyful piping, which would last until the following February; thereafter the pipes would be silent until the next *umkosi*.[64]

Naturally, the ritual harvest songs, playing such an important part in the lives of some North American Indian tribes, are confined to a definite season.

Our 10th group, "instruments and music which are confined to a given place," does not have to be examined separately, because as a rule it coincides with the 2nd and the 4th group, comprising, respectively, instruments and compositions reserved for special ceremonies and institutions. These are usually confined also to a permanent place (temple, palace, sacred menhouse, etc.).

Of the 11th category, "instruments which should be played only by the owner himself," ethnologist John Niles provides a characteristic example. He found that the flutes belonging to the men of the Kumaon tribe in the highlands of Eastern New Guinea are only to be played by the owner or possibly by a very close relative. These flutes are supposed to represent a kind of family guardian spirit. It happens occasionally that another man, not belonging to the family, plays the flute. However, this is done to punish the owner for an offense. The playing of the flute by another person is felt as an intrusion upon the property which has the effect of exacting punishment.

Among the Koryaks of Siberia, according to Mrs. Drinker, every woman has her own drum and her own individual drumbeat.

A 12th category could be added to the preceding eleven groups, music characterized by the fact that its being reserved for special persons, places and occasions is not because of the special right to these songs, or because of the special nature of the place or the moment of performance, but because of the nature of the melodies and texts themselves. I am referring to the group of magic songs and formulas so prominent in cultural history. In fact, if sufficient data were at our disposal, we would presumably find that many if not all restrictions as regards performance and use, characterizing the phenomena examined, have sprung from the conviction that the way of singing or the tone of the instrument had a powerful magical influence, beneficial to the person or group claiming exclusive right. On this subject, interesting as it is, I cannot now go into any further detail. However, if this should cause any disappointment amongst my readers, I may refer to a work by Jules Combarieu, *La Musique et la Magie*. Although the book was published in 1909, it is still of value.[65]

To conclude—I have made it clear, I hope, that it is *not* these remarkable sociological restrictions and reservations that form an exception; on the contrary, it is modern Western musical art and its relative freedom from regulation and privacy that may be said to be exceptional.

NOTES

1. Grove, Sir George, *Grove's Dictionary of Music and Musicians,* Fifth edition, London, Macmillan and Co., Ltd., 1954. Vol. 5, p. 1016a.
   See also:
   Crevel, Marcus van, *Adrianus Petit Coclico,* The Hague, Martinus Nijhoff, 1940; p. 393ff.
2. As was pointed out to me from various directions, the ties, as referred to here, have not been so completely destroyed in European culture as I thought. Alex de Jong, an organist of the Old Catholic Church, drew my attention to various examples of restricted music in the Roman-, Old-, Free-, and Greek-Catholic liturgies. For instance the "Gloria"—a mass hymn—is sung only at ordinary and festive services. It is not to be sung on days of mourning, *i. e.,* during Advent, Lent, and during the obsequies. When, in a sung service, the Bishop gives his blessing, he will do this to a melody sung by him only. During the Silent Week, the organ is not to be played at all.
   The former director of the Music Department of the Belgian National Institute for Radio Broadcasting, Paul Collaer, told me this: "In Neerfeste, near Brussels, we have recorded shepherds' voices. An 80-year-old man still knew cries for the rounding up of sheep and cattle. However, he did not much like our recording these cries. A 40-year-old man told us that he, too, knew these cries, but he refused to sing them for us as they were the old man's property. Said he: 'If I were to sing them, all his cows and sheep would join mine'—old magic."
3. Sachs, Curt, *Handbuch der Musikinstrumentenkunde,* Leipzig, Breitkopf und Härtel, 1920; p. 85.
4. Joinville, Jean de, *Memoires de Jean, Sire de Joinville, ou Histoire de Très-Chrétien Roi, Saint Louis,* (ed. Francisque Michel), Paris, Didot, 1858; p. 47.
5. Sachs, *op. cit.,* pp. 276ff.
   See on this subject also:
   Lach, Robert, "Zur Geschichte der musikalischen Zunftwesens", in *"Sitzungs-Berichte der Akademie der Wissenschaft in Wien"* (Phil.-hist. Klasse, No. 199, Bd. 3, 1923; pp. 31ff), where many more particulars are to be found concerning the special position of kettle-drummers and trumpeters, namely among the ancient Hebrews, in Rome, and in the German Middle Ages. I refer further to:
   Schaeffner, André, "Timbales et longues trompettes", in *Bulletin de l'Institut français d'Afrique noire,* (XIV, October, 1952; pp. 1466ff.)

6. Kunst, Jaap, *Music in Java*, The Hague, Martinus Nijhoff, 1949.; Vol. I, pp. 259, 262.
7. *ibid.*, p. 265ff.
8. Kunst, Jaap *and* Kunst van Wely, C. J. C., *De Toonkunst van Bali*, Weltevreden, G. Kolff & Co., 1925; Vol. II, pp. 437ff.
9. Korn, Victor Emanuel, *De dorpsrepubliek Tnganan Pagringsingan*, Santpoort, C. A. Mees, 1933; p. 159.
10. Meyer, D. H., "De spleettrom", in *Tijdschrift voor Indische Taal-, Land-en Volkenkunde*, Vol. LXXIX, No. 2, 1939; pp. 415–446.
11. Devrocy, Egide *and* van der Linden, R., *Le lac Kivu*, Brussels, van Campenhout, 1939; fig. 7.
12. Boone, Olga, *Les tambours du Congo belge et du Ruanda-Urungi*, Tervuren, Annales du musée du Congo belge, 1951; p. 74–75.
13. Denis Roosevelt expedition, recordings 7, 8 and 9, issued by the Institut des Parcs nationaux du Congo belge, Brussels; and Decca L. F. 1120 (Music of Africa, Nos. 3 and 4)
14. Grove, *op. cit.;* Vol. 4, p. 529a.
15. Pauwels, Marcel, "La magie au Ruanda", in *Grands Lacs*, Vol. LXV, No. 1, 1949; p. 47.
16. Trowell, Margaret *and* Wachsmann, K. P., *Tribal Crafts of Uganda*, London, New York, Oxford University Press, 1953; pp. 326–327.
17. *ibid.* p. 314.
18. *ibid.* pp. 366ff.
19. Hickmann, Hans, *La Trompette dans l'Égypte ancienne* (Annales du Service des antiquités de l'Égypte, cahier No. 1), Cairo, l'Institute français d'archéologie orientale, 1946.
    See also the same author's "Die kultische Verwendung der altägyptischen Trompete", in *Die Welt des Orients* for 1950, (Vol. V, pp. 351–355).
20. Hickmann, Hans *Cymbales et crotales dans l'Égypte ancienne* (Service des antiquités de l'Égypte), Cairo, L'Institut français d'Archéologie orientale, 1949.
21. Read, K. E., "Nama Cult of the Central Highlands, New Guinea", in *Oceania*, (Vol. XXIII, No. 1, 1952; p. 5.)
22. Schaeffner, André, *Les Kissi, une société noire et ses instruments de musique* (Actualités scientifiques et industrielles, No. 1139, Paris, 1951; pp. 22ff.)
23. *ibid.*, pp. 74ff.
24. Neff, Edwin D., "The Vanishing Tribes of Brazil", in *Natural History*, (Vol. LX, No. 2, 1951; p. 77.)
25. Soulié, Charles Georges, *La Musique en Chine*, (Extrait du Bulletin de l'Association france-chinoise), Paris, Ernest Leroux, 1911; p. 87.

See also:

Courant, Maurice, "Chine et Corée", in Lavignac, Albert, (ed.) *Encyclopédie de la musique*, Paris, Delagrave, 1913; Part I, Vol. 1, p. 147.

26. Kunst, Jaap, *Terschellinger volksleven*, 3rd ed. The Hague, H. P. Leopold, 1951. pp. 84ff.

27. Kunst, Jaap, *Music in Flores*, (Internationales Archiv für Ethnographie, Vol. XLII, Supplement), Leyden, E. J. Brill, 1942; pp. 150ff.

28. Van der Tuuk, H. N., ed., *Bataksch-Nederduitsch woordenboek*, Amsterdam, F. Muller, 1861; p. 152a.

29. Sachs, Curt, *Geist und Werden der Musikinstrumente*, Berlin, D. Reimer, 1929; pp. 49ff.

30. Kunst, Jaap, *Music in Nias*, (Internationales Archiv für Ethnographie, Vol. XXXVIII, Fasc. 1–3) Leyden, E. J. Brill, 1939; p. 23.

31. Kurosawa, Takatomo, "Takasago Bunun-zoku no kyukin to godan onki hassei no shijun (The Musical Bow of the Bunun Tribe on Formosa and Some Suggestions Regarding the Origin of the Pentatonic Scale)," in *Toyo Ongaku Kenkyu*, December, 1952 (No. 10/11); pp. 18–32.

32. Kirby, Percival R., *The Musical Instruments of the Native Races of South Africa*, London, Oxford University Press, 1934; p. 168.

33. Meyer, D. H., "De spleettrom", in *Tijdschrift van het Bataviaasch Genootschap* (LXXIX, 1917; p. 415.)

34. Drinker, Sophie, *Music and Women*, New York, Coward-McCann, 1948; p. 57.

35. Schaeffner, André, *Op. cit.;* p. 9.

36. Trowell *and* Wachsmann, *Op. cit.;* p. 325.

37. Deacon, Arthur Bernard, *Malekula, a Vanishing People in the New Hebrides*, London, George Routledge & Sons, 1934; p. 42.

38. Schneider, Marius, "Australien und Austronesien", in Blume, Friedrich, (ed.) *Die Musik in Geschichte und Gegenwart*, Kassel and Basel; Bärenreiter, 1949–1951. Vol. I; col 869–878.

39. The southeast Asiatic bronze drums also are supposed—at least many of them—to have served for *Regenzauber*, i. e. rain magic.

40. Hübner, Herbert, *Die Musik im Bismarck-Archipel (Schriften zur Volksliedkunde und völkerkundlichen Musikwissenschaft*, ed. Werner Danckert, Vol. I; Berlin; Bernhard Hahnefeld, 1938); pp. 17ff. Also chart on pp. 110–111 and the musical examples 15, 16 and 17.

41. Hornbostel, Erich M. von, review of Walter König-Beyer's *Völkerkunde im Lichte vergleichender Musikwissenschaft*, in *Baessler-Archiv*, Vol. XV, Fasc. I, Berlin, D. Reimer, 1932; p. 56.

42. Kunst, Jaap, *A Study on Papuan Music*, Weltevreden, The Netherlands East Indies Committee for Scientific Research, 1931; p. 8.

43. Estreicher, Zygmunt "La musique des Esquimaux-Caribous", in *Bulletin de la Société neuchâteloise de géographie,* (Vol. LIV, 1948; p. 3.)

44. Preuss, Konrad Theodor, *Lehrbuch der Völkerkunde,* Stuttgart, Ferdinand Enke, 1939; p. 130.

45. As I learned from the spoken commentary to some recordings of Papuan songs, brought back, some time ago, by Miss A. W. Landberg from the Schouten Islands (Biak and Supiori).

46. B. C. in *Die Huisgenoot* (Capetown, August 10, 1934, No. 646; p. 47.)

47. Driberg, Jack H., *The Lango,* London, T. Fisher Unwin, 1923; pp. 124–125.

48. Howard, John Tasker, "American Indian Music", in Apel, Willi (ed.) *Harvard Dictionary of Music,* Cambridge, Mass., Harvard University Press, 1944; p. 27.

49. Roberts, Helen H. *and* Swadesh, Morris, "Songs of the Nootka", in *Transactions of the American Philosophical Society,* June, 1955, (Vol. XLV, part 3; pp. 201–202.)

50. Densmore, Frances, "For the Sake of Indian Song", in *The Masterkey,* January–February, 1955 (Vol. XXIX, No. 1, pp. 27ff.)

51. Spencer, Sir Baldwin, *and* Gillen, Francis James, *The Native Tribes of Central Australia,* London, Macmillan and Co., Ltd., 1889; p. 281.

52. Roth, Walter E. *Ethnological Studies among the North-West-Central Queensland Aborigines,* Brisbane and London, Edmund Gregory, 1897; pp. 117ff.

53. Schmidt, Wilhelm, "Über Musik und Gesänge der Karesau-Papuas, Deutsch Neu-Guinea," abstract in *III. Kongress der internationalen Musikgesellschaft. . . . Bericht. . . .* Vienna, Artaria & Co., Leipzig, Breitkopf & Haertel, 1909; p. 298.

54. Myers, Charles S., "Music", in *Reports of the Cambridge Anthropological Expedition to the Torres Straits,* IV, 1912; p. 238.

55. Schmidt-Ernsthausen, Victor, Über die Musik der Eingeborenen von Deutsch Neu-Guinea', in *Vierteljahrsschrift für Musikwissenschaft.* Vol. VI, 1890; p. 268.

56. Guppy, Henry B. *The Solomon Islands and Their Natives,* London, Swan Sonnenschein, Lowrey & Co., 1887; p. 141.

57. Seligmann, Charles, G. *The Melanesians of British New Guinea,* Cambridge, University Press, 1910; p. 152.

58. Kunst, Jaap, *Op. cit.;* p. 38.

59. Lach, Robert, *Op. cit.;* p. 10.

60. Kunst, Jaap, *Music in Java,* The Hague, Martinus Nijhoff, 1949; pp. 338, 344.
    See also: Hood, Mantle, *The Nuclear Theme as a Determinant of Patet in Javanese Music,* Groningen, Djakarta, J. B. Wolters, 1954.

61. Labberton, Dirk van Hinloopen, "Raden Marta Hardjana's Pepakem Sapanti Sakoentala, met een Nederlandsche vertaling en vergelijkende aanteekeningen," in *Widya Poestaka* (No. 1, 1912; pp. 64ff.)
62. Fox Strangways, A. H. *The Music of Hindostan*, Oxford, The Clarendon Press, 1914; p. 153.
63. Arndt, P. P., "Die Religion der Nad'a," in *Anthropos* (Vol. XXVI, Fasc. 3, May-August, 1931; pp. 356–7.
64. Kirby, Percival R., *Op. cit.;* p. 116.
65. As other references, in general, I may mention Chapter X of the recent work by Marcel Belvianes, *Sociologie de la musique* (Paris, Payot, 1951); further, Kurt Blaukopf, *Musiksoziologie,* (Vienna, W. Verkauf, 1951); Frank Howes, *Man, Mind and Music* (London, Secker and Warburg, 1948); Betty Wang, "Folk-Songs as a Means of Social Control" (*Sociology and Social Research,* XIX, 1934; pp. 64ff.); *ibid.* "Folk Songs as Regulators of Politics", (*ibid.,* XX, 1935, pp. 161ff.); and Max Weber, *Die Rationalen und soziologischen Grundlagen der Musik,* Munich, Drei Masken Verlag, 1924 (2nd ed.).

THE LIBRARY OF CONGRESS

THE LOUIS CHARLES ELSON MEMORIAL FUND

THE ORIGINS OF SCHÖNBERG'S TWELVE-TONE SYSTEM

A LECTURE DELIVERED BY

EGON WELLESZ

Fellow of Lincoln College, Oxford

IN

THE WHITTALL PAVILION

OF THE LIBRARY OF CONGRESS

JANUARY 10, 1957

Washington : 1958

THE ORIGINS OF SCHÖNBERG'S TWELVE-TONE SYSTEM

I AM afraid I accepted too lightheartedly the invitation to talk to you about the origins of twelve-tone composition. The more I try to recapture the memory of those days in my mind, the more difficult I find it to talk about an artistic movement the rise of which I myself experienced, and in which, in the beginning at least, I took an active part.

It is not an easy task to conjure up the days of one's youth, when expectations run high, when every work of a young composer seems to hold the promise of future, important development.

What finally helped me to overcome my doubts and hesitations about talking to you of musical events which began half a century ago, and are yet as near to me as if they had happened yesterday, is the simple fact that I am almost the last surviving composer of the small group which was formed by the first pupils of Schönberg.

The technical side of the subject of my talk has been discussed extensively in books and articles, and it is even included in the courses on musical theory in the universities, colleges and conservatories, here and on the Continent.

In this lecture I do not intend to go into technical details, which must be left to the classroom, but I want to spread before you the facts which I still remember. They range from the days in Vienna in 1904 and 1905, when we, Berg, Webern and I, took lessons with Schönberg, down to the time when he abandoned the tonal system and, after years of experimenting, finally worked out the twelve-tone technique.

You all know how fascinating his music is. Whether we like it or not, we feel that a powerful personality speaks to us. You may imagine what influence the contact with such a teacher had on all of us in those formative years.

At that time Schönberg was still unknown as a composer; only his sextet, *Verklärte Nacht,* had been performed in the Wiener Tonkünstler Verein, a musicians' club, and I was too young to have heard it. But while I was still at the Gymnasium I had heard from a friend, who was a few years older than I, about Schönberg's fascinating way of teaching, and also about Professor Adler's newly founded Music-Historical Institute in the University.

I wanted to become a composer; but in those days it was even more difficult than at present to earn one's living as a composer, and most of my friends tried to find posts either as private music teachers or as conductors. I dreaded the usual career of a conductor who, at that time, had to spend his best years working on small operatic stages. I dreaded also the academic way in which musical theory was taught at the Vienna Conservatorium. My friend's suggestion appealed to me, and I decided to study musicology with Guido Adler and to have private lessons with Schönberg.

To understand this decision it is necessary to have an idea of the musical atmosphere in Vienna at the beginning of the century. Vienna was still one of the great musical centers of Europe. It had acquired this position at the beginning of the 19th century when, after the Napoleonic wars, all the great aristocratic families had concerts in their palaces and the patrician circles followed their example. The Philharmonic concerts began, concert halls were opened. In order to be recognized all over Europe, composers had to be performed in Vienna, and conductors, singers and virtuosos had to get favorable reviews in the Vienna papers, which devoted large columns to musical events. The dictatorial position which the music critics had acquired in Vienna by the end of the 19th century had an unfavorable effect upon the development of progressive music. The majority of critics accepted Hanslick's leadership in condemning music which did not conform to his aesthetic doctrines, and only a few younger ones accepted the *Ars Nova*, the new music, which just at that time began to find recognition in other countries; also, the Vienna musical atmosphere was troubled by the antagonism between the adherents of the two greatest representatives of opposing tendencies, Brahms and Bruckner.

But at the moment when our story begins, the great creative period which had lasted for more than 150 years seemed to have come to an end.

Brahms and Bruckner had died only a few years before. Hugo Wolf's work had come to a standstill; he was still alive, but confined in a lunatic asylum. Mahler, though he had written his first symphonies, was for the Viennese primarily the Director of the Vienna Opera and admired as a conductor. His recognition as a great symphonic composer began in Germany.

At that time a new orchestra was founded, the Vienna Symphony Orchestra. Its conductor was a pupil of Bruckner and he was the first to perform all the nine symphonies of his master, the symphonic poems of Richard Strauss, and some of the orchestral works of Max Reger. Also, for the first time, modern French music was heard. Debussy came and conducted with that orchestra some of his works, including *Iberia*.

In 1904/5 the Verein Schaffender Tonkünstler, the Association of Creative Musicians, under the chairmanship of Alexander von Zemlinsky and Arnold Schönberg, performed among other works Strauss's *Symphonia Domestica*, conducted by Mahler, and asked Mahler to conduct his *Kindertotenlieder*. Schönberg conducted the first performance of his own symphonic poem *Pelleas and Melisande*.

Today we can put all these works into their historical pigeonholes. In those days, however, each of them meant something new and very exciting to us. You must realize that even Mahler's performances of Mozart operas, given for the first time on a simple stage, very modern in design, with a small body of strings and with the secco recitatives played on a harpsichord by Mahler himself, met with violent opposition from a part of the conservative public, and particularly from some of the critics. Small wonder that the performances of these new orchestral works were passionately discussed and brought Schönberg, when he was performed, into conflict with the general public.

Today it now seems unbelievable that a work of his, like the string sextet *Verklärte Nacht,* should meet with the most violent opposition at its first performance because of its "daring harmonies." But we should not blame the public for its attitude. I have come to understand that to the general public no innovation is at first so repellent as a new dissonance, yet nothing is so quickly assimilated and accepted by the ear.

To give an example: I once came to Schönberg to take a lesson and found him glancing at the first page of the piano score of Richard Strauss's *Salome,* which had just been published. He tried to analyze the harmonies and said to me: "In twenty years' time we shall perhaps be able to grasp the logical sequence of these harmonies."

That was said at the time when he was composing his first *Chamber Symphony.* A few years afterwards, he himself had written works which surpassed in daring dissonances anything Strauss had ever written.

The explanation of this paradox may be that the composer, following the command of his creative mind, writes music which he would find it difficult to accept aesthetically.

In order to understand Schönberg's unique musical personality we must bear in mind that he was a self-taught man with an unusually quick and controversial mind. He liked to speak in paradoxes and to refer commonplace words to their original meaning, a fact which makes it nearly impossible to translate his German into English. The tendency to think musically in opposites, jumping from high to low pitch and so on, does not emerge so much from his early works, but becomes apparent in those of his second, his so-called "atonal" period. The term "atonal," by the way, was coined by the Viennese critics. Schönberg himself called the term nonsensical. "Music without tones—what does that mean? The right expression," he said, "would be 'a-tonical,' a music without the dominance of one tonic center."

Studying the compositions of his early period one will easily discover their connection with other works of the late 19th century. In his early works he is influenced by Wagner's *Tristan,* by Strauss in his orchestral works, and by Wolf in his songs. This can be seen from his *Gurrelieder.* But the composer who influenced him decisively throughout his life, and whom he rated highest among modern composers, was Brahms. It was Brahms whose way of constructing and developing a theme, of making an unnoticeable transition from the first theme to the second, influenced him in his *Sextet* and in his string quartets. I well remember Schönberg analyzing the first movement of one of Brahms' string quartets and laying particular stress on the way in which the characteristics of the first theme disappeared step by step, while the entry of the second theme was prepared. This was actually his own method. We can notice it best in the transition section from the first to the second theme in his D-minor Quartet (bars 85—98).

Another feature of Brahms' technique, which Schönberg took over, is the combination of a 4-beat rhythm with triplets in the viola or the cello, which produces a kind of *clair-obscur,* a manner of writing which, particularly in the first Quartet in D minor, makes it difficult to follow the music at a first hearing. All these traits are noticeable also in his first, purely orchestral work, the symphonic poem *Pelleas and Melisande,* which carried the Liszt-Strauss technique to a climax. It is the only symphonic poem he wrote and, for many years to come, his last big orchestral work.

Why did this happen?

Schönberg, who had explored new and striking sonorities, must have felt that the Grand Orchestra was for him not the proper means of expressing in sound what he aimed at. He was in his heart of hearts a composer of chamber music, and his mind worked too quickly to find the appropriate realization of his inner vision in the heavy sound of the orchestra.

He was certainly influenced in his decision to concentrate on small combinations of instruments by Anton von Webern, his most devoted adherent and friend. His association with him was of a deeper nature than with any of his other pupils, even Alban Berg. In these years Berg prepared the piano score of Franz Schreker's opera, *Der*

[4]
173

Measures 85—98 of Schönberg's first String Quartet, Op. 7.

ferne Klang,[1] a work whose instrumentation had a lasting influence upon him; but not the instrumentation only, if we remember that the second act of *Der ferne Klang* was written in sonata form, a form which is taken up in Berg's *Wozzeck*. There is also the piano which is supposed to be out of tune. For Webern, his master Schönberg was an authority whom he followed fanatically. But soon Schönberg was influenced by Webern, who confirmed him in his intransigent attitude. It is my conviction that it was Webern who convinced him that the Liszt-Strauss orchestral technique had outlived itself and that it was Schönberg's task to write a new kind of music that would be as different from that of his contemporaries as the paintings of the so-called "Pointillists" were from those of their predecessors.

This new style becomes apparent in the last movement of Schönberg's sceond Quartet in F-sharp minor, op. 10, composed in 1907–08. This movement is the first atonal composition he wrote, and it is significant that in this movement the soprano begins with the words: "Ich fühle Luft von anderen Planeten" ("I feel air from other spheres").

Here we have the decisive break with the harmonic development which began in the Romantic era with the introduction of the chord of the diminished seventh, first on the dominant, as a dramatic effect, but soon as a means to underline melodic tension. When diminished seventh chords on the dominant had lost the effect of surprise, composers after the middle of the 19th century built them up on the mediant and finally on every tone of the scale. The next step was the use of dissonances without a resolution, and composers like Max Reger—I remind you of his great *Inferno–Fantasia and Fugue for Organ*—used clusters of diminished sevenths, rolling chromatically up and down, as middle parts. At the same time, Debussy used clusters of unresolved ninths diatonically, thus re-creating the effect of the 12th- and early 13th-century *organa*.

---

[1] *Der ferne Klang*, composed 1903–9, was performed on most German operatic stages between 1912 and 1914. The piano score is by Alban Berg. From about 1924 Schreker's fame in Germany declined. On 3 February 1957 *Der ferne Klang* was broadcast by the Third Programme of the British Broadcasting Corporation.

The result of both lines of harmonic development was the replacement of the tonic-dominant effect of the cadence and, with it, of classical modulation, by an oscillating harmonic texture which left the musical development in suspense. Such a procedure, of course, affected the melodic line, which became subservient to the harmonic progressions.

The ultimate result of this process was the replacement of a dynamic harmonic movement, with its modulations through several keys, by oscillating harmonies without a center. It led to the opposite effect from what the composer had aimed at; through the lack of distinct harmonic progressions it created a static harmonic effect.

Though Schönberg had great admiration for Reger on the one hand and Debussy on the other, he was not the man to accept either of the lines of development here indicated.

For him, melody and harmony had to be of a piece. I remember how often he turned sarcastically against those who tried to embellish a diatonic melody by chromatic harmonies in order to make the piece sound more "modern." Basing his teaching of harmony on the chorales of Bach, he always stressed the point that a melodic highpoint must coincide with a harmonic highpoint, even if the old cadential effect of tonic and dominant were replaced by other means which created a similar effect. This tendency was worked out by him first in the *Three Piano Pieces,* op. 11, in which no triads are used, but the dissonances are treated as if they were common chords. I regard the *Three Piano Pieces* and the following *Six Short Piano Pieces,* op. 19, as something like the sketches of a painter who, in order to train his hand, tries out a new technique on a small scale before embarking upon the final work. In fact, the change in Schönberg's style coincides with his attempt to paint, and the pictures which he painted in this period reveal the inferno through which he must have gone in those years.

It is always a dangerous undertaking to find an explanation for the crisis in the creative work of a composer. To base one's hypothesis on a single factor is to oversimplify and it may miss the real cause. So much, however, may be said: Vienna was in those days still the capital of a great realm, the Austro-Hungarian monarchy—but one felt the approaching storm. The creative artist—if his path lies clearly designed before him—may turn away from what goes on in the world, as was the case with Richard Strauss, who wrote during the war his most serene work, *Ariadne auf Naxos.*

Schönberg, however, a more sensitive composer, acted like a seismograph which registers the cosmic disturbances. He finished in 1912 his *Pierrot Lunaire,* a work in which he displayed his mastery of all devices of counterpoint; and the *Four Melodies for Voice and Orchestra* in 1913–14. What he experienced is expressed in the words and music of the last piece of *Pierrot Lunaire,* in the nostalgic mood of "O alter Duft aus Märchenzeit." He felt that a great period of civilization was coming to an end, the world of his youth.

The war came, and Schönberg remained silent as a composer until 1923, when his *Five Pieces for Piano,* op. 23, was published, the first work in which he consciously applied a new technique: the composition of a work based upon a series of tones ("Reihenkomposition" or "serial composition").

This was the first step towards the twelve-tone technique, which one finds for the first time fully developed in a movement of his *Serenade for Bass and Seven Instruments,* op. 24, in the movement "Theme and Variations." Let us now consider how Schönberg arrived at the development and use of the new technique.

It was in 1916 that I received the visit of a soldier who was sent to me by my friend, Rudolph Reti, a Viennese composer whose important book *The Thematic Process in Music* you may have read. This soldier was an elementary-school teacher whom the military medical authorities considered too high-strung for active service. His name was Josef Matthias Hauer. He showed me some of his works. I had never seen such a mixture of amateurish writing, without any training in harmony and counterpoint, and of passages of undisputed originality. He told me that he wanted to write music like the ancient Greeks. He showed me his compositions. All were very short. Each piece represented a *Nomos,* and the *Nomos* consisted of twelve tones, divided into four sections of three tones. This meant that each melody represented the whole compass

21. O alter Duft.

First page of "O alter Duft," from Schönberg's *Pierrot Lunaire*. Copyright 1914 by Universal Edition, Vienna; renewed 1942 by Arnold Schönberg. Used by permission of Associated Music Publishers, Inc.

of the chromatic scale, but the tones were chosen in such a clever way that the layout of a row sounded almost diatonic. The music was easily singable. Hauer's compositions became known in our small circle and were brought to Schönberg, who, at that time, had occasionally made use of the serial technique. But undoubtedly Hauer's twelve-tone compositions showed him the way out of his crisis; they came to him as the right impulse at the right moment.

You will remember that there is a parallel to this event in the meeting between Erik Satie and Claude Debussy. It was Erik Satie who freed himself from the Wagnerian influence, who was the first French composer to introduce chains of unresolved sevenths and ninths, and who drew Debussy's attention to Maeterlinck's play, *Pelléas et Mélisande,* which he himself had wanted to set to music, but had not the means to buy the libretto. It was, however, Debussy who succeeded in developing all the elements which were in Satie's music, and in writing to this libretto an opera which was the supreme achievement of a great composer.

Something similar happened with regard to Hauer's twelve-tone music. He succeeded in composing a choral work which, in 1924, caused a sensation at the music festival in Frankfurt. But in spite of his great talent he was prevented by his lack of technique from becoming a great composer. However, he provided Schönberg with the principal idea, the row of twelve tones as a new principle of composition.

What is the row of twelve tones, in the hands of Schönberg and of his school?

I should like to call it the creative idea of the work, its essence. In fact, the composition depends upon the use one can make of the row, just as in the former, traditional music the effect of a work depends upon the theme. A row can be as ineffective as a dull theme of a fugue, and the composer will try in vain to make it alive by his technical skill. It needs more than that in a twelve-tone composition to turn its Platonic idea into the sphere of musical reality.

The basic problem of that kind of music, however, is still open to question and I must confess that I have not, so far, found a satisfactory answer: Does music consist of tones or does it consist of intervals?

I myself am convinced that it consists of intervals. If, for instance, we take an interval of great tension, the interval of the augmented seventh, c′–b′ natural, how is it possible to turn it by mirror movement into the interval of a minor second, *i.e.*, c′–b natural, the interval of the smallest tension, without destroying the portrait of the melody in the mirror? This question is not of paramount importance if we listen to Schönberg, whose melodic lines have a great power of motion. Here we may assume that the ear corrects the intervals, just as happens in the Ninth Symphony of Beethoven, where the ear automatically corrects a run of the flute which starts on a lower b″-flat, and leaps up to an a‴-flat only because in Beethoven's days in the flute players had difficulty in starting on the higher b-flat.

The question, however, becomes urgent where compositions of Webern are concerned, which often consist of single tones, interrupted by pauses, and of crossing parts which make it impossible for the ear to catch the flow of the melody, to separate the single parts, and to follow their course. There, we must just take in what we can hear and trust the composer when we are unable to disentangle a chord which is not meant to form a harmony, but is an aggregation of tones. The real importance of the twelve-tone system lies, to my mind, in its structural possibilities. It combines the inherent potentialities of the theme of a movement in sonata form with those of the theme of a fugue and of variations. It creates a coherent texture throughout the single movements and the work as a whole. Needless to say that this kind of coherence can also be achieved in serial compositions, that is in movements in which not the full row of twelve tones, but only seven or eight or nine tones, form the basic row.

It took Schönberg a long time to work out the new technique. This happened in the years 1917–20, after he had left unfinished the composition of his oratorio, *Die Jakobsleiter*. The coming into being of the system which he called "composition with twelve tones," as he worked it out, is the logical consequence of that trend in late 19th-century composition which had its roots in Wagner's *Tristan*, and which led to the various unsuccessful attempts to substitute twenty-four quarter-tones for the existing twelve half-tones. Schönberg never went so far; his aim was, first, to create several harmonic centers instead of the one tonic center; and, finally, he aimed at creating twelve centers of equal importance, a harmonic development by which the old system based on harmonic progressions is replaced by a new kind of part writing, in which the harmonies are parts of a line, but sounding simultaneously.

Is the basic idea of the new technique a completely new one, justifying the controversy between Hauer's and Schönberg's adherents when Schönberg proclaimed his first twelve-tone composition and the theoretical explanation of the technique?

Looking back, it is interesting to find that the principle of the series of tones and the twelve-tone row is not an entirely new system, which Schönberg or Hauer invented, but the revival of the technique of formulas which originated in the East, came to the West with plain-chant, and is one of the basic principles of early medieval polyphonic music. These formulas in Byzantine and Gregorian chant do not, as I have shown, presuppose a scale, but are melodic archetypes. Their presence in a melody determines its belonging to a certain group of chants.

If one works out this principle of composition and transfers it from diatonic to chromatic rows of tones, one finally arrives at Schönberg's twelve-tone system.

When, in August 1911, I wrote the first essay about Schönberg in a musical journal, the *Zeitschrift der Internationalen Musikgesellschaft*, I compared him with Gesualdo, Principe da Venosa, who, in his madrigals, went further in applying chromatic harmonies than any other composer of that period. I think I was right in my evaluation, perhaps more so than I was able to see at that time. The feeling for widening the harmonic horizon was certainly innate in both composers.

If the twelve-tone system is attacked by some critics as an arbitrary system, this is not the fault of the composers whose works are written in it, but of some fanatical twelve-tone commentators who raise opposition by proclaiming that the new technique would, in future, be the only possible basis of composition. It is perfectly understandable that at one time Schönberg himself expressed that view. This was in the days when, after years of experimenting, he had finished the first work in the new technique and was overwhelmed by the inspiring effect which the application of the twelve-tone row had on his creative faculty. But he continued to teach theory on the traditional basis and he himself wrote several works in the traditional style of composition, just as Wagner, when he had written *Tristan,* went back in the *Meistersinger* to a harmonic style based on Bach, or as Strauss, after *Don Quixote,* wrote *Ein Heldenleben* and the *Sinfonia Domestica.*

The great composer can never be subservient to any existing theory, but follows his inner ear. It is the business of the interpreter to find out the theoretical basis of his style of composition and his technique.

The transition from the late Romantic style of composition to atonal composition with the abandoning of a single tonic center was a necessity at a certain historic moment in the development of music. The break with the post-Wagnerian and post-Brahmsian style freed us from the fetters of a routine which had become unbearable. When the minds of the composers began to concentrate on the creation of a structure, as the backbone of their music, the twelve-tone system saved it from becoming rhapsodic and incoherent. Thus Schönberg and the dodecaphonist school preferred writing variations, because themes and variations and eventually fugues were the given means for building up a work upon a row of tones.

It was only at a later stage that Schönberg returned to writing quartets, Berg to writing his violin concerto, and Webern his symphony.

To give just one example illustrating Schönberg's twelve-tone technique I choose the Fourth Quartet, opus 37. Let us first turn to the beginning of the third movement, the *Adagio,* in which the row is spread out in the *unisono* of the four instruments like a theme for variations.

III

Opening of the third movement of Schönberg's fourth String Quartet, Op. 37. Copyright, 1939, by G. Schirmer, Inc.; international copyright secured. Used by permission of G. Schirmer, Inc.

And now we turn to the beginning of the first movement. Here the same row is given in the first violin in a different rhythm and a different mood. The row is turned into a first theme which has the perfect shape of the theme of a string quartet. In bar 10 the first violin intones the retrograde version. The handling of the theme is so masterly that nobody needs to know anything about the technical side of the composition.

Fourth String Quartet

Arnold Schoenberg, Op. 37

Opening of Schönberg's fourth String Quartet, Op. 37. Copyright, 1939, by G. Schirmer, Inc.; international copyright secured. Used by permission of G. Schirmer, Inc.

This analysis will help the musician to understand how Schönberg's mind worked; the listener will feel—without this knowledge—that he hears a piece of music whose inner logic impresses his mind by its unabating flow. All is of one piece.

Down to the end of the first quarter of this century twelve-tone composition remained confined to Schönberg, Berg, Webern, and the small group of their pupils in Vienna. Composers outside the group remained unaffected by the movement which started in the century's first decade. Among the majority of them, all over the world, was a growing tendency to concentrate on structural problems, which presupposed a turning away from harmonic and contrapuntal subtleties and the return of melody and rhythm to the place which they held in music before the introduction of the twelve-tone technique, although, seen in retrospect, it is my personal experience that one writes even triads differently if one has passed through a phase of writing music without a definite tonic center: they have now acquired a strong structural element.

Recently, however, we have experienced that in countries which have not yet taken part in the modern movement, composers turn to the twelve-tone technique in its most rigid form. Will this movement grow and find more and more adherents?

Predictions as to the course an artistic development is going to take are always idle speculations. However, from what I know other composers are doing, and from my own experience, I would venture to say that both the serial principle and, occasionally, the twelve-tone system, will keep its place in the near future—but only if composers feel the urge to express themselves in that way. Art must be convincing. If the composer creates a work in which the twelve-tone technique appears unavoidable, he will succeed and will carry with him those who will listen to his music. If, however, the plan of a composition which is taking shape in his mind needs the diatonic system he should not hesitate to apply the traditional technique.

Schönberg, who regarded himself as a traditionalist, may serve as an example. One of his last works, the *Variations on a Recitative,* opus 40, for organ, is composed in D minor, and there are many sections in his later works in which the twelve-tone technique is used very freely, so freely indeed, that these works are criticized by the ultra-modernists of today.

In his memoirs Darius Milhaud records a visit to Schönberg in Los Angeles. He told him that he had many fervent admirers in France, all very uncompromising adherents of the twelve-tone system. Schönberg answered: "Uncompromising adherents . . . hm, do they also put some music into the twelve tones?"

Nothing is more abhorrent than modernism turned into academic intransigence. It is my conviction that the composer must have absolute freedom in choosing the means to transform his inner vision into sound.

All technical devices are nothing else but means to that end.

THE LIBRARY OF CONGRESS

THE LOUIS CHARLES ELSON MEMORIAL FUND

MUSICAL CREATION

A LECTURE DELIVERED BY

MARC PINCHERLE

Honorary President of the Société Française de Musicologie

IN

THE WHITTALL PAVILION

OF THE LIBRARY OF CONGRESS

OCTOBER 4, 1960

Washington: 1961

MUSICAL CREATION

THE WAY MUSIC has evolved since the beginning of the present century, at more and more accelerated pace during the past twenty years, brings to mind many problems that one might think had already been resolved. At the same time, this rapid evolution seems still to postpone the solution of other problems obviously unsolved until now. One of these is the problem of musical creation, but I want to declare immediately that I do not propose to offer a solution. My ambition is, at best, to present the problem as it stands today in view of the recent orientations to which I have just referred.

This will not be a scholarly dissertation. I have based my survey chiefly on the utterances of composers or of their biographers; many of them are widely known, but they are important and far from negligible.

I have, moreover, made a very limited use of philosophical theories, those of Plato, the wise men of ancient China, also of Dr. Julius Bahle's *Der musikalische Schaffensprozess* and of *Esthétique et création musicale* by my distinguished compatriot Gisèle Brelet. Actually, in such matters, the most high-flown aesthetic or metaphysical systems are often more likely to bring additional complications rather than fuller enlightenment. For example, when Nietzsche, following numerous predecessors, considers music as "the immediate idea of eternal life," when Schopenhauer writes "the composer discloses to us the inward essence of the world, he expresses the deepest wisdom in a language that his reason does not understand," one cannot help asking: what music, what composer do they mean?

Let us put aside the differences of appreciation (arising from remoteness in place or time) which make traditional Chinese music sound like noise to the non-initiated occidental listener, which explain why a great fifteenth-century musician was, in the opinion of a great sixteenth-century musician, as barbarous as the latter was in the opinion of a great musician of the seventeenth century. Today, because of the rapid changes sweeping us along, a great musician of the year 1930 is definitely outmoded in 1960.

These are puzzles that can be ignored. Let us consider today's music only, the music of 1960. To which category of musical works shall we turn to find the revelation of "the inward essence of the world" promised by Schopenhauer? Is this a privilege reserved to so-called "pure" music—the symphony, the sonata, the quartet? Is opera to be admitted? Are we to go so far as to include operetta?— even the popular song, the street song, or rock-and-roll?

On the assumption that every type of music is accepted, what is the minimum degree of formal perfection, of originality, of achievement that must be attained in order to be in accord with Nietzsche and Schopenhauer?

This question of limits, which I have carried to the absurd, is closely concerned with the problem of creation, but it goes much further. It involves, indeed, the whole of musical aesthetics. You will understand, of course, that I deem it rather risky even to have alluded to it, and I now descend from these heights to more down-to-earth considerations, to what Anglo-American musicology very cleverly calls *the composer's workshop*: the question of learning how the musical work springs into existence or, to use another phrase, how it is fabricated.

But remember, to enter this composer's workshop with full freedom of spirit, it would be necessary first to have answered another very delicate question, that of musical heredity or non-heredity. In contrast to the impressive dynasties of the Bachs and the Couperins, to the many composers whose parents were good musicians in their own right, there stands the enigma of Berlioz, Debussy, Fauré, and so many others born of non-musical parents who were sometimes totally unresponsive to music.

Perhaps an opinion could be formed by means of statistics, but I shall not attempt it. I should like to recall, however, for the sake of curiosity, the information that some people thought could be drawn from musicians' physical constitutions—by means of chiromancy, phrenology, and other sciences more or less dependent on intuition.

On August 22, 1834, a Doctor Fossati, vice president of the Phrenological Society of Paris, addressed to his colleagues a voluminous communication concerning composers.[1] I have extracted a few passages, the first of which is about Weber.

"Here is the mask of Weber. A strong musical organization and educability or perfectibility, revealed by the development of the middle inferior part of the forehead, are the most remarkable of his features. It is this organization that most predisposes a composer to work and makes it possible for him to teach himself, also to learn from work previously done by others. Thus Weber's music shows the influence of science; we recognize, in addition to his native genius, how much he attained by study."

Concerning Bellini: "Bellini, who joins to the organ of music the organ of over-developed kindness, will always make expressive, pathetic, dramatic music whenever he wishes to express in sound the sensations passing through his mind . . .

"The plaintive, passionate tones already will have resounded in his soul before he is able to think of the effect that they will produce on others. Because of his personal constitution, I am inclined to believe that his compositions will always convey song and melody rather than instrumentation and harmony."

Concerning Rossini: "I have only a word to say about Rossini. His enormous head will show you that assembled within him are all the organs, all the qualities sufficient to make an extraordinary genius. The lateral-anterior development of his head explains the great extension that he has given to instrumental music in musical drama. . . ."

I shall stop here with these quotations. As you see, these texts, dating from 1834, reveal no more than a certain cleverness in explaining the past. They leave untouched the phenomenon of the

[1] *Journal de la Société Phrénologique,* Paris, 1835, p. 95

birth of the musical work. This phenomenon has almost always been accounted for, at least up to very recent times, by the intervention of a *deus ex machina* called *inspiration*. Nowadays we tend to minimize the importance of this mysterious power, or even to deny that it exists. Let us take a closer look.

No one has proclaimed more clearly than Goethe, in his *Talks with Eckermann*,[2] the omnipotence of inspiration in musical creation. "Composition!" he says, "a repugnant word, which we owe to the French, and which we must strive to liquidate as soon as possible. How can one say that Mozart 'composed' *Don Giovanni* . . . as if it were a question of a piece of cake produced by kneading together eggs, flour, and sugar! It is a spiritual creation in which the details, as well as the whole, are the product of a single spirit, animated by the breath of a single life. Because of this the creator had no need to experiment, to sew pieces together, to follow his fantasy; he was entirely in the hands of his *inner daemon*, acting according to its orders."

To what extent this *inner daemon* controls the composer—absolutely, or leaving to him a larger or smaller part of initiative—may be open to discussion. But, until quite recent times, those most directly concerned (I mean the composers) have almost unanimously admitted its existence. If they concede some importance to technique, to free will, to the desire to build something, in their judgment it is *inspiration* that has by far the leading part. Such is the meaning of Rameau's well-known words, uttered in his old age: "Every day I acquire taste, but I have no more genius." [3]

Young Georges Bizet asserts the same idea when, just twenty years old, he compares his present way of composing to that of his student days when he was content to apply the rules he had learned. Thus he writes to his mother: "I feel that all my musical skill and application are of no further use to me; I can write nothing without an inspiring idea. . . ." [4]

---

[2] June 20, 1831.
[3] Quoted by Chabanon, *Eloge de M. Rameau,* Paris, 1764, p. 54.
[4] Translated by Edward Lockspeiser, *The Literary Clef, London,* 1958, p. 40.

If, down to our days, there has been almost unanimous agreement concerning the reality of inspiration, this agreement disappears when we approach the mechanics of creation, the way in which this inspiration manifests itself, and the way in which the work takes form in the composer's mind and on his music paper.

For some it is a sudden illumination, for others a long and laborious task. I need not dwell on the example of Beethoven, who sometimes struggled through ten, fifteen, or twenty successive sketches to his final theme, the ultimate realization of which for a long time he had only vaguely foreseen. Both "rhythms" of creation may alternate in the same composer. Berlioz spends three weeks in writing the *Scène aux champs* of the *Symphonie fantastique,* yet completes the *Marche au supplice* in one night.

Nearly always, once the first idea is expressed, the materialization of the work on paper continues at a slower tempo. For certain gifted musicians, however, endowed with a strong power of concentration, the composition is practically completed in the mind before anything is written down. This seems to be the case with J. S. Bach and his masterworks. Certain of our contemporaries who compose in cold blood, as if laying out a plan, pretend to find in him a precedent and a model. Nothing could be more inaccurate. According to Spitta, who thoroughly studied the process of Bach's inspiration, his music in its best moments springs forth with great spontaneity. Usually when he begins to write, his general plan is already settled. His manuscripts eloquently reveal the excitement of his inspiration. Likewise they show when inspiration is weakening, as in those sequential developments which Constant Lambert disrespectfully speaks of as the Bach "sewing machine."

Wagner, among others, conceives large portions of his works before writing the poem and score. He tells Carl Gallard, in a letter of January 30, 1844: "Before I sit down to write in verse, even before trying to draft a scene, I am already bewitched by the musical perfume of my creation. I have all the melodies in my head, all the characteristic themes, so that once the verse is concluded and the scenes elaborated, the opera is, practically, finished. The detailed working out only depends thenceforth on patience and reflection; these follow after creation itself."

With Mozart this faculty of mentally conceiving a total work becomes prodigious. Everyone knows about the overture to *Don Giovanni,* written in a half-doze as if under dictation. And we know of similar illustrations. At four and a half years of age little Camille Saint-Saëns wants to compose a song, and he is given a poem by Marceline Desbordes-Valmore. He composes his music mentally, then plays it on the piano, and finally writes it down on paper. The same process operates with Benjamin Britten: "Usually, I have the music complete in my head before putting pen to paper.[5]

The case remains where music comes to the composer spontaneously, but he dares not accept such a gift of inspiration. He examines it critically, then reworks it in a state of concern bordering on distress. George Sand (*History of My Life*) describes Chopin's workshop as follows: "His creation was miraculous. He found without looking for it, without foreseeing it. Music came out of his piano, complete, sublime, or it sang in his head during a walk, and he was in a hurry to hear it himself by playing it on his instrument. But then began the most heart-rending labour that I have ever seen . . ." and she describes the torments, the indecisions, sometimes prolonged for weeks, concerning a single page which he would finally re-establish in the exact form it had come to him at first.

Honegger, too, knew such agonies, though he flattered himself for not being a *romantique*: "When I am full of the joy of discovery, my guardian angel whispers in my ear, 'it is not possible, it is a reminiscence or an empty dream; all is going to collapse.' Imagine the gold miner—from early morning on he digs with his pick, he perspires, he is exhausted, he will never find anything, and suddenly there is the nugget; he cannot believe his eyes . . . In such a situation great courage is necessary to keep from changing what one has just written." [6]

---

[5] In the *Observer,* London, Oct. 27, 1946.
[6] Honegger, *Je suis compositeur,* Paris, 1951, p. 120.

Sometimes it happens that, without the composer's knowledge and in a completely painless manner, a long process of maturation takes place. Richard Strauss describes this with great accuracy: "It usually takes two years before a composition begins to assume form with me. At first there comes to me an idea—a theme. This rests with me for months; I think of other things and busy myself with everything but it; but the idea is fermenting of its own accord. Sometimes I bring it to mind, or play the theme on the piano, just to see how far it has progressed—and finally it is ready for use. You see, therein lies the real art of creation—to know exactly when an idea is ripe, when one can use, must use it. More and more I cling to the belief that we conscious people have no control over our creative power. For instance, I slave over a melody and encounter an obstacle which I cannot surmount however I try. This during the course of an evening; but the next morning the difficulty has surrendered itself, just as though my creative forces had toiled at it overnight." [7]

The phenomenon of inspiration, of course, does not leave all composers as calm as Strauss. Without going back to a mythical age, when the musician-magician was literally "possessed" by his art, we find in more recent times certain creators whose inspiration is accompanied by characteristic emotional symptoms, occasionally sufficiently pronounced to suggest some kind of "twilight state." We can discover many such examples in the Renaissance. Adrien Petit Coclico, transmitting the doctrine of Josquin des Prés, declares (in 1552): "The composer must be compelled to write by an imperative inner impulse, to the point of forgetting thirst and hunger as long as the piece is not completed. Under such conditions one does more in an hour than otherwise in an entire month." [8]

---

[7] Quoted by J. G. Huneker, *Overtones,* London, 1904, pp. 33–34.

[8] *Compendium musices,* Nuremberg, 1552—"[Compositor] . . . ad componendum magno ducatur desiderio, ac impetu quodam naturali ad compositionem pellatur, adeo ut nec cibus nec potus ei sapiat, ante absolutam cantilenam, nam una hora plus conficitur, cum impetus ille naturalis sic urget, quam alias in integro mense."

This resembles Ronsard's attitude when, in his *Preface au Mellange de Chansons tant des vieux Autheurs que des modernes* (1572), he writes: ". . . The divine furies of Music, Poetry and Painting do not come by degrees of perfection, like the other sciences, but by impulses, like flashes of lightning which appear here and there in various countries—then suddenly disappear."

Händel often composed in a state of extreme exaltation. His biographer Victor Schoelcher recalls different traits: "When he was composing, his excitement would rise to such a pitch that he would burst into tears:—'It is said, that a friend calling upon the great musician when in the act of setting these pathetic words, "He was despised, and rejected of men," found him absolutely *sobbing*.' 'I have heard it related,' says Shield, 'that when Händel's servant used to bring him his chocolate in the morning, he often stood with silent astonishment to see his master's tears mixing with the ink, as he penned his divine notes.' " [9] Even Grétry, whose music today seems so reassuringly placid, told his young colleague Désaugiers that "in order for him to work, he had to warm his imagination for eight days; consequently it caused pimples to appear on his face, his chest was aching with sharp pains, unexpectedly fever came, and then he could compose." [10] Grétry's own *Mémoires* confirm this: "I read, I re-read twenty times the words that I want to express in sounds; I need several days to warm my head. At last I lose my appetite, my eyes take fire, my imagination rises; then I make an opera in three weeks or a month." [11]

Beethoven, more justifiably, becomes exalted, and he describes this exaltation to Bettina von Arnim, who relates to Goethe, among the "beautiful things" the composer told her, his utterances about musical inspiration: "Not only because of their contents, but also because of their rhythm, Goethe's poems have great power over me, I am tuned up and stimulated to composition by this language which

---

[9] Victor Schoelcher, *The Life of Händel*, London, 1857, p. 378.
[10] Letter from M. A. Désaugiers, Oct. 18, 1774, in M. Pincherle, *Musiciens peints par eux-mêmes*, Paris, 1939, p. 10.
[11] Grétry, *Mémoires; ou, Essai sur la musique*, Paris, 1789, pp. 28–29.

builds itself into higher orders as if through the work of spirits and already bears in itself the mystery of the harmonies.

"Then from the focus of enthusiasm I must discharge melody in all directions; I pursue it, capture it again passionately; I see it flying away and disappearing in the mass of varied agitations; now I seize upon it again with renewed passion; I cannot tear myself from it; I am impelled with hurried modulations to multiply it, and, at length I conquer it:—behold, a symphony!" [12]

As for Schubert, his intimates had the impression of a dual personality. "Whoever has seen him just once, in the morning, in the heat of composing, his eyes sparkling, even speaking in a quite different manner, will never forget it . . . I consider unquestionable that the excitement in which he composed his most beautiful *Lieder,* particularly his *Winterreise,* contributed to hastening his death." [13]

Many composers try to arouse this excitement by means of methods more or less peculiarly their own. We have already seen Grétry, Beethoven, and Wagner warming their imagination by reading again and again a poem or by meditating on the subject they mean to set to music. Tartini, too, when planning to compose a sonata or a concerto, usually sought a stimulus in some lines of Metastasio, which he would write down under the staves of his score. From a curious scruple of circumspection, he employed for this purpose a cryptography of his own, the key to which was discovered twenty-five years ago by our Greek colleague, Minos Dounias.[14]

I shall not burden you with a catalog of the many stimuli, sometimes quite unexpected, said to have been used by certain well-known masters. Felice Blangini, in his *Souvenirs,*[15] gives us a copious if not absolutely reliable list. Some find help in generous wines, in good cheer; others need agitation, noise, or the presence of some pet object or animal.

---

[12] Bettina von Arnim, letter to Goethe, May 28, 1810, in Thayer-Krehbiel, II, p. 188.

[13] Josef von Spaun's diary (1827).

[14] M. Dounias, *Die Violinkonzerte G. Tartini's,* Wolfenbüttel, 1935, pp. 90–98.

[15] Paris, 1834, pp. 364–67 (plagiarized by Albert Cler, *Physiologie du musicien,* Paris, 1841).

Among these various aids, of course, the piano is the most natural, the one most frequently required. Many composers use it not only to check on their harmonies but also as a source of inspiration. We are told that Wagner, deprived of a piano for one month during his first stay in Paris, was radically stopped in his work for that entire period; and when he succeeded in renting an instrument, he expressed to a friend his joy in discovering that (I quote his own words) "the ability to compose was not dead." It was then, in fact, that he completed *The Flying Dutchman.*

Were it not for fear of lengthening this lecture, the role of the hand in musical invention would deserve close study. How many discoveries in the field of melody, of harmony, rhythm, and tone-color, result from the careless, almost unconscious wandering of the fingers preluding on the keyboard? Three centuries ago the Reverend Father Mersenne wrote, with regard to the lute: "The art, or science, and skill of the hand are so great that some people have called it one of the principal instruments of wisdom and reason . . . Without dwelling on all of its accomplishments, it is sufficient to consider the way it moves on the lute and on all the other instruments; because these movements are so wonderful that reason often must admit that it is unable to understand their lightness and swiftness, which defy the quickest imagination in the world." [16]

Strawinsky echoes Father Mersenne when, speaking of his *Piano-Rag-Music,* he says: "What interested me especially was the fact that the various rhythmic episodes of this piece were dictated to me by the fingers themselves. . . . We must not despise the fingers: they are great inspirers and, being in direct contact with the raw sound itself, they often awaken in you subconscious ideas which otherwise would not, perhaps have been revealed." [17]

We may observe that Weber also recognized this suggestive power of the hands, but he condemned it as an impediment to the free inspiration of the composer: "These hands, these cursed fingers of

[16] *Harmonie universelle,* Paris, 1636; Livre second, Des Instruments, proposition IX.
[17] *Chroniques de ma vie,* I, p. 178.

the pianists, with their endless practice, have developed a certain independence so that, like unconscious tyrants, they influence creative activity."

What is to be thought of the action of great emotional crises on inspiration? There is no denying this with respect to Beethoven, and the whole romantic world considered such crises of prime importance. According to Lacépède, writing in 1785, "pleasure gave rise to the song, but it is only to sorrow and melancholy that we owe true music." [18]

There are exceptions, however. Berlioz, the hyper-romantic, sees a real danger in emotions when they rise to a paroxysm. When feeling too deeply the sentiments he wants his heroes to express, he becomes paralyzed; he writes: "Passionate subjects must be dealt with in cold blood." [19] Likewise Debussy: "I have never been able to compose anything at the very moment that something happened in my life; this, I believe, makes for the superiority of recollection [as a source of inspiration]: from it one is able to draw valuable emotions. But people who cry when writing masterpieces are insolent jokers." [20]

In a correspondence to which I shall refer again, Tchaikovsky is still more explicit: "When he is creating, the artist must have calm . . . those are mistaken who believe the artist can use his talent to relieve himself of specific feelings of the moment. The sad or happy emotions which he expresses are always and invariably retrospective. With no especial reason for rejoicing, I can experience a happy creative mood, and conversely among the happiest surroundings I may write music suffused with darkness and despair. In brief, the artist lives a double life, an everyday human one and an artistic one, and these two lives do not always coincide." [21]

---

[18] *La Poëtique de la musique,* Paris, 1785.
[19] Letter to the Princess Carolyn von Sayn Wittgenstein, Aug. 12, 1856 (about the opera *Les Troyens*).
[20] Letter to Pierre Louÿs, March 27, 1898.
[21] Letter to Nadejda von Meck, July 6, 1878, quoted by Catherine Drinker Bowen and Barbara von Meck in *"Beloved Friend,"* New York, 1937, p. 247.

This fragment of self-analysis leads us to a category of statements possibly more substantial than the sporadic quotations I have offered so far. Some composers have attempted to describe quite methodically their creative process. For a long while the model of such descriptions was considered to be a lengthy and indeed fascinating letter in which Mozart minutely explored the mechanism of his creation. This letter, dated October 12, 1790, and addressed to a certain Baron von Aufsess, was first published in 1815 in the *Allgemeine musikalische Zeitung* [22] of Leipzig, reprinted in 1904 in the *Leipziger neueste Nachrichten,* and issued again on September 25 of the same year in *Le Guide musical* of Brussels. It was accepted as genuine and widely exploited until about 1920. Unfortunately no trace has ever been found of Mozart's autograph, and today the opinion of the experts, principally Dr. Wilhelm A. Bauer and Dr. Otto Erich Deutsch (preparing the complete edition of Mozart's correspondence), is that the letter is a forgery of the too ingenious Rochlitz, a forgery which seems, however, to be based on rather plausible data.

But more reliable documents are available, such as those I have already quoted by Richard Strauss, Honegger, Tchaikovsky. I shall have recourse again to the last-named, who makes us more conscious of the psychophysiological complexity of the creative process. In his correspondence of February–March 1878 with Nadejda von Meck, to which I alluded above, there is an extensive passage of the utmost importance. I am not the first to appreciate its value, but I feel that it cannot be neglected. Tchaikovsky says: "Usually the seed of a future musical creation germinates instantaneously and most unexpectedly. If the soil is eager, if there is a disposition to work, that seed takes root with amazing power and speed, appears above ground as a little stalk which puts forth leaves and branches and finally, flowers. This simile is as near as I can come to a description of the creative process. If the seed appears at a favorable moment, the main difficulty is past. The rest grows of itself.

---

[22] XVII, No. 34.

"Words are vain to tell you the boundless joy that comes over me when a new idea is conceived and begins to take definite shape. One forgets everything; one is a madman, trembling and quivering in every organ, with scarcely time to outline the sketches, so rapidly does one idea pursue another. Sometimes in the midst of this magic process an outside shock wakes one from this state of somnambulism. The bell rings, the servant enters, the clock strikes, reminding one that the business of the day must be attended to. These interruptions are inexpressibly trying. Sometimes, inspiration takes flight, one has to seek it again—often in vain. Frequently one must rely here upon a quite cold, deliberate technical process of work. Perhaps such moments are responsible, in the works of the Great Masters, for those places where the organic coherence fails and where one can trace artificial coherence, seams and patches. But this is unavoidable. If that spiritual condition of the artist called inspiration, which I have tried to describe, should continue uninterrupted, the artist could not survive a single day. The strings would snap and the instrument fly to pieces. One thing however is indispensable: the main idea of the piece, together with a general outline of the separate parts, must not be found through searching but must simply appear—a result of that supernatural, incomprehensible and never-analysed power called inspiration." [23]

"Do not believe those who tried to persuade you that musical creation is a cold, purely mental exercise. Only the music that pours from the depths of an artistic soul, moved by inspiration, can touch and take possession of the hearer. There is no doubt that even the greatest musical genius has sometimes worked unwarmed by inspiration. It is a guest that does not come on first invitation. In the meantime one must work, and an honest artist cannot sit with his hands crossed because he is not inclined to compose. . . . One must hold fast and have faith, and inspiration will come.

"This happened to me only today. I wrote you that I had been working regularly, but without enthusiasm. If I had given way to

---

[23] Bowen-Von Meck, *op. cit.*, p. 206.

a lack of inclination, I would surely not have accomplished anything for a long time. But faith and patience never desert me, and today, ever since morning I have been possessed by the inexplicable, mysterious fire of inspiration." [24]

When the composer is in good disposition "then work proceeds with the strangest ease. One forgets everything, the spirit quivers with sweet excitement, and before one has time to follow the swift flight to its end, time has gone by unperceived. In this state is something somnambulistic, *'on ne s'entend pas vivre.'* " [25]

I shall end this review of composers who believe in that mysterious power which Goethe called the *inner daemon* with a profession of faith of Debussy, in an interview granted to a reporter in 1911, a few weeks before the first performance of *Le Martyre de Saint-Sébastien*: "Who can penetrate the secret of musical composition? The noise of the sea, the curve of the horizon, the wind in the foliage, the chirp of a bird awaken in us many impressions. And suddenly, without the slightest assent from ourselves, one of these remembrances springs out of us and expresses itself in music. It bears its harmony in itself. Whatever you may try to do, you will not be able to find anything more just and sincere. Only thus will a heart predestined to music make its most beautiful discoveries"—and here Debussy merely develops a thought expressed a few years earlier (1907) to his friend Victor Segalen: "Art is occultism. Whence does it come?"

* * * * *

Today a directly opposite conception is gaining more and more adherents in musical circles. This conception puts the emphasis on intelligence and industry and regards musical composition as an objective activity in which the leading role is played by technique.

It was Jacques Ibert, I believe, who transferred to musical composition the definition Thomas Edison gave of genius: one percent

---

[24] Letter of March 17, *ibid.*, p. 217.
[25] Letter of July 6, *ibid.*, p. 247.

inspiration, ninety-nine percent perspiration. This was semifacetious. But Strawinsky is perfectly serious in declaring: "The phenomenon of music is given to us for the sole purpose of establishing order in things, and chiefly between *man* and *time*. Such purpose requires necessarily and exclusively a construction. This construction being achieved, order being attained, everything is said. It would be useless to search or wait for something else. It is precisely this construction, this order, which produces in us an emotion of a quite special character, thoroughly different from our customary sensations and reactions springing from impressions of everyday life. One cannot define more clearly the sensation generated by music than by identifying it with that which we feel at the sight of architectural forms." [26]

This is the same idea, in fact, that Mersenne attempted to carry to its ultimate consequences in a *proposition* of his *Harmonie universelle,* entitled "To determine if it is possible to compose the best of all songs that can be invented." [27] To form this perfect structure he tried countless combinations and permutations of notes—until he was obliged to give up and renounce this visionary goal.

It so happens—and this is a mere parenthesis—that nowadays some people are, indeed, working in a way not so different from that which Mersenne proposed. But they base their work on mathematical probability, the laws of Fischer, Laplace-Gauss, Maxwell-Boltzmann, and so on. Two and even three centuries ago composers already were attempting to exploit the laws of chance, but in a much more naïve or even frivolous way. Some of them devised musical games in which dice, dominoes, or lottos were thrown haphazardly. Whatever number came up represented a phrase of music, and the result, accidental as it might be, was always a perfectly acceptable, logical composition which conformed to the rules. Thus, anyone

---

[26] Igor Strawinsky, *Chroniques de ma vie,* I, pp. 117–18.
[27] *Harmonie universelle,* Livre second, Des Chants, Proposition VII.

could "compose without knowing a single note of music." [28]   Even
the very learned Abbé Stadler amused himself with such fancies.
His *Tabelle, aus welcher man Menueten und Trio herauswürfeln
kann,* published in Vienna in 1781, has often been reprinted—under
Mozart's name!

To return to Strawinsky, however: some other texts of his seem
to admit the existence of inspiration, but how restricted in its at-
tributions! "The layman," he writes, "imagines that it is necessary,
in order to create, to wait for inspiration. On the contrary, it is a
propulsive force found in any human activity, and is not at all the
monopoly of artists. But this power is only disclosed when put into
action by an effort, and this effort is termed *work*. Just as appetite
comes in eating, so it is equally true that working summons inspiration
if it did not show itself at the beginning. But it is not only the inspiration that matters: it is the result, in other words, the product." [29]

It seems advisable to point out here that the *Chronicles of My
Life* dates from 1935, quite some time after the extraordinary
creative period in which Strawinsky composed, at a stretch, the
Firebird, Petrushka, Le Sacre du printemps, Noces, and *L'Histoire
du soldat.* More recently, less and less dependent on the *inner*

---

[28] For the sake of curiosity I shall mention the *Secret pour composer en musique
par un art nouveau, si facile que ceux-mêmes qui ne sçavent pas chanter pourront
en moins d'un jour composer à quatre parties sur toute sorte de basses* by Du
Reneau, Paris 1658 (actually only a method to realize, by means of tables of
letters and numbers, counterpoints of the first species on a given bass) ; the *Ludus
melothedicus; ou, Le jeu de dez harmonique,* sold at La Chevardière, 1757 ; the
Domino musical; ou, L'Art du musicien mis en jeu by Avocat [N. Bigant], 1779 ;
a *Tabular system whereby any person, without the least knowledge of Musick,
may compose ten thousand different minuets,* by Welcker, a London music publisher *ca.* 1775 ; the *Musikalisches Charten-Spiel . . . wobey man allezeit ein
musikalisches Stück gewinnet* of Michael J. F. Wiedeburg, Aurich, 1788 ; the
Gioco pitagorico-musicale of Calegari, Venice, 1801 ; the *Quadrille Melodist* of
J. Clinton, London, *ca.* 1850 (a set of 62 cards supposedly able to produce
214,000,000 quadrilles and melodies)—but all these inventions were by far trans-
cended by the surprising *Componium* built by Winkel in 1821, an instrument
really able to give out variations *ad infinitum* upon a given theme (a specimen,
perhaps the only one extant, belongs to the Museum of the Brussels Conserva-
toire).

[29] Strawinsky, *op. cit.,* II, pp. 186–87.

daemon, he has increasingly staked almost everything on research, experimentation; each new score has been the solution of a new problem in writing, in form, in orchestration, dramaturgy, or aesthetics.

It is interesting to compare Strawinsky's point of view with that of another composer, Maurice Ravel, to whom for a long time (and quite erroneously) critics ascribed an attitude similar to the Russian's. The precision of Ravel's writing deceived the commentators, persuading them to see him as nothing more than a patient adjuster of micrometric mechanisms. But what did he himself say? In 1910, in an article on Chopin, we read: *"Architecture! What an inane comparison!* There exist rules which tell us how to make a building stand up, but there is nothing of the sort to show us how to link up a chain of modulations. Or rather, yes, one thing— inspiration." [30]

On another occasion, attacking the formula of Buffon that *genius is no more than steadfast patience,* Ravel said: "That *steadfast patience,* or will-power which unfortunately Buffon thought constituted the very essence of genius, is in reality no more than an accessory to it. The principle of *genius,* that is to say, of artistic invention, can only be established by instinct or sensitivity. What was intended by Buffon as nothing more than a witty remark has given rise to a fatal, and relatively modern, error, an error that leads people to think that the artistic instinct is directed by the will. . . . In art, craftsmanship [métier] in the absolute sense of the word cannot exist. In the harmonious proportions of a work, in the elegance of its unfolding, inspiration plays an almost unlimited role. The *will* to develop can only be sterile." [31]

This point of view is not entirely extinct today, even among masters considered innocent of conservatism. Witness Messiaen: "I believe in musical inspiration—not in the sense of an abrupt invasion by some Dionysian ecstasy, but rather as a slow, imper-

---

[30] "Impressions" in *Le Courrier musical,* Paris, Jan. 1, 1910, p. 32.
[31] *Revue S. I. M.,* Paris, March 15, 1912, p. 50.

ceptible process which goes on despite ourselves. We can control it to a certain extent, but we have no absolute power over it." [32]

Nor can I forget that, in this very hall, in the course of a lecture in this same series in which it is an honor to appear, my eminent colleague Egon Wellesz spoke on Schoenberg and concluded: "The great composer can never be subservient to any existing theory, but follows his inner ear." [33]

We cannot deny, however, that in recent times a lively opposition has arisen—and not only in the realm of music—against the dogma of inspiration as a spontaneous manifestation more or less subject to the subconscious. For these new theorists the primary conditions of creation are: a) the composer's becoming aware of his own position in the evolution of music, and b) his wish to introduce something new. In an article leveled against Strawinsky (before musicians of the younger generation decided once again that he had some genius) René Leibowitz wrote: "I do not believe in musical genius in itself, or rather, I do not believe that there exists in man an inspired nature which permits him to achieve at certain times and, so to speak, despite himself works of genius. The musician of genius is he who becomes conscious of the totality of the problems resulting from the evolution of polyphony in the period in which he lives, problems which he poses to himself of his own accord and which he proceeds to resolve with prodigious gifts and with an irresistible force of character. In this sense there is no more an element of chance in the act of creation than in the evolution of an artist. In the final analysis one must choose his path and commit himself to it entirely." [34]

In a less belligerent manner these same ideas are developed in Gisèle Brelet's *Esthétique et création musicale*, which derives in part

---

[32] "L'Inspiration musicale" in *Opéra*, Dec. 19, 1945.

[33] *The Origins of Schönberg's Twelve-Tone System*, Washington, Library of Congress, 1958.

[34] "Igor Strawinsky, ou Le choix de la misère musicale" in *Les Temps Modernes*, Paris, April 1, 1946, p. 1336.

from the theories of Dr. Julius Bahle.[35] I should like to quote a few passages that are particularly explicit: "The artistic will of the musician can only arise in the first place from the consciousness of his historical destiny. We have already said that the history of musical thought seems to develop according to some internal logic beyond the psychological personalities of the various composers. Now, to become aware of this internal logic, to know how to introduce one's own creative personality into the historical curve to which the art of music is committed—these seem to be the primary conditions for a fruitful creativity. . . . The creator can only achieve a fertile creation if he becomes conscious of the historical moment when his personality is called upon to manifest itself. . . . The profound will of the artist is dominated by a struggle to conquer new forms and sensations of sound, which are linked to one another. . . .

"In the depths of himself the musician expresses the wish to be *original,* to raise and to solve new problems in the realm of musical thought." [36]

If I devoted to these ideas the attention they deserve, it would be necessary here to go beyond the particular problem of the "composer's workshop" and to attack the even vaster and thornier problem of contemporary musical evolution. But that would require another lecture, or two or ten, and at that there would be faint hope of exhausting the subject. In these new doctrines I must limit myself to the appearance of two elements which, throughout many centuries, have scarcely been considered by composers: first, the desire to become conscious of their place in the evolution of music; and second, the deliberate wish to present something new.

In the past, as you know, things were far simpler. With very rare exceptions the creator followed the teachings of one composer or another whom he specially admired. He considered himself a success when he resembled his master as closely as possible. When his own genius stirred him to innovation, it was because of an inner

---

[35] *Der musikalische Schaffensprozess,* Leipzig, 1936.
[36] Gisèle Brelet, *op. cit.,* pp. 15–17.

impulse to which he did not always willingly abandon himself—
since those around him were hardly likely to applaud such heresy.
To surpass others in technic (everyone's aim today) was considered
rather a handicap. Most people thought that genius does not go
together necessarily with daring, that, instead, it is to be found (as
believed by most of the composers I have mentioned) in those
regions which elude our conscious control. If further proof were
needed, it would suffice to think of Mozart. Certainly there are
innovations in many of his works, but far more numerous and
equally, or even more, admired are those pieces written in a style
no more advanced than that of Wranitzky, Dittersdorf, or Wanhal.
Should not this make those who believe the most important thing is
to pose new problems stop and reconsider?

Perhaps we, too, we critics, musicologists, aestheticians are partly
responsible for this. I should like to recall—and this will be my
last quotation—the diatribe of a great French composer who was,
at the same time, probably our greatest music critic, Paul Dukas.
Early in this century he lashed out against those commentators on
Wagner who thought that they had explained everything when they
had taken apart, bit by bit, all of his *Leitmotivs*. They create, he
said, "an illusion which profits most those who like to 'take stock'—
the statisticians of sixteenth-notes, the accountants of reminiscences,
those who are enchanted that music becomes, in some way, an art
about which one can reason as if it were a thing without mystery,
with precise examples, footnotes and numbers. By leaving nothing
unexplained, by giving a translation of almost every bar, these
inveterate commentators have made of Wagner's music a purely
analytic art from which we shall only painfully be able to free ourselves. At the same time, and this is the delicate and serious point
of the matter, they have at last offered unbelievable facilities to
mediocre composers. A reading of their anatomical dissections
must have convinced many musicians . . . that a powerful art was
within their grasp, since skill counted for more than imagination,

patience more than emotion, and since, too, it was only necessary to labor sufficiently in order to win a spotless glory.

"Thus it is that the misunderstanding found throughout the history of our art has assumed a new guise, and not the least curious one. Thus it is that we have embarked upon a particularly interesting phase of the struggle which has been going on ever since the Middle Ages, between the notes themselves and the music. This has resulted from the confusion of the writing and the thought, the letter and the spirit, the means and the end." [37]

Dukas really seems to condemn, by anticipation (in 1901) those tendencies which have gained common currency in our times. What he could not foresee was the extraordinary development they would undergo, a development which has forced us to embrace, under the same term *music*, two fundamentally different arts, despite all the verbal acrobatics that certain people indulge in as they attempt to harmonize them. On the one hand there is a music which goes back to remotest times and which, despite many trials, despite so many abrupt changes that might be dignified as revolutions, has permanently preserved two essential characteristics: a) it was related to the composer's desire, to an instinct if you wish, which impelled him to express in the language of sounds what we call (for lack of a less equivocal term) musical ideas, those concepts which in reality are sensations and which, moreover, obey other laws or follow a logic differing from that of spoken language; b) this music fulfilled its task with the utmost regard for the ear, for the affinities and repulsions existing between sonorities, for the evolution of our aural keenness or tolerance, which constantly enlarges our conception of dissonance, or rhythmic symmetry, and of association of instrumental timbres.

Opposed to this music, to which Schoenberg and his first disciples once subscribed, another music arose, or rather many others, diversified in their aims and in their means of expression but having in

---

[37] P. Dukas, "Les Notes et la musique" in *La Revue hebdomadaire*, October 1901, pp. 255–256.

common the same absolute confidence in intelligence, in reasoning, in will-power, aided and abetted in certain cases by pure chance (as in the case of Mr. Janis Xénakis). Here the process of musical creation nonchalantly ignores the *inner daemon* invoked by Goethe, and there are no mysteries behind its façade.

There are—at least one may fear so—two distinct universes. Is it possible to reconcile them, as attempted sometimes by certain daring young composers, troubled by their own boldness and seeking reassurance by placing themselves under the retrospective sponsorship of Johann Sebastian Bach, who is no longer present to straighten things out?

In an article recently published in the magazine *Théâtre* I find this utterance: "Discovering in 1948 the resources offered by manipulations of sounds after recording, Pierre Schaeffer completely upset [the French *bascule complètement* is coarser] the traditional procedure of musical creation." [38] I am not convinced of its accuracy. Quite different is musical creation, quite different that creation which consists of calmly, objectively fabricating assemblages of sounds. One system cannot be discarded in favor of the other. One is the privilege of genius (in varying degrees of power); stemming from the profoundest depths of human thought and feeling it can act upon mankind with a force the untold examples of which I need not recall. The other is an activity, academically as well as financially burdensome, the future of which is not yet easy to foresee, but for which the best hope is that it will become a devoted auxiliary of the first. Is this possible?

I shall do no more than pose the question, having, as I admitted to you earlier, only very modest ambitions and not at all the gift of prophecy.

This may seem a slight harvest after such a long talk, and I am embarrassed that, in order to reach this point, I had to shield myself behind such a profusion of quotations. It was through neither

---

[38] Sophie Brunet, in *Théâtre*, Paris, July 1960, p. 16.

laziness nor cowardice, but simply because it would be improper to neglect what greater authorities than I have contributed to a subject that engrosses me. And it was also the means of presenting to you, thanks to their assistance, a sufficient number of judgments of tested value to be sure of not vainly having seduced you away from either your work or your leisure.

THE LIBRARY OF CONGRESS

THE LOUIS CHARLES ELSON MEMORIAL FUND

DISCREPANCIES IN HAYDN
BIOGRAPHIES

A LECTURE DELIVERED BY

ANTHONY van HOBOKEN

Dr. Phil. honoris causa, Christian-Albrechts-Universität, Kiel
Dr. honoris causa, Rijksuniversiteit, Utrecht

IN

THE WHITTALL PAVILION

OF THE LIBRARY OF CONGRESS

MAY 18, 1962

Translated by Donald Mintz

Washington : 1962

DISCREPANCIES
IN
HAYDN BIOGRAPHIES

A NYONE WHO READS a Haydn biography of some scope will
soon notice that the greater part of the book is not about Haydn
himself. The reader will find detailed descriptions of persons and
circumstances that have only a loose connection with Haydn—if
indeed they have any at all! The recounting of Haydn's life is the
smallest portion of these biographies—and this portion, in turn, is
75 percent anecdotal.

As a matter of fact, we do not really know very much about
Haydn's life. And it is remarkable how many of the sources concerned with it—sources parts of which older biographers were able
to employ—have been lost. A few examples will suffice. The
Weimar collection used by Gerber at the beginning of the nineteenth
century was burned in 1825. A collection belonging to the Bishops
of Passau was similarly destroyed by fire some years earlier. "A
Traveler" writing in the *Allgemeine musikalische Zeitung* in 1827
claimed to have seen a large number of opera scores in Eisenstadt,
but today only a small quantity of such scores can still be found in
the Esterházy Archives, which have since been moved to Budapest.
The holdings of Lippe-Detmold, which Brahms diligently studied,
have subsequently vanished from the face of the earth, and the
Breitkopf Collection, of which Pohl made exhaustive use for his
biography of Haydn, likewise no longer exists.

Fortunately, there has survived an autobiographical sketch, written by Haydn at Esterháza Castle on July 6, 1776. There are two
extant autographs of this document. One is located in the Széchényi
Library in Budapest; the other, a fair copy of the first, is in my library. There is a third copy in Budapest, but it is not in Haydn's
hand. Excerpts from this sketch were inaccurately published in
1778 in the periodical *Das gelehrte Österreich*. It was not until
1836 that the *Wiener Zeitschrift für Literatur und Mode* published
it in its entirety, but this publication was based on a vanished copy

which did not correspond exactly with the original. In this form the sketch was taken over by Pohl and printed (1878) in the appendix to the first volume of his biography of Haydn.

The autobiographical sketch at least gives us some information about Haydn's youth, but this early document obviously can tell us nothing about the crucial later period of the composer's life. Haydn's letters, insofar as they have survived, are as silent about this period as are the London notebooks, which are restricted to events of the years directly in question.

Through more recent research in the Esterházy Archives in Budapest, letters from the 1760's and 70's have been found and published. These give us an idea of the obligations placed on Haydn in connection with his position as *Kapellmeister,* but for more biographical details we depend primarily on reminiscences which Haydn, as an old man, considered sufficiently noteworthy to be transmitted.

These reminiscences were first told to Georg August Griesinger, secretary of the embassy of the Electorate of Saxony in Vienna. As Griesinger himself writes, he had the good fortune to have maintained an unbroken relationship with and to have been honored with the confidence of Joseph Haydn in the last years of the master's life. This was possible because, from 1799 on, Griesinger acted as business agent for the Leipzig music publishers, Breitkopf and Härtel, in their dealings with Haydn. Griesinger's recollections of what Haydn told him first appeared in 1809 in the *Allgemeine musikalische Zeitung* and then, a year later, in book form as *Biographische Notizen über Joseph Haydn.* His description became a foundation of Haydn research and was newly reprinted a few years ago.

The biographical notes of Albert Christian Dies follow directly those of Griesinger. According to his own testimony Dies, a landscape artist, poet, and musician, paid homage as a dilettante to more than one muse. He visited Haydn between 1805 and 1808. At first Haydn parried with the comment that "his life story could not be of interest to anyone." This remark, perhaps, attacks by innuendo the writing of high-toned autobiographies, a product which was then becoming fashionable. But Haydn nevertheless admitted his admirer, and the *Biographische Nachrichten von Joseph Haydn,*

nach muendlichen Erzaehlungen desselben entworfen und herausge-
geben von Albert Christoph Dies resulted from these visits. Dies'
delineation is far more artful and sensitive than Griesinger's, and it
is unjust that less attention is paid to it. It, too, has recently been
reissued.

It is not uninteresting to consider the reciprocal effect of these
two biographies. In 1806, when Dies asked Haydn to whom he
should submit his work, Haydn referred him to Griesinger. After
he had made the latter's acquaintance, Dies wrote that for several
years Griesinger, without Haydn's knowledge, had been quietly
assembling material for a biography of the master, which means that
Griesinger did not question Haydn as Dies had done. At whatever
time Griesinger may have seen Dies' manuscript describing his first
visit with Haydn, it is entirely plausible that he used it for his final
biography. As I shall show later, by 1806 he had hardly gotten past
the very beginnings. Dies, on the other hand, mentions Griesinger's
series of articles in the *Allgemeine musikalische Zeitung,* which he
found especially useful for the description of Haydn's earlier
development.

Comparison of these two biographies shows that, in general, what
they have to tell us about Haydn's youth coincides fairly well with
Haydn's own report. When they are not always consonant with one
another regarding the later periods, I am convinced this is due, to
a considerable extent, to the different temperaments of the two biographers, which, in turn, may have caused Haydn to become freer
and more communicative with one than the other.

I should now like to adduce several examples to show the extent
to which these two biographies agree, disagree, and supplement one
another in reporting a number of individual events. Many episodes
that one reads about in these two books were not only taken over
but were even extended by later biographers.

Discrepancies begin directly with Haydn's childhood. Griesinger
tells us how the young Haydn accompanied the singing of his parents on an imaginary violin with such rhythmic accuracy that they
decided he had musical talent and sent him to a cousin in Hainburg
for further training. Haydn himself reports in his autobiographical

sketch that as a boy of five he could correctly repeat all his father's simple songs. This was surely the better proof of his musical talent and certainly the source of the quotations of the folksongs in the works he wrote in London so far from his home. Griesinger confirms this when he writes that the melodies of these songs had engraved themselves so deeply in Haydn's memory that he still remembered them in his latest years. This must have been the talent that caused his father to send the boy to his relative, the headmaster Frank in Hainburg. Three years later, continues Griesinger, the choirmaster of St. Stephen's in Vienna, Georg Reutter the younger, on a tour looking for new choir boys, visited Hainburg, examined young Haydn in sight-singing, and offered him a handful of cherries. Dies' report is similar, but he gives no date and has Reutter presenting the boy a coin.

In the first volume of his Haydn biography, Carl Ferdinand Pohl describes a touching farewell scene in which Haydn's seven-year-old sister beholds her five-year-old brother in an almost ceremonious fashion, while the father, turned towards the worried mother, gestures in the direction of a cradle prepared for the reception of a new offspring. Since Joseph had become five on March 31, 1737, and his brother Michael was born on September 13 of that year, this farewell must have taken place toward the end of August 1737. In his book about Haydn's ancestors, Ernst Fritz Schmid corrects this by pointing out that Joseph was present at the baptism of his brother on September 14.

Accordingly, Haydn's father would have gone with him to Hainburg at about the time when, even today, children in rural areas first go to school, namely, after the end of the summer's work in the fields. And so those fantasies collapse, fantasies according to which Haydn went through the fields of ripe grain, through the *Heidentor* near Petronell, and on to Hainburg while the happy lark chirped above him. The more sober version, however, agrees with the autobiographical sketch, in which Haydn reports how, in his seventh year, he boldly sang several masses from the choirloft in Hainburg. Both biographers leave Haydn in Hainburg until the end of his eighth year, that is, April 1740, when he went to the choir school of St. Stephen's in Vienna. But while, in Griesinger's view, Haydn received his discharge at the age of 17 because his voice broke, Dies has him remain at the choir school until the age of 18.

Haydn himself says of his time at the choir school that he learned a good deal and that he sang soprano until his eighteenth year when he finally lost his voice. Correspondingly, Dies writes that when the Empress Maria Theresa heard the boys in Klosterneuberg on the Feast of St. Leopold she said that Haydn no longer sang, but cawed! As Haydn became 18 in March 1750, this event must have occurred on November 15, 1749, and he must have been discharged shortly thereafter.

The anecdote of the ominous castration that Reutter is supposed to have urged on Haydn in order to preserve his voice is reported only by Griesinger. According to the story, Haydn received the suggestion with unmitigated joy until, by chance, his father intervened. Griesinger specifically notes that he did not hear the story from Haydn himself but learned it from a third person. This third person was presumably Pleyel, who spread abroad a good deal of incorrect information about Haydn but left no writings concerning him.

The two biographers come together again in the depiction of a pilgrimage which Haydn is said to have made to Mariazell. When, on applying to the choirmaster of the church, he was denied permission to sing in the choir there, he is supposed unhesitatingly to have bribed the soloist, torn the music from his hand, and sung so beautifully that the attention of everyone was drawn to him. The chapter is supposed to have boarded him for a week and even to have given him money for his return to Vienna.

How that episode can be brought into agreement with the breaking of his voice, which was the cause of his discharge from St. Stephen's, is not explained, and it is still arousing confusion in the mind of the modern biographer. There is another discrepancy regarding the time of this pilgrimage. Griesinger has Haydn undertake it shortly after his departure from the choir school; Dies, however, places it in the following spring. In his book on Haydn's

Masses, Carl Maria Brand tells us that, in general, pilgrims first came to Mariazell in July, and that it was by no means unusual for the needy among them to be boarded gratis.

Haydn himself writes little about the years after his departure from St. Stephen's. In his autobiographical sketch we are merely told that he composed diligently but without a secure foundation, until he finally had the good fortune to learn the true basis of composition from the famous maestro Porpora, that he later obtained a position as music director to Count Morzin on the recommendation of Baron von Fürnberg, and that from there he went to the position of *Kapellmeister* in the service of Prince Esterházy.

Apparently it was with the greatest pleasure that Haydn told his visitors about the composition of his first opera, *Der krumme Teufel,* which he wrote for the comedian Kurz-Bernardon. Here again we encounter a discrepancy. Griesinger writes that Haydn was 19 years old when he composed the opera; Dies places the work in Haydn's twenty-first year. The opera, unfortunately, has disappeared. And though Griesinger writes further of the pleasure with which Haydn loitered before the shops of the music dealers where one or another of his works was displayed in print, these prints, too, have not yet been rediscovered. To be sure, Haydn, as he later confesses, had given away many autographs which could then have been copied and sold; yet such early copies are also unknown to Haydn researchers.

We read in Dies how Haydn acquired Carl Philipp Emanuel Bach's *Versuch ueber die wahre Art das Clavier zu spielen.* This could have been as early as 1753, since the first part of the book appeared in that year. Dies is the only one who mentions Haydn's opinions about Mattheson's *Der vollkommene Capellmeister* and Fux' *Gradus ad Parnassum.* The German translation of the latter had been available since 1742. But Dies also offers Haydn's views on Kirnberger's writings, which did not appear until much later and which Haydn could not have studied at that time. The judgment falls without reservation in favor of C. P. E. Bach.

A little-known event was reported in the *Neue Berliner Musikzeitung* under the title "Blosse Füsse und seidene Strümpfe." According to the story, Haydn was polishing Porpora's boots when, through the open window, he heard Regina Mingotti sing one of his arias. Now, Mingotti could very well have been in Vienna, traveling from an engagement in Dresden to another in Madrid. She could surely have visited her old teacher and director, Nicolo Porpora, who at the age of 65 had been pensioned on January 1, 1752, and had moved to Vienna. An aria by Haydn is certainly conceivable at that time and indeed is mentioned by Wendschuh in his dissertation on Haydn's operas. But the question is whether Haydn would have found it necessary to polish Porpora's boots—which Dies also refers to—or otherwise to be Porpora's servant, as, for example, during the excursion to Mannersdorf. We know from Ernst Fritz Schmid's book about the master's ancestors that Haydn's father was by no means to be counted among the poorest inhabitants of the village of Rohrau. He had been a market judge since 1741, and by 1749 he was a farmer who had considerable land holdings. From Jančik's biography of Michael Haydn, we know of a letter from the father in which he announces that he will send a carriage to Vienna so that Michael, Joseph, and a friend can come to Rohrau. One might well think that he was also in a position to protect his son in Vienna from the direst poverty.

But aside from this, we read again and again of other sources of income that Joseph possessed. A businessman named Buchholz lent him 150 Gulden, and by 1751 Haydn was in a position to repay him. He gave music lessons for which he received first two and later five Gulden. This and the admittedly small sums he received as an organist in various chapels could have brought him perhaps the same annual sum that Reutter received for each choirboy, a sum on which he could have been able to live. In any case, he brought savings of 1,000 Gulden to his marriage in 1760. Yet in the last year of his life Haydn emphasized over and over to visitors that he had had a very difficult youth.

In this period there is also mention of a Countess Thun who saw Haydn's early sonatas and thereupon sent for him and gave him 25 ducats. The person in question here is probably Philippine Aloisia von Thun, the widow of Count Johann Franz Joseph von Thun-

Hohenstein, *née* von Harrach. As a fourth-degree cousin of Count Karl Anton von Harrach, she had good reason for concerning herself about the young man who was born on her cousin's estate. She is not, however, the Countess Thun referred to by Pohl and who, according to Count Zinsendorf's diary, played a Haydn Sonata in 1775.

With regard to the rest of the time in Vienna, Dies mentions the friendship of Haydn and Dittersdorf, who together played many a merry prank. It is striking that on one occasion Dies describes an incident in which Dittersdorf, who was seven and a half years younger, physically protected the older Haydn. Dittersdorf says nothing about this in his autobiography, where he mentions his connection with Haydn as having first occurred in 1763.

Griesinger, for his part, tells of Baron von Fürnberg at whose house Haydn played quartets and also composed his own first string quartet. Griesinger gives the date 1750 for the latter event. This is definitely too early. Then an admittedly quasi-legendary figure, Major Weirach, who fell into Austrian captivity during the Seven Years' War, offered a judgment on the first quartets. According to the original document, the Major heard them at the home of the nobleman on whose estates Haydn was born or lived at the time. As a consequence this discrepancy shows that one modern Haydn biographer has the quartets played in Rohrau where Haydn was indeed born in 1732, while another places the event in von Fürnberg's Schloss Weinzierl. Haydn was actually the guest of von Fürnberg in whose residence he composed and played his first quartets.

The two biographers differ also in locating Haydn's quarters. Both agree in mentioning the garret room in the Michaelerhaus, but Griesinger has him move from there to the Seilerstätte where all his worldly possessions were stolen. Dies, on the other hand, takes him to a miserable room in the home of a stocking worker's family, where he met his future father-in-law, the wigmaker Keller.

Haydn's entry upon his duties as *Kapellmeister* to Count Morzin is generally placed in the year 1759. Pohl, however, feels that this date, too, must be considered an assumption. At least the composition of Haydn's first symphony, written while he was in Morzin's service, is placed in this year. The Quartet No. 5 which, supplied with oboes and horns, was originally also a symphony, is evidently not included in this calculation.

We do not regain firm ground until Haydn's marriage to Anna Aloysia Appollonia Keller. This took place at a public ceremony in the presence of witnesses at St. Stephen's Cathedral in November 1760. Accordingly there can be no question of the possibility that the marriage was kept secret from Count Morzin, who wanted only unmarried musicians in his service. Yet this "secret marriage" is common in the biographies. Rather, it should be assumed that, at this time, Morzin had already dissolved or considerably reduced his musical establishment, and that Haydn was no longer in his service. He had not yet taken up his position with Prince Esterházy, for the decree appointing him was signed in Vienna on May 1, 1761. It seems reasonable to assume that this was the period during which Haydn moved to the Kellers. In any case, he did not do so immediately after his discharge from the choir school, as Carpani maintains.

Haydn's rise to fame began in Eisenstadt where the Princes Esterházy resided. In 1766, the same year that Prince Nicolaus inaugurated his new castle, Esterháza, the newspaper *Wiener Diarium* referred to Haydn as "the nation's favorite" and said that he was to music what Gellert was to poetry. Despite this public recognition, little is known about Haydn's daily life during the 30 years he spent at the Esterházy court. Visitors, who were drawn in ever-increasing numbers as Haydn's fame grew, have reported almost nothing about it. Johann Abraham Peter Schulz, who visited Haydn in 1770, makes a touching remark about his piety while at work. Burney, who was in Vienna briefly during his musical journey in the fall of 1772, did not meet Haydn there, nor did he travel to Hungary in order to visit him, although the court of Nicolaus the Magnificent, as well as Haydn himself, already enjoyed international renown. Burney came to know Haydn for the first time years later in London.

Bernhard Schott, a music publisher from Mainz, was among the visitors of the 1770's, but business connections probably did not arise from that meeting, for the first Haydn works published by Schott appeared in the second half of the 1780's, and these are not first editions. Maximilian Stadler—not yet an abbot—visited Haydn in 1781, and remained his friend for life, but he left no memoirs. We learn the most from Michael Kelly, who was a tenor at the Royal Opera in Vienna from 1783 to 1787, and who apparently met Haydn frequently. Kelly met him again in London and once had dinner with him. Since descriptions of Castle Esterháza also contain little about Haydn's daily life, it is not surprising that Haydn biographers so often stray into peripheral areas.

So for the first 60 years of Haydn's life we find ourselves back with the first two biographies, and it is precisely for this period that they are not very productive. Both agree in mentioning the anecdote of the *Farewell Symphony,* as well as the story of the sly poodle. Accordingly, these are to be traced back to Haydn himself. On the other hand, Griesinger tells us of only one fire that occurred in Haydn's house in Eisenstadt, and that manuscripts of operas were lost in it. Here Dies is better informed. Haydn's house burned down twice, first in 1768 and then in July 1776. Prince Nicolaus had it rebuilt both times. Pleyel later said that the autograph of the opera *Armida* was lost in the fire of 1776, and that the work itself survived only because he had previously copied the score in secret. The discrepancy of this story is immediately apparent from the fact that *Armida* was not composed until seven years later. Moreover, Pleyel never copied it, and the original holograph is still extant; a part of it is even in this country.

Haydn sold the house two years later. The biographers do not tell us where he lived after that. If one reads Pohl's description of Haydn's rural life at Castle Esterháza, one assumes that Haydn lived there all year round. The extant letters of the period convey the same impression, for all of them, written in the depth of winter, are dated from Esterháza. Haydn once complained that a letter failed to reach him because it was addressed to Eisenstadt. His continuous residence at Esterháza was possible only so long as the princely household was also in continuous residence and the opera steadily at work. In a recently published book, *Haydn als Opernkapell-meister,* Dr. Dénes Bartha and László Somfai report in detail on Haydn's activities in the opera house. They show how he made arbitrary cuts in the works to be performed, transposed and altered arias, and from time to time composed his own. This last action was undertaken largely to favor the soprano, Luigia Polzelli, with whom he was very intimate at the time. The book does not contain much about Haydn's working conditions outside of the princely establishment and his occasional appearances as conductor in other cities—Graz and Vienna, for example. In January 1790 a letter is suddenly dated "Vienna, at home." We do not know how long Haydn owned this dwelling or whether his wife, of whom one finds no mention, lived there. She was not likely to have been with him at Esterháza.

The period of Haydn's life following Prince Nicolaus' death is far easier to survey than that during which he was bound exclusively to Eisenstadt and Esterháza. In London he kept the notebooks mentioned earlier, documents of which his first two biographers made advantageous use. The greatest discrepancy between the two lies in the varying transcriptions of an index to the works that Haydn composed in England, which was added to a notebook for the second English journey. This index, which also includes works composed in Vienna between the two trips to England, is given in different versions by the two biographers. While Dies prints the index in English, the language in which one supposes Haydn wrote it, Griesinger translates it into German. His version contains one entry less than that of Dies, but in compensation he adds to each entry the number of pages in the autograph. It can easily be shown, however, from the autographs that are still extant that these page-counts are not correct. In spite of this, later biographers generally take over Griesinger's information. They appear to consider that Griesinger, as the confidant of a large publishing house, was a better hand at figures than the artist Dies. Which version is correct can no longer be shown, for the notebook that allegedly contains the index has been lost.

The third biographer, who published reminiscences of Haydn as if he had heard them from the subject himself, was surely less successful in this respect. Giuseppe Carpani was an active man of letters in Milan, but he was obliged to leave the city when it was entered by the French Revolutionary armies under General Bonaparte. He went to Vienna with Archduke Ferdinand, the Austrian governor of Lombardy. There Emperor Franz entrusted him with the censorship of the theater and paid him an honorarium. At the desire of the Empress, Carpani translated *The Creation* into Italian, and this task no doubt brought him into contact with Haydn. But Haydn did not have sufficient confidence in Carpani to turn to him for the Italian translation of *The Seven Last Words*. While Pohl says that Carpani came and went at Haydn's house, proof is lacking, but we do have such proof for the visits of the Swedish diplomat Silverstolpe, for example. We know from Bertuch, however, who visited Haydn in 1806, that, aside from Griesinger, Dies was among the very few persons the venerable old man saw from time to time.

Carpani's biography, *Le Haydine,* appeared for the first time in 1812. A single fact suffices to show that the letters are supplied with fictitious dates—on September 25, 1811, he complains that he has not heard from Haydn for a long time. Haydn had been dead for more than two years! At the beginning of the biography Carpani drops every name imaginable. This would not have been necessary had he been able to draw on information obtained from Haydn himself. Furthermore, he never even mentions a single Haydn letter. He would certainly have made such reference had it been in his power to do so. Despite Carpani's long residence in Vienna, he could not be said to have mastered the German language, as can be seen in his erroneous transcription of the text of a canon. This is further confirmed by Zelter, who met him in Vienna in 1819. So Haydn would have had to tell his reminiscences to Carpani in Italian!

Carpani seldom calls on Haydn's authority when he is retailing his improbable anecdotes and incidents. And the nicknames he attaches to Haydn's symphonies—names like "Bella Circassa," "Elena Grece," "Solitario," "Persiana," and "Poltrone"—cannot possibly have come from Haydn. Today we do not even know the symphonies to which they refer. Surely Carpani cannot have used any words of Haydn for his literary outpourings about the symphonies.

As compensation for all this, he is the first to mention Haydn's friend, the singer Luigia Polzelli, about whom the other early biographers tell us nothing. Yet Carpani cannot have gotten his information about the lady from Haydn himself, for he calls her "Boselli" and maintains that her death was the cause of Haydn's first journey to England in 1790. In reality, Polzelli was still alive as Carpani was writing, and she had nothing whatever to do with Haydn's trip. Towards the end of his biography, when he wishes to coin a special distinction for his hero, Carpani compares him with Field Marshal Loudon and calls them "two illustrious idiots."

Marie Henri Beyle, later known as Stendhal, was the next of Haydn's biographers. His *Lettres écrites de Vienne en Autriche, sur le célèbre compositeur J? Haydn,* published under the pseudonym of Louis-Alexandre-César Bombet, is based primarily on Carpani's *Haydine.* Large sections of Carpani's book are translated verbatim into French. Sometimes he shoots past the mark, as for example when he copies from Carpani the supposed fact that he (Beyle) paid Haydn several visits in 1808, whereas Beyle first arrived in Vienna on May 10, 1809, as an officer in Napoleon's army. In this capacity he may have attended Haydn's funeral mass, at which Carpani was not present, having fled for the second time before the approaching French army of Napoleon.

Beyle, like Carpani, gives his letters fictitious dates, and in so doing he commits the fatal error of referring to Napoleon's Russian campaign of 1814 in a letter dated June 2, 1809. But his biography may not be written off simply as a plagiarism. Beyle revised Carpani's work, and he shortened, turned about, and improved many of its sentences, a fact to which Larousse's *Dictionnaire universel du XIX⁰ siècle* has already called attention.

In this matter Carpani had another opinion. In two open letters of August 1815 to the *Giornale dell' italiana letteratura* he vigorously attacks Bombet, denies that he was personally acquainted with Haydn, and accuses him of lying and of stealing intellectual property. Bombet, for his part, accuses Carpani of plagiarism in a reply to the journal *Constitutionel,* and in his last response goes so far as to represent himself as his own brother who was too old and too gouty to concern himself further with music and Carpani.

Despite the many discrepancies, these two biographies must not be rejected *in toto*. The remark that in *The Creation* the pizzicato that precedes the line "und es ward Licht" (and there was light) represents the Eternal Father striking flint against stone and producing a spark in the darkness can certainly be attributed to Haydn. All that Carpani says of Haydn's ancestors is that they were born, lived, and then died, but this brief account is plainer and more concise than everything that is written on the subject today, however good it may be. Genius cannot be explained by heredity.

Though Stendhal saw only Haydn's catafalque, Carl Bertuch met the master, while he was still alive on a trip to Vienna in 1805–6. In 1806 he visited Haydn 12 times, and in 1808 at Weimar he published his *Bemerkungen* about these meetings. During his last visit, on December 20, Haydn promised him a catalog of his works. This is the well-known Elssler Catalog. At the end of Bertuch's version we find 400 minuets and German dances that are to be found neither in the original nor in any of the copies, but Bertuch cannot have invented it himself. He then offers a brief biographical sketch that agrees with the beginning of Griesinger's notice. This is the reason why I earlier expressed the opinion that by 1806 Griesinger himself had not progressed further with his biography.

In the program booklet for a performance of *The Creation* that he conducted during Lent 1809, in Bergamo, Giovanni Simone Mayr wrote a brief notice about Haydn's life and works. This performance, incidentally, was the first occasion on which the work was heard in Italy in its entirety. The notice itself was the first biographical sketch of Haydn. In it Mayr maintained that Haydn had told him that the degree of skill which caused Count Morzin to hire him had been reached only through tireless diligence exerted without the aid of a teacher or master. This does not agree with his mention of Porpora as his teacher in his autobiographical sketch. The date when Mayr met Haydn has not yet been determined. In any case, Mayr is not among the visitors of the last years of Haydn's life who are listed by Botstiber in the third volume of the Pohl biography.

If, in situations in which a direct contact between Haydn and an author can be proved, statements are made that cannot be clarified, how much worse is the situation with regard to the utterances of writers who did not know Haydn personally! We can show this by examining the orations delivered in his memory at the Institut de France, of which Haydn was a foreign member. De Framery and Le Breton delivered addresses which, aside from a few already well-known facts about Haydn's life, consisted entirely of anecdotes based primarily on oral statements by Pleyel and Neukomm. Yet in both of them we already find mention of Spangler, who is said to have harbored Haydn after his discharge from the choir school. Pohl later repeated this.

The Institut speeches were published in 1810. Griesinger, reviewing Le Breton's address in the *Allgemeine musikalische Zeitung* of February 20, 1811, makes the important remark that many of the anecdotes, as Haydn told them himself, sounded completely different from the subsequent versions. Dies also remarks that Haydn, when telling stories of his life, gave his mood of the moment free play. These stories were thus subject to variation! But this is no excuse for Carpani's bombastic decorations. Fantastic rumors occurred even during Haydn's lifetime. As the Newberry Library in Chicago informed me the other day, *Poulson's American Daily Advertiser* for March 7, 1805, carried this announcement in Philadelphia: "Died, at Vienna, the beginning of December, the celebrated composer, Haydn, in the 79th year of his age." Haydn lived until 1809 but did not reach the age of 79!

In the next 65 years there appeared larger and smaller biographies of Haydn, some of which I have been able to study in the Music Division of this Library. One of these, the work of Franz Joseph Fröhlich, was published in the Ersch and Gruber encyclopedia of 1820. It contains the crudest falsifications; yet Sandberger reprinted it in 1936 at a time when no one was yet thinking about new editions of the vastly more important biographies by Griesinger and Dies. The other biographies, among which are those by C. Albert Ludwig and H. Barbedette (appearing when Pohl had already begun work on his Haydn biography), are as good as forgotten.

Scholarly Haydn research dates its true beginning from 1878, when the first volume of the biography by Carl Ferdinand Pohl appeared. He went back to the sources and winnowed the available material according to strict historical criteria. His biography of Haydn was conceived on a wide scale. It is the first such study to devote attention to Haydn's wife and his circle of friends, two matters about which Haydn himself did not report. Beyond this, Pohl reserved considerable space for discussions of the musical life of the time and general social relationships, as indeed he had done in an earlier special study of Haydn's London period. Although he gives detailed descriptions of Vienna, Eisenstadt, and Esterháza, and the kind of life led by the reigning princes, Haydn is always at the center of the story.

Though Pohl errs in the exact date of that touching farewell scene that I have already discussed, he sets Haydn's departure for Hainburg in the right year, 1737. This was the year in which Michael Haydn was born, and it is the year in which Haydn himself placed the trip in his autobiographical sketch. Then Pohl shows that Reutter could not have come to Hainburg prior to 1739 because he did not take over the supervision of the choirboys until the death of his father in the fall of 1738. Since Griesinger associates the encounter of Reutter and Haydn with cherries, it must have taken place early in the summer.

In the autobiographical sketch Haydn writes: "When I was seven years old the late Herr Kapellmeister von Reutter fortuitously learned of my weak but pleasant voice." But we must bear in mind that in this sketch Haydn placed his birth date one year too late. When Reutter heard him, he must therefore have been not seven but eight years old, the age he would indeed have been in 1739. Haydn then continues: "He [Reutter] immediately took me into the choir school." Pohl corrects this. Haydn did not go to Vienna until the end of his eighth year—that is, in 1740.

Pohl places Haydn's discharge from St. Stephen's in 1749. He then has Haydn meet the tenor Spangler, who takes him into his poor quarters until Haydn sets out on his pilgrimage to Mariazell. Haydn did not mention Spangler in his conversations with his visitors, but 40 years later he supported Spangler's children, which indicates that he was obligated to the singer. Even in his old age, Haydn never forgot the good deeds done him in his youth, a fact also proved by his will.

Pohl writes that he had the greatest difficulty with the chronological order of events in the years immediately following Haydn's discharge from St. Stephen's. We are still in the same position today, and we must not find fault with Pohl for not having always succeeded in reconciling the crisscrossing contradictions of the earlier biographies. He carefully examined all of these biographies and pointed out many discrepancies. But he himself fell victim to several, for example, that regarding Haydn's visit in Bad Mannersdorf.

Porpora traveled to Bad Mannersdorf in the company of the Venetian ambassador Correr and his mistress whose singing teacher he was. Porpora is supposed to have brought Haydn along as his servant to function as accompanist for these singing lessons. In Mannersdorf, Haydn, who was then about 20 years old, is supposed to have met Gluck and Wagenseil and to have had a meeting with Dittersdorf. In a concert given by the Prince of Sachsen-Hildburghausen, Dittersdorf is said to have hoaxed the ambassador while he was playing the violin. In Dittersdorf's autobiography this event takes place several years later in the fall during the vintage. In summer the Prince of Sachsen-Hildburghausen resided and gave concerts on his estate, Schlosshof, until he sold it to Emperor Franz.

Pohl's biography also tells how, at a rehearsal in Paris in 1789, Gyrowetz placed before the orchestra a symphony of his own which had previously been known under Haydn's name. Many years later Gyrowetz wrote in his autobiography that the symphony in question had been published by Schlesinger. Pohl accepts this supposed fact without objection, though in 1789 there was no music publishing house of Schlesinger. About 10 years later in Munich, Gyrowetz again heard the symphony and again it was offered as a work by Haydn. I have not been able to identify the symphony in question.

Pohl is also in error when he lists Willmann among the Paris publishers of Haydn's works and has Haydn act as his own publisher for the piano sonatas nos. 40, 41, and 42. In the first volume of my Haydn catalog I have corrected all this, as well as Pohl's erroneous assertion that the published parts of the first version of *The Seven Last Words* contain the introductory bass recitatives. These recitatives are part of Frieberth's arrangement of the work, an arrangement that Haydn heard in Passau while on his second journey to England.

Pohl describes in detail this journey as well as Haydn's first trip to London, when he traveled via Bonn. We do not know when Haydn began the return voyage from his first stay in London. In his letters he repeatedly wrote that he intended to leave at the end of June 1792. But the last of the letters that Mrs. Schroeter wrote to him can be interpreted to mean that he was still in London on July 2, for in it Mrs. Schroeter invites him to dinner on that day.

The trip to Bonn would have taken six or seven days. He met the music publisher Simrock there and negotiated with him about the publication of symphonies. Botstiber's assumption that the Elector's orchestra tendered Haydn a dinner on this occasion in the Redoutensaal of the neighboring town of Godesberg—a dinner at which he is supposed to have met Beethoven—probably rests on a confusion with the dinner Prince-Elector Maximilian Franz gave Haydn in Bonn, when he passed through this city in December 1790 on his first journey to London. I could find no evidence of such a Godesberg dinner in contemporary local papers as far as they are preserved. Besides this, Pohl does not mention such a dinner in his essay on Haydn in London. As for Beethoven, by the summer of 1790 he had finished the cantata on the death of Emperor Joseph II, which he is supposed to have shown to Haydn during that dinner. He is more likely to have shown Haydn the cantata in December of that same year than on Haydn's return from England two years later. Moreover, Beethoven's cantata on the elevation of Emperor Leopold II was also completed in 1790.

In another letter Haydn writes that he wants to travel to Frankfurt am Main because his Prince expects him there for the coronation of Emperor Franz II on July 14. It was not the then reigning Prince Paul Anton who went to Frankfurt, but his son, the later Nicolaus II. Nicolaus took with him only a small part of the musical organization and would scarcely have needed Haydn. On the other hand, there is a letter of the Mainz publisher Bernhard Schott, who had already visited Haydn in Bonn on the journey to England. According to this letter, Schott met Haydn in Biebrich on July 17, after having been notified of Haydn's arrival by Simrock in Bonn. But if Haydn, traveling from Bonn, first arrived in Biebrich on July 17, he cannot have been at the coronation in Frankfurt on July 14. The rest of his route is not known. In any case, he was back in Vienna on July 24.

On the second return trip Haydn traveled via Hamburg but not to visit C. P. E. Bach, as we are told, for Bach had died on December 14, 1788, and Haydn must have definitely been aware of this. Furthermore, he had been expected in Hamburg by the bookdealer Westphal ever since his first English trip. He is supposed to have presented to the Hamburgers a melody for trumpet which thereafter was played from the tower of a church. But this may also be merely an anecdote.

Haydn left London on August 15, 1795, and a notice in a Hamburg paper states that he arrived in that city on August 19. This arrival would have taken place in the evening, for the correspondent of an English paper did not report the event to London until the following day. Since Haydn could not have taken the Calais route because of the Franco-Austrian war, he must have traveled by sea. As it happens there left, on that very day, a direct passenger ship from Harwich to Hamburg. However, direct proof has not been discovered that Haydn was actually aboard this ship, together with his amanuensis Elssler, who had accompanied him on his second journey, and presumably also the parrot he was given in England.

Despite many errors and gaps, Pohl's biography remains the single fundamental work on which all subsequent serious Haydn biographies are based. Thus it is incomprehensible that four years after the publication of Pohl's first volume there appeared *Joseph Haydn, ein Lebensbild* by Franz von Seeburg (a pseudonym for Franz Hacker), a book that makes a mockery of all the preceding biographies. Seeburg alters previous depictions—insofar as he makes use of them at all—completely mixes up all matters of chronology, has events occur in the wrong places, and reduces them to sentimentality. The chapter headings show this: "Poor days—good hearts," "It should not have been," "Beggar and bridegroom," "Poor as a churchmouse," "It is all in God's hands," "The shimmering bubble of luck bursts," and many more. This book, which later appeared with the subtitle "The Novel of an Artist," went into its seventh edition as late as 1929. In 1888 it was translated into French, and within two years this translation went through four editions.

After the recent war the book was made available in condensed form in the series *Deutsches Gut,* but it was shortly replaced by a popular novel by Heinrich Eduard Jacob. Though more soundly based and better written than Seeburg's book, Jacob's novel also contains freely invented sentimental episodes which follow in Carpani's steps. Jacob even outdoes Carpani in citing the names of artists. The anecdotes are expanded to short stories, and at the very outset the book offers an anecdote that was not previously heard. According to this tale, a poor Austrian farmer set about bringing his cow into her stall on a warm summer day in 1735. He shrank back when he clearly heard a mooing in the stable and perceived that something was moving in the straw. He thought that the devil had conjured a second cow, crossed himself, and fled in terror to the priest. The priest examined the stable and found not magic, but a three-year-old child playing cow. The excited reader is surprised by the *dénouement.* The child is none other than Joseph Haydn who, in his earliest youth, is clearly adumbrating the animal imitations of his late, great oratorios. This book first appeared in New York in 1950. A year later it was translated into French, accompanied by a laudatory preface by Thomas Mann which also accompanies the German edition of 1952. Then it was brought out by the Gutenberg Book Club, and ever since it has been among the most discussed books about Haydn.

[20]

I should not have mentioned these two books were it not for the fact that they have definitely contributed to a diminution of the picture of Haydn among a wide circle of readers and thereby increased public preference for pieces like the "Toy Symphony," the Ox-Minuet (which Griesinger had attacked), or the serenade from the so-called Opus 3, the authenticity of which is by no means established. But these books at least show a certain love for Father Haydn. This love is completely absent in the historical and psychological study based on an analysis of Haydn's string quartets, published in London in 1951 by Robert Sondheimer. The author disintegrates the quartets into tiny melodic scraps to prove that these are all to be found in works by earlier composers, who, moreover, use them in a more coherent fashion. He then accuses Haydn of having combined these scraps for mercantile reasons into works of rhythmical ebullience, after having drained them of their intense emotional poetry—thus is it expressed in the English version of this study, which was translated from the German.

It is inconceivable that Haydn should be accused of such a thing, for he especially made derogatory comments about contemporaries who put one little bit of music after another and broke off when they scarcely had begun.

Sondheimer further pretends that Haydn's string quartets first led the way in music to the ominous separation of Art and Life, and that they are no longer "fraught with immense feelings as in the pre-classics" who, in Sondheimer's own words, sought essential nature and not external splendor in music. Considering, according to Haydn's own words, that a musical composition should consist of flowing song and integrated ideas in order to reach the hearer's heart through its continuity, one might conclude that he would not have had much use for the "immense feelings" that Sondheimer misses in his music.

In conclusion, I return to the beginning of my lecture and the remark I made that we really know very little about Haydn's life, at least in comparison with what we know about the lives of Mozart, Beethoven, Schubert, and other composers. Our first glimpse into Haydn's private life comes from his correspondence with Frau von

Genzinger, which begins with a letter of June 10, 1789, when he was 57 years old. The correspondence becomes ever more ardent on Haydn's side. On one occasion he even felt obliged to reassure the noble lady that a letter to her, which went astray, did not contain anything that could compromise her.

Haydn carried on this correspondence during his first stay in London, but his most ardent letters from that period are addressed to Luigia Polzelli. She was engaged at the Esterházy opera in 1779 but was soon dismissed because of her mediocrity as a singer. It was through Haydn's own special request that Prince Nicolaus kept her at Esterháza. As a result we have been bestowed with several fine arias which Haydn especially composed for her as insertions in operas that were performed there under his direction.

In one of the letters to Polzelli, Haydn calls his wife an infernal beast. Probably she had communicated to him some unpleasant things about Polzelli, and she may have been perfectly right in doing so. The Italian singer directed much of her attention towards money, and a few weeks after Haydn's death she attempted to obtain an annuity from his estate on the basis of a declaration made by him nine years earlier. Haydn, however, revoked this declaration and had her cut out of his last will. He probably decided that she had already obtained enough from him during his lifetime.

Although we do not know much about Haydn's mistress, we know still less about his wife. He married her after the termination of his employment with Count Morzin and before he entered the service of Prince Esterházy. He had really wanted to marry her sister who, however, became a nun. But if, on the one hand, Haydn's wife is accused of bigotry and extravagance and of having rolled up Haydn's autographs in order to use them as hair curlers, other biographers write that she well and truly accompanied him on his trips to Vienna.

As I have said, we do not know where she stayed or what she did while Haydn was at Esterháza with Polzelli. Even the latest research, done for me on this point in Vienna, brought no results. After the death of Prince Nicolaus, Haydn moved to an apartment which his wife is supposed to have occupied in Vienna. He lived with her there between his two English journeys, and they moved together into his house in Gumpendorf after he remodeled it. He also carried on a correspondence with her from London. It is another remarkable fate of Haydn research that, while letters to Frau von Genzinger and Luigia Polzelli have been preserved, there is no trace whatever of Haydn's correspondence with his wife.

Judged by her will, she was more primitive than malicious or evil. On one occasion Haydn refused a present intended for her. He loved his wife, he argued, but she wanted for nothing and had performed no service that warranted recompense. On another occasion he is supposed to have said of her that it would have been all the same to her whether her husband had been a composer or a shoemaker. He kept a picture of her until his death, but the picture has disappeared. He showed it to one of his last visitors with the comment: "That is my wife. She has often enraged me," which, in general, is not so uncommon.

I could go on for a considerable time telling you about discrepancies I have found in Haydn biographies while consulting them during my researches for my Haydn catalog. This would come very near to the scope of a new Haydn biography which, however, I do not intend to write. I must finish the catalog; but I hope I have shown you to what extent biographical researches are necessary before completion can be contemplated.

THE LIBRARY OF CONGRESS

THE LOUIS CHARLES ELSON MEMORIAL FUND

MUSIC—ITS PAST AND ITS PRESENT

A LECTURE DELIVERED BY

SIR JACK WESTRUP

IN

THE WHITTALL PAVILION

OF THE LIBRARY OF CONGRESS

SEPTEMBER 3, 1963

Washington : 1964

MUSIC—ITS PAST AND
ITS PRESENT

When Charles Burney published the first volume of his *General History of Music* in 1776, he envisaged the possibility that his work might "fall into the hands of persons wholly unacquainted with the elements of Music." The possibility might seem to us remote. Burney accepted it and, for the benefit of such readers, prefixed his work with a few definitions. The first of these, describing music as "an innocent luxury," [1] is so well known that it would be impertinent to use it as a text for this or any other lecture. I prefer to quote the last, which refers to "excellence of Style and Composition." It runs as follows: "It may perhaps be said that to practised ears the most pleasing Music is such as has the merit of novelty, added to refinement, and ingenious contrivance; and to the ignorant, such as is most familiar and common." [2] To which the peevish reader might reply: "And what, pray, about music which is neither novel nor familiar?" The author's answer might well have been: "Read my book." We can spare ourselves that delightful labour by turning to his conclusion at the end of Volume IV. I would gladly quote it all, but I shall content myself with the last two paragraphs:

It may be thought a useless labour by some to have drawn from the tomb the names of so many obscure and barbarous authors, whose insipid productions, if preserved, would but degrade human nature, and shew the imbecility of their endeavours at distinction; but the progress of science, and the principles of its declension, can only be discovered by tracing the steps by which it has advanced towards perfection or tended to corruption.

---

[1] Op. cit., I, p. xvii.
[2] Ibid., p. xviii.

Many specimens of melody and harmony are given, not as models of perfection, but reliques of barbarism, and indisputable vouchers that mankind was delighted with bad Music, before good had been heard; and I have spoken of some musicians whose fame is now so much faded, that it is perhaps the last time they will ever be mentioned. Yet though I have constantly treated old masters with reverence, it has never been at the expence of the modern. Indeed, respect for the dead should not annihilate all kindness for the living, who are in much greater want of patronage. The artist who is suffered to linger in want and obscurity, is made but small amends by posthumous honours and commemorations.[3]

These are strong words. If they offer no help for the solution of our present discontents, at least they throw light on a prevalent attitude to music in the eighteenth century—an age when "Gothic" was a term of abuse.

We are often told that we should listen to older music with "historical" ears—that Beethoven should come to us direct, without any associations that may filter into the mind from Wagner, Strauss, Debussy or Stravinsky. This is sound advice, so far as it goes. It may help us to accept as dramatic what might otherwise appear insipid, to borrow Burney's word. It may induce us to believe that the frenetic reiteration of a tonic chord is as exciting as anything in the *Symphony of Psalms*. But even if this exercise in historical imagination were completely possible, which it is not, it would still not be sufficient. It would not be enough to listen with eighteenth- or early nineteenth-century ears. We should have to approach the music with minds conditioned by Beethoven's environment. If by some miracle we could be transported back in time and could actually be present at the first performance of a Beethoven symphony, we should not merely have to get used to mechanical oddities, such as the different sounds made by the instruments, we should also find ourselves sitting among people whose outlook was entirely different from ours, except in one respect—that they expected to derive pleasure from what they heard.

---

[3] Op. cit., IV, p. 685.

The possibility that music may give pleasure does not normally enter into the minds of modern historians. It is sufficient for them that the music exists. Burney did not make this mistake. He recognized that "mankind was delighted with bad Music, before good had been heard." But he could not very well pursue the question without getting involved in a string of sophistries. If men were delighted with music in the past, was it a different delight from ours, and if not, was it morally reprehensible that they should be delighted with what was bad? It would have been agreeable to have Burney's answer to this question. We should then go on to press him by asking what he meant by "bad." And we should know, even before we asked the question, what the answer would be. "Bad" music is music by obscure and barbarous authors. In Burney's defense it should be said that he did not relegate all old music to this category. He says of Josquin des Prés: "I have never seen, among all his productions that I have scored, a single movement which is not stamped with some mark of the great master." And again: "There is such a manifest superiority in his powers, such a simple majesty in his ideas, and such dignity of design, as wholly justify the homage he received." [4] This is high praise; yet there is little here to suggest that the music might give pleasure if sung. What Burney admired in Josquin was the gravity of the style, the purity of the harmony, and above all the mastery of counterpoint and canon. The latter, he argues, are by no means to be despised. "Before the cultivation of Dramatic Music," he says, "as Canon and Fugue were universally studied and reverenced, they were brought to such a degree of perfection, as is wonderful; and though good taste has long banished them from the Theatre, yet the Church and Chamber still, occasionally, retain them, with great propriety; in the church they preclude levity, and in the Chamber exercise ingenuity." [5]

There is something almost defensive about this statement, as though Burney were apologizing for disloyalty to his own principles. Perhaps he had doubts, as we all do when we start investigating our opinions. But any doubts he may have had about *Sumer is icumen*

---

[4] Op. cit., II, p. 509.
[5] Loc. cit.

in were firmly stifled. The piece, he says, "is very ingeniously contrived, and has not only more melody, but is in better harmony than I have hitherto found of so early a period; yet, in point of composition though its defects may not be discovered by every *Ear* during the performance, it is hardly clean and pure enough to satisfy the *Eye,* in score: as many liquors may be tolerably palatable, and yet not bear a glass." [6] If anyone had asked him whether he judged the music of his own time by its appearance on the printed page, he might have found it difficult to give a convincing answer. I have quoted from Burney at this length, not in order to poke fun at a man whose extraordinary industry must win the admiration of all who have followed him, but rather to show how strongly judgments of the past are affected by awareness of the present. We may very well say that we are not the victims of such a gross historical error. Yet if our attitude to the music of the remote past is more liberal than Burney's, it is only in comparatively recent years that it has become so. In the early years of this century historians were still discussing early medieval music as though the intervals employed in polyphonic music were the chief subject of interest. Melody and rhythm as vital elements in a composition were largely ignored. Yet melody is of paramount importance in plainsong; and whatever interpretation of troubadour songs we adopt, we cannot very well resign ourselves to supposing that they were unrhythmical. Another weakness in discussing the music of this period was an excessive reliance on the works of theoretical writers. If historians insist on writing a chapter or two about Greek music, we may allow them to argue with each other about what the theorists meant, since there is virtually no music to talk about. But in the Middle Ages there is a great deal of music to talk about, even if it is only a fraction of what was actually written.

Theorists are very dangerous people. They may be ultraconservative, in which case they will lay down the law to their more progressive contemporaries. They may agree with each other because they have copied from each other or are too supine to think matters out for themselves. They may disagree with each other, not from any

---

[6] Ibid., p. 406.

profound conviction that they are right but simply from a natural inclination to think that someone else is wrong. In the case of medieval theorists we cannot always be certain that the texts adequately represent what they said. Lecture notes are rarely models of accuracy, as every lecturer who has stumbled on a pupil's notebook knows to his cost. And even progressive theorists are reluctant to turn their backs completely on the past. In the interests of completeness, they stuff their pages with antiquated matter which may once have been useful but has long since ceased to have any validity. Skim through the pages of Thomas Morley's *A Plaine and Easie Introduction to Practicall Musicke* and consider how much of it would have been entirely useless to his younger contemporaries.

Theorists, however, command respect. They seem to speak with the voice of authority. And that authority has a habit of growing as it becomes enveloped in the mists of time. Rameau's theoretical writings have enjoyed far more repute since his death than they ever did in his lifetime. In spite of the fact that his views have done more harm to the study of harmony than those of any other individual writer, they are still the basis of many of the textbooks of our own time. Young people who might acquire an intelligent grasp of harmony, as Bach's pupils did by studying figured bass, are brought up on the monstrous theory of inversions which does not correspond to anything they hear and which, if carried to its logical conclusion, ends in nonsense. All this we may note and even approve. But it is not simply a matter that concerns the study of history or of elementary harmony. We have theorists with us today who follow in the footsteps of their predecessors by laying down the law about contemporary music. There seems, however, to be a difference. In the past composers were not much concerned with what the theorists had to say. In a paragraph added to Bach's obituary, Lorenz Christoph Mizler observed that the composer "did not . . . occupy himself with deep theoretical speculations on music, but was all the stronger in the practice of the art." [7] Today, however, not only do theorists tell composers what they ought to do, but they are listened

---

[7] *The Bach Reader*, ed. by Hans T. David and Arthur Mendel (New York, 1948), p. 224.

to with apparent respect.　Composers themselves lay down the law; and even if the most eminent insist that they have no wish to impose their methods on others, their pupils and followers ignore the modest disclaimer and proudly flaunt a banner which others refuse to follow at their peril.

It is almost as though composers formed a trade union, the purpose of which, like many other trade unions, is not so much to protect their interests as to make things uncomfortable for those who are unwilling to join them.　Perhaps it would be more accurate to say that there are several unions.　There is the twelve-tone union, the more specialized Webern union, the electronic union, and what for simplicity's sake may be called the sheer-nonsense union.　The last of these is perhaps the most dangerous.　Nonsense allied to fun does no harm to music, and many composers have exploited it in the past. If their efforts are now almost entirely forgotten, that does not mean that they failed to win appreciation in the past.　But the nonsense music of our own time is deadly serious.　No doubt all music should be serious in intention, but there is no need for it to be deadly.　Queen Victoria's remark "We are not amused" was an expression of disapproval.　But a failure to be amused may not necessarily imply disapproval.　It may simply be a natural reaction to something which is not funny; and, as every comedian knows, that is a form of unspoken criticism against which there is no defense and to which there is no reply.　I had at one time intended to call my lecture "What Lessons Can Music Learn From the Past?"　I abandoned it because I should have felt bound to offer an answer.　But if that had been my theme, the danger of paying attention to theorists would have been one of the lessons.　I cannot on the present occasion very well say that there is too much talking about music; but I can and do say that there is too much writing about it.　Burney's criterion for the music of his own day was good taste.　He expected the older composers to obey what he imagined to be "the rules."　When they did not, he was grieved and even affronted.　Today there is no such thing as good taste.　It is the rules that are paramount; and everywhere there are pocket dictators to tell us what they are.

I said earlier that the older historians were little concerned with melody and rhythm when they were writing about medieval music. Yet anyone who is not purblind can see at once that these meant as much to composers of the time as they do to us. Intelligent appreciation of a thirteenth-century motet does not depend on the number of times the composer uses thirds and sixths but on the beauty of the individual melodic lines and on the subtleties within a pervasive rhythm. The old idea that Josquin was the first "artistic" composer is now so completely dead that younger people would probably be surprised to learn that it ever existed. Yet its death is comparatively recent. Even music later that Josquin was often viewed with suspicion. Palestrina was regarded with reverence because he was supposed to have saved church music and because his polyphony was "pure," though it is difficult for the uninitiated to understand how technical processes can be either pure or impure. Monteverdi's chief claim to inclusion in the roll of fame was the traditional assertion that he was the first to use the chord of the dominant seventh unprepared. No one stopped to enquire why this, even if it were true, should inspire respect; and needless to say no one bothered to perform his music. I cannot say what conditions were like in other countries, but I know that in England, when Monteverdi's *Orfeo* was performed for the first time in 1925, it came as a revelation—not only to critics, whose reactions are not of much importance, but to the ordinary music lover. The discovery that music, which had hitherto been the preserve of the historian, was actually delightful to listen to was something that no one seems to have foreseen. It was about the same time that the Germans started reviving Handel's operas. Till then it had been accepted as a matter of course that they were undramatic and would make no effect on the stage. "Concerts in costume" was the parrot cry. Today we know better. As opera after opera is rescued from limbo, traditional historians, if there are any still left, rub their eyes in surprise as they observe a public enthusiasm which they would not have thought possible. As for Monteverdi, he is now a household word. Every Tom, Dick, and Harry can reel off the names of his works and even sing some of the tunes; his madrigals are the staple fare of amateurs and pro-

fessionals alike.   To a large extent this is due to the activities of recording companies, but not entirely.   Recording companies are com-
mercial organizations and rarely issue what they do not expect to
sell.   Their way has been made easier by the tremendous growth
of broadcasting, which has shown a praiseworthy desire to explore
the whole field of music, ancient and modern.   But even this activity
would not have occurred if it had not been for the efforts of pioneers
who were at work before broadcasting began or while it was still in its
infancy.   I am not thinking of scholars who published old music at
a time when no one seemed likely to want it.   The publication of the
Bach Gesellschaft was an article of faith.   So was Chrysander's monumental edition of Handel, the most remarkable example of an undertaking promoted by a single man.   But these editions would have
remained on library shelves if it had not been for men, Chrysander
himself among them, who believed that this was music that was
worth hearing.   The tide was modest at the beginning, but it gathered momentum and ended by sweeping all before it.   Musicologists
struggled in the deep waters and continued to argue about principles
of editing which interested no one but themselves.   The performers
ignored them, issued their own practical editions, and insisted that
the music should be heard.   The very term "practical edition" is a
commentary on this stage of development.   What use is an edition
which is not practical?   Bach and Handel would have laughed at
the idea.

Eventually the inevitable happened.   A new race of musicologists
arose who were themselves performers.   They were as expert as
their predecessors and as enthusiastic as the pioneers.   They valued
accuracy and were able to avoid some of the mistakes which had
been due to amateur enthusiasm; but they also believed that performances should be alive.   Musical instruments were no longer
objects to be revered in a museum.   They were brought out into
the light of day and played.   Expert craftsmen learned to copy them,
and a new industry grew up which has brought profit to many and
pleasure to even more.   Thousands of children all over the world
are playing on recorders today without realizing that thirty-five years
ago only a handful of enthusiasts had ever heard the instrument.

I assume that the purpose of reviving old music is to give pleasure. That it does give pleasure is evident from the reactions of those who listen to it. People who have had no historical training have been known to listen entranced to *organa* of the Notre Dame school. To historians, reluctant to admit that pleasure matters and suspicious of aesthetic judgments, this new development is apt to be puzzling. Some of them still seem barely aware of it. They dutifully begin their chapters on early polyphony by quoting examples from *Musica Enchiriadis* but fail to emphasize the fact that this is a theoretical work or to explain that there is no certain evidence that any group of people ever sang in this way. This is a particularly flagrant example of misguided respect for theorists. The error is perhaps natural. Since there is no music, the historians would say, we are compelled to rely on theoretical writings. But we have only to compare the music of later times with contemporary theorists to see how dangerous this attitude can be. If we had to depend on theorists for our knowledge of ninteenth-century music, should we be in a position to guess what the works of Brahms and Wagner must have been like? The very fact that Artusi criticized Monteverdi is sufficient indication of the gulf that so often existed between theory and practice in the past.

Burney would have been puzzled by the pleasure that we derive from music which he thought barbarous. The ignorant listener, he maintained, is pleased by music which is most familiar and common. But medieval music is neither familiar nor common to the ignorant listener today. Much of it might be said, in Burney's words, to have "the merit of novelty," except that to him "novelty" implied music that had recently been composed. He would have found it hard to accept as novel something that had been written several hundred years ago. And he would not only have been puzzled by the pleasure we derive from it, he would have been suspicious. He grudgingly admits that the defects of *Sumer is icumen in* "may not be discovered by every *Ear* during the performance," but is quick to point out that it will not satisfy the eye in score. This is an attitude which has bedeviled a good deal of critical writing since Burney and has often provoked rebellion against a teacher. It has

[9]

even led to the absurd suggestion that critics of Berlioz disapprove of what they see on the printed page, whereas the truth is much simpler: they dislike what they hear. This might at first sight appear to be the reason for Artusi's attack on Monteverdi, since he speaks of offences against the ear. But as the argument proceeds it is evident that the appeal is rather to reason. "The ear," says Artusi, "is so taken up with the other parts that it does not fully perceive the offense committed against it . . . , while reason, which knows and distinguishes the good from the bad, perceives right well that a deception is wrought on the sense . . ." [8] We are back in the dilemma which faced Burney when he studied *Sumer is icumen in.* "It sounds all right," the pedants seem to say, "but it ought not to."

In this matter I am on the side of the angels; and the angels are those who, hearing music, enjoy it. What is the nature of this pleasure, and how far is it constant through the centuries? The first part of this question is one that every listener must answer for himself. It is easy for us, as we sit in the concert hall, to imagine that our neighbours on either side are experiencing the same enjoyment as ourselves. Our applause may be equally enthusiastic, but our reactions may be totally different. What does a dog hear when he listens to music? Without being a dog I cannot say; and a hundred experiments with dogs will not make me any wiser. And dogs differ one from another as much as human beings do. To some extent my neighbour is as much a mystery to me as a dog would be. Perhaps he has virtuously attended a course on musical appreciation and has come primed with the stock recipes for sonata form. But if we are both listening to the first movement of Mozart's G minor Symphony, does the change from the tonic to the relative major mean as much to him as it does to me? And if he can follow this, can he also find his way through the modulations in the development? Does he know that the recapitulation has started because he recognizes the opening tune, or does he foresee its appearance because he realizes that the music is moving inexorably back to the tonic key? Or again, let us suppose that we are listening to the

---

[8] I quote from the translation by Oliver Strunk in *Source Readings in Music History* (New York, 1950), p. 399.

finale of Schubert's C major Symphony. Does he want to cry, like Humpty Dumpty, "There's glory for you," when the recapitulation starts in E flat major, or is he so oblivious of key that he notices nothing unusual and merely recognizes the theme? Quite apart from details of this kind, does my neighbour enjoy the composition as a whole, or is he merely pleased with certain incidents—the tunes from the symphonies which he can buy in a music shop, conveniently arranged for the modest pianist? If he is watching *Götterdämmerung,* does he wait patiently for "Siegfried's Journey to the Rhine," the "Funeral March," and the final scene and leave the theatre content because he has heard these three? To all these questions there is no positive answer. A nationwide questionnaire might enable us to give some sort of answer to the question "What do you enjoy?," but we should still want to know "Why do you enjoy it?"— and that would not be easy to determine.

The other question—"How far is pleasure in music constant through the centuries?"—is equally difficult but for a different reason. Theorists, like historians, are not normally concerned with pleasure. They occasionally refer to beauty, but without defining it, which is understandable. Franco says that if you want to write a *conductus* you must first invent a melody as beautiful as possible.[9] Another medieval theorist tells us that accidentals are introduced into music for two reasons: *causa necessitudinis* and *causa pulchritudinis.*[10] The first is ambiguous, since what necessity can there be other than the obligation to please the ear? The second allows a good deal of latitude: the composer may have one idea of what is beautiful, his listeners another. Medieval and Renaissance writers often express admiration for outstanding composers of their time, but generally on account of the skill which they show in the exercise of their craft. It is unusual to find the kind of appreciation expressed by Joannes de Tinctoris in the dedication of his *Liber de arte contrapuncti* of 1477. Citing the names of living composers whom he admired, he says of their works: "I never hear them, I never

---

[9] Op. cit., p. 155.
[10] Coussemaker, Edmond de, *Scriptorum de musica medii aevi novam seriem,* Vol. I (Paris, 1864), p. 312.

examine them, without coming away happier and more enlightened." [11]   That music makes one happier is a sentiment often expressed by poets, though not all of them have been qualified to utter it.   When the sentiment is expressed by someone who is both poet and musician, like Guillaume de Machaut, it naturally carries more weight.   But in spite of Tinctoris and Machaut it is more often the amateurs who convey to us some of the pleasure that music can give. Perhaps it is not quite fair to describe St. Augustine as an amateur, but at least music was not his chief concern.   When he confesses to a feeling of guilt at enjoying the music in church more than the message, we have an insight into his reactions which is probably more valuable than any poetic rhapsody.   Here, as so often, it is the casual remark that is most revealing to the historian.   Pepys never intended his diary for the public eye, and for that reason his recorded ecstasy at hearing wind music in the theatre is all the more moving.   This is the state of mind which we have all experienced at one time or another.   We feel ourselves in the presence of a kindred spirit.   The question "Did they enjoy music as much as we do?" becomes academic.   We cannot prove that the pleasure which music affords is one and indivisible, but our heart assures us that it must be so.

This still leaves uncertain whether the things that please us would have pleased them, and vice versa.   Conditions of performance have changed so much in the course of years, and evidence is not always as straightforward as it might appear at first sight.   Chaucer's Prioress "entunéd in hir nose ful semely." [12]   Was that the way they sang in church?   Clerics are not unknown at the present day who seem to be afflicted with permanent catarrh.   Or was Chaucer making fun of her?   It is difficult to say.   There is a strange oriental quality about Léonin's *organa* which suggests that the singers may have learned something from the Arabs.   Contact between East and West was much closer then than it is today.   It is by no means impossible that a style of singing was cultivated and admired which we should find tedious if not intolerable.   One of the most frustrating

---

[11] Strunk, op. cit., p. 199.
[12] *Canterbury Tales*, Prologue, line 123.

tasks in the history of music is to try to find out what was considered to be beautiful singing. The theorists do not help us; they are too busy teaching their readers how to improvise counterpoints. We are told that two girls sang a *ballata* by Landini so beautifully that even the birds in the trees began to sing more sweetly. Bird song can hardly have changed from that day to this, but human beings are less consistent. Should we be as delighted as that aristocratic audience if the girls could come back to us and sing again? The enormous popularity of opera in the eighteenth century was due as much to fine singing as to the quality of the music. "Damn her! she has got a nest of nightingales in her belly" cried a voice from the gallery when Cuzzoni was singing in London. The tribute seems to have been spontaneous; it could be illuminating if only we knew what she sounded like. But though writers of the time tell us a good deal about the technical prowess of singers, we are left to imagine their tone. According to Quantz, Cuzzoni had "a pure intonation, and a fine shake; . . . her graces . . . took possession of the soul of every auditor, by her tender and touching expression." Faustina, says the same author, had "a flexible throat for divisions, with so beautiful and quick a shake that she could put it in motion upon short notice, just when she would." [13] The information is agreeable but falls far short of what we should like to know. And if we could hear *castrati* today should we admire them as much as our forefathers did? Is it just possible that there was once in the world a beauty of sound which we shall never know?

With instruments we are on safer ground up to a point. Old organs have survived in working order, and the sound they make is not only apt to the music that was written for them but attractive to the ear. If we knew exactly how violins were played in the old days, we could say the same of them. Even without this exact knowledge we can hear that they are capable of producing an exquisite tone, though ears accustomed to a perpetual vibrato might be puzzled by a method of performance which used this device merely as an occasional means of expression. Wind instruments may present further problems. Seventeenth- and eighteenth-century writers

---

[13] Burney, op. cit., IV., pp. 318–319.

speak of the oboe as delicate.   A tradition which is securely ensconced in popular textbooks asserts that it was a coarse instrument.   Instinct and acquaintance with the music rejects this tradition as mere assumption; but it cannot be conclusively disproved.   We have the instruments but not the reeds, and without them we are not really in a position to judge.

Learned writers of today have much to tell us about what, in the jargon of musicologists, is called "performance practice."   What they rarely emphasize is that composers frequently allowed for a wide range of possibilities.   It is reasonable that we should not use a flute when the score says "recorder," if we have a recorder available.   But Monteverdi wrote a piece in which he prescribes either flute or recorder—you can take your choice.   Other alternatives are common: cello or bass viol, bass viol or trombone, and so on. The one thing which is foreign to the spirit of Baroque music is a rigid attitude to resources.   "Make do with what you have got" might have been the motto of musicians in the seventeenth and eighteenth centuries.   It does not necessarily mean that we have to make do with what Bach had got.   His protest against the resources available at St. Thomas's, Leipzig, makes it pretty clear that he was far from satisfied.   People sometimes express the sentimental wish that they could return to eighteenth-century Leipzig and hear a performance of one of the cantatas under the composer's direction.   I am not sure that I share that wish.   With the best will in the world it is hardly possible to suppose that these performances were as subtle or as polished as we should expect them to be today, though there is no reason to suppose that they were hopelessly inefficient.   If they had been, Bach would hardly have continued to write music which makes serious demands on expert choirs today.   My own wish would be to hear Bach directing the *collegium musicum,* partly because the conditions would be similar to those I am familiar with in university music, and partly because this was music that everyone could hear and enjoy.   Our historians are apt to lay too much stress on the dominance of patronage in the eighteenth century.   They forget the people who came to hear Bach's young men making music, the crowds who flocked to Ranelagh to hear Handel's concertos, and other manifestations of the same kind. The new wind that was blowing through the world of music did not have to wait for the French Revolution.

The sheer mass of music that was written during the course of the eighteenth century is staggering in its bulk. It is true that only a fraction of it found its way into print, but even that fraction is substantial. During the last war there were notices outside railroad stations in England saying: "Is your journey really necessary?" It would be tempting to ask: "Was all this music really necessary?" The eighteenth-century composer would have countered with the further question "Necessary for what?" An opera composer was not forced to go on turning out new works; but if he failed to do so he would win neither money nor reputation. The court employee had no choice. Amateurs were constantly asking for something new. Burney took it for granted that novelty was a merit that would be most appreciated by practised ears. The demand is still with us, but it is less general and less pressing. Churches, choral groups, school orchestras, opera workshops—all these are on the lookout for new material that they can get their teeth into and perform with a reasonable chance of success. But the composers who supply this demand are not necessarily those best qualified to do so. The better composers have loftier aims in view but less chance of achieving them. They operate to a large extent in an area where ignorant ears prefer what is familiar or common. We are all the victims of our reverence for the past. Outside the church, the eighteenth-century musicians were not interested in the past. They had a virgin field to plough, and they ploughed it to the extent of thousands of concertos, suites, and symphonies—not to mention the many operas that survive only in an index.

The ploughing was not merely a matter of covering sheets of manuscript paper with notes; it involved performance as well. A *Kapellmeister* was expected to compose; a composer who held aloof from practical musicmaking was a rarity. "I was forced to become original," said Haydn of his years of servitude. In a way it was too modest a statement. Haydn would have been an original composer whatever his career had been. But it does underline the circumstances in which may eighteenth-century musicians found themselves. Compelled to find a substantial part of their repertory from their own resources, they could hardly help developing a personality which can be discerned even through the most threadbare clichés of the time. Pious inscriptions like "Laus Deo" might record their acknowledgement to the Deity. But Heaven helps those who help themselves; and they were helping themselves all the time, though they were generally too busy to notice it. It is not easy to say exactly when the change occurred. Beethoven is obviously a key figure, partly because he was too independent to be a *Kapellmeister* and partly because his deafness made him a hopeless conductor. His successors were not bound to imitate him. Some of them did not. Mendelssohn and Wagner, in their different ways, were both accomplished conductors. Composers who were also virtuosos continued to show their skill in performance, but they did not generally make music with others, as Vivaldi had done. Liszt was an exception; but then he was an exception in everything. Physical injury prevented Schumann from becoming a pianist, but it did not prevent him from conducting. His utter incapacity as a conductor is in a way a symbol of the times; it might be regarded simply as a weak spot in the armour of a gifted musician, but it also derived from an attitude of mind. Romantic composers were not, like Haydn, forced to be original; they tried to be original. It was natural for them to withdraw into a dream world remote from the practical mechanism of performance. This did not necessarily prevent them from conducting their own works, but the results often showed how complete was the separation of the two activities. Tchaikovsky and Debussy were both hopeless on the podium. In Mahler, who was both composer and conductor, there was a conflict between two personalities. The fact that Strauss and Elgar frequently conducted their own works would not be worth mentioning if it had not been unusual.

In a way the Romantics seem curiously remote from our own times, even more remote than their immediate predecessors. This is partly due to a natural reaction against their idioms and partly a tendency to undervalue what we do not understand. We cannot see how people could faint at a Liszt recital or have convulsions when they heard a Beethoven symphony. These people seem to belong to a different race of beings. In the same way, younger musicians particularly find it difficulty to understand how Romantic composers could express themselves in the way they did: their self-consciousness is embarrassing, their ardour sounds manufactured, their heroics are empty. Perhaps we should understand them better if we could hear those who were also conductors directing their own works. Unfortunately, most of them have passed beyond our ken. I was taught the side drum by an old man who had played the cornet under Wagner, but I was too young to think of asking what he was like as a conductor. Later Romantics fall within living memory, and here perhaps there may be one or two clues. I recall a dazzling performance under Strauss of *Don Juan* which was unlike anything I have heard from any other conductor. Elgar was not technically a good conductor; but when he directed his own works they sounded different, as if he were creating them as he went along.

It is this union between the conductor and the composer that is too often lacking at the present day. It would be possible to argue that those who compose electronic music are also in charge of its performance, but the parallel is not exact. Performance is not something that can be stereotyped in a laboratory. It involves physical contact with human beings and a combination of technical skill and imagination strong enough to stand up to the nervous strain of a public appearance. "Von Herzen—möge es wieder zu Herzen gehen" wrote Beethoven over the Kyrie of his *Missa solemnis*. It is a prayer that every sincere composer must echo. But how can music reach the heart if there is no one to offer it and no awareness of anyone to receive it? The achievements of electronic music are not to be despised. They are often stimulating, they can be impressive; but they are not part of the world of music as I understand it. In that world the gulf between composing and performing has widened to an alarming extent. We need not pay too much attention to stories of composers, rehearsing their own works, who are unable to say whether the orchestral parts are right or wrong or who are even capable of playing through an entire movement without realizing that the clarinetist has the wrong instrument. Some of these stories are malicious inventions; a few I can vouch for myself as authentic. But they are significant only if they draw our attention to the fact that the difficulties which performers have to face are too often the result of a lack of any practical acquaintance on the part of composers with the problems of practical musicmaking.

This is particularly true in the field of choral music. We may accept the fact that instrumentalists can now play anything; but it is not equally true that chorus singers can sing anything. For one thing they have to keep the pitch—a problem which does not worry instrumental players. Anyone who has conducted a choir knows how difficult it is to maintain the pitch in any unaccompanied work. But the majority of composers today have never conducted a choir and are blissfully unaware of this difficulty. I cannot help wondering whether, when they hear their own works, they are conscious of any fluctuation of pitch or whether they regard such details as relatively unimportant. It is obvious that the difficulty of maintaining the pitch is enormously increased if the singers are asked to sing awkward intervals. In theory a singer should be able to pitch any interval with complete confidence, and in practice a near approach to accuracy can be achieved by laborious rehearsal. But there must always be a lurking doubt as to whether labour brings any commensurate reward. Leopold Mozart, finding his infant son writing a concerto, remarked that it was too difficult to be played. "That is why it is a concerto," replied the little man. "It must be practised." [14] In a sense all music is difficult, but there are degrees of difficulty. It may be true that the labour we delight in physics pain, but what of the labour we loathe? The pleasure of the performers is not something that can be wholly disregarded; nor is a performance that is achieved only by grim and tormenting struggles with intractable material likely to give much pleasure to those who listen.

The composer who accepts the limitations of performers is not cramping his invention. Limitations of any kind are a stimulus to

---

[14] O. E. Deutsch, *Mozart; die Dokumente seines Lebens* (Kassel, 1961), p. 396.

a creative artist, and there are some which even the most obstinate composers are compelled to endure. It is possible to insist that a woodwind player go at least one note higher than he ever has before or than anyone has ever thought feasible, but you cannot very well make him go one note lower than his bottom note unless you are prepared to pay for mechanical alterations to his instrument. Furthermore, a composer who bears his performers in mind is much more likely to get a good performance. Eighteenth-century musicians wrote solo music for particular singers or particular players whose capabilities they knew; and when they wrote for an ensemble they took good care that the music was within the grasp of the forces they were directing. Bach's cantatas are often difficult; but the difficulties tend to lie more in the solo numbers than in the choruses. In any case, his singers were presented with music in an idiom which they understood and which was the basis of their training. The choirs which valiantly perform contemporary music today are not likely to feel that the idioms they are required to sing are second nature to them; for one thing there are so many different idioms.

The pleasure which music affords can affect the listener, the performer, and the composer. The composer hopes to please the listener. He is less worried about the performer; and he is enormously concerned about himself. The eighteenth-century idea that his music might be necessary to anyone but himself will hardly occur to him. His job is not to provide for the needs of others but to find a satisfactory means of self-expression. This might be condemned as mere selfishness; but it is rather the natural heritage of Romanticism. The composer does not necessarily wish to remain aloof, but society seems to offer him no other choice. The obvious way for him to break down the barrier is to leave his ivory tower and plunge into the hurly-burly of practical musicmaking. Some contemporary composers have done this—with a benefit to their work which they would be the first to recognize. It is not essential that the composer work with professional groups. On the contrary, it will do him a great deal of good to work with amateurs. Bach was not too proud to conduct the students of Leipzig University.

This would not involve any lowering of standards. Amateurs, particularly young amateurs, are often extraordinarily competent and are prepared to tackle any difficulties which are not virtually insurmountable. In the days when I was an amateur horn player the works that I enjoyed most were those in which there was a challenge of some kind to my imperfect technique. There is a passage in the finale of Mozart's Clarinet Concerto which I practised for hours on end, because it did not always come quite right, and I wanted it to be right every time. It looks simple enough on paper, and the ordinary music lover would probably never notice it; but every horn player knows where it comes. In later works I had to tackle passages more spectacular in appearance than this but belonging to the same category; they could be mastered and one felt that they were worth mastering. The composer would be able to count on finding among his amateurs a boundless enthusiasm, and he would soon discover how far he could trust that enthusiasm to conquer the technical demands which he made. He would not have the opportunity, as the eighteenth-century *Kapellmeister* did, to write hundreds of symphonies, but he would know that he was writing music that was wanted, and with a little experience he could be fairly certain that it was playable.

A good performance and a rapturous reception are what every normal composer dreams of. It would be natural to say that he cannot expect the latter without the former. But there have been occasions, as most composers know, when the performance was marred by errors known only to him and the conductor; yet the audience, conscious of vitality and imagination, responded warmly without bothering about details of which they were ignorant. Conversely, many good performances have been coldly received. Coldness is anathema to composers. A riot would at least be stimulating; they would have something to fight against. Even random hisses would be better than nothing. But polite handclapping from a few well-disposed persons is enough to damp the spirits of any creative artists. Yet what else is an audience to do? There are plently of works that arouse neither violent antipathy nor warm appreciation. The cause may be the novelty which, according to Burney, should appeal to

[20]
260

practised ears. But even practised ears are sometimes puzzled by idioms which evoke no associations. We sometimes need to get the right wavelength before we can hear the composer talking to us.

Let us suppose that all the conditions are favourable for the listener. The music gives him pleasure. What precisely is it that pleases him? It is easier to give a negative than a positive answer to this question. The pleasure certainly does not depend on awareness of the composer's technical processes. This may seem to conflict with what I said earlier about the recognition of key and modulation. But these I do not call technical processes. They are part of the language of music, and the least one can expect of a serious listener is that he should know the language. The processes to which I refer are the mechanical devices by which a composer binds his music together—imitation, canon, inversion, ostinato, and the like. Anyone who is studying composition needs to have these things pointed out to him, since they are part of the craft which he is trying to master. But to the listener they are quite unimportant. It will do him no harm if he notices them, but equally he will not suffer if he does not. It is possible to derive immense enjoyment from a fugue without noticing every entry of the subject, much less the occurrence of stretto, augmentation, and all the other tricks of the trade. A seventeenth-century composer would have been horrified if he knew that an audience was concentrating on every recurrence of a ground bass: it was the melody above it that he wanted them to hear. One might as well expect appreciation of a Renaissance painting to be enhanced by the discovery that it was based on a geometrical pattern. As for wildcat theories like the one which claims that Bach composed in golden sections, the less said about them the better. A composer may plan his work according to a mathematical formula or he may subconsciously cast it into a form which will submit to mathematical analysis. But all this is of no interest to the listener.

It was only in the present century that the existence of an elaborate system of construction, now known as isorhythm, was discovered in the music of fourteenth- and fifteenth-century composers. The fact that no one had noticed it before does not seem to have

[21]

hampered appreciation of these works. I doubt very much whether any contemporary listener would have been aware of the means employed to achieve coherence. And at the present day can anyone who listens to Dunstable's *Veni sancte Spiritus* honestly say that he enjoys it any better for knowing that its structure is isorhythmic? A great deal of harm has been done by books, supposedly dealing with musical appreciation, which delude the innocent reader into thinking that these things matter. Program notes often fall into the same error. I see no objection to quoting the principal themes of a work or a movement: they serve as a kind of sketchmap or preview which gives the listener some idea of what he is to hear. But even this is not essential. It is far better to listen with a mind unencumbered with foreknowledge. And it is pointless to follow a performance with a score unless you know the work well and want to see if the performance is adequate. Scores are for students who want to know how music is made. The listener is concerned only with the finished article.

Contemporary music has not escaped the analyst's probing eye. In fact, it might almost be said to be the analyst's paradise. What joy to be able to parade before the untutored listener the raw materials of a serial composition, to draw his attention to unsuspected ingenuities, or to explain that the last movement is the first one played backwards. We are back again in the realm of the theorists who not only tell composers what to do but triumphantly point out how faithfully their prescriptions have been followed. It is only occasionally that a note of sadness creeps in, when a composer has chosen to ignore the rules of the game. Theorists do not confine their activities to composers and listeners. They feel that students should also be instructed in the mysteries. There is a strong school of thought today which claims that conventional harmony teaching is out of date and that the teaching of serial composition should be an essential part of the curriculum. This seems to me misguided. The technique of serialism is childishly simple; the difficulty is to use it with imagination, but that applies to any kind of composition. The conventional teaching of harmony and counterpoint, assuming it is reasonably enlightened, does not say "This is good, that is bad."

It aims at showing how acknowledged masters have used the raw material of music. No sensible person teaches any particular kind of composition; he simply teaches composition—that is, in essence, how to go on and how to be consistent. Any great master of the past, whatever his idiom, will teach one how to go on—and none better than Handel, who never seems to put a foot wrong and whose music is at the same time full of surprises. Consistency may be regarded as the supreme virtue; it is the one thing that budding composers find hard to achieve. Indeed there are plenty of young composers active today who have not achieved it, either from some defect of temperament or more probably because they have never submitted to the severe discipline on which the older composers built their unassailable technique.

Leafing through the analyses, the instructions, the propaganda, the whole corpus of didactic pedantry, we ask ourselves wearily: "To what purpose is this waste?" We come back again to our opening theme. Music was meant to be enjoyed. What advantage have we gained from the gradual extension of musical experience to the public at large—an extension which began as far back as the seventeenth century—if so little of what is now produced is enjoyed by so few? The hungry sheep are waiting; they only ask to be fed. Composers, aware that their potential audience is small, sometimes defend themselves by saying that they hope to be appreciated in fifty years' time. I am not sure that it is not presumptuous to assume that they will be remembered in fifty years. In any case, it is not their function to compose for the future which they cannot possibly foresee. As members of our human society, they should be writing for us here and now. They should feel themselves part of an organization dedicated to providing pleasure for their fellowmen. The word "pleasure" may seem too soft and comfortable a term. That is not how I understand it. I am on the side of the philosophers who regard pleasure as a good. It is not the equivalent of wallowing in a warm bath, with the rosy assurance that all is for the best in the best of all possible worlds. It is a tonic for the mind and can be a tonic for the body. We have only to recall those occasions, rare but memorable, when we emerged from a concert hall and seemed to feel no solid ground beneath our feet. At such moments we feel not merely a strange exaltation but also a disposition to show unwonted kindness to other people. Handel, so the story goes, was complimented by a noble lord, after a performance of *Messiah,* on "the noble entertainment which he had lately given the town." "My Lord," he replied, "I should be sorry if I only entertained them, I wish to make them better." [15] Cynics may retort that "better" is an ambiguous word; but every musician will know what Handel meant.

---

[15] O. E. Deutsch, *Handel; a Documentary Biography* (London, 1955), p. 855.